The Complete Id... Refere...

(You Mean ... This Book, and You're Not Going to Read It?)

Cool Tip #1

If you know which document you want to use before starting WordPerfect, include its name in the startup command to open it automatically. For example, to start WordPerfect and open RUTABAGA.DOC, type **wp rutabaga.doc**.

Cool Tip #2

Need to rehighlight a block in a hurry? No problemo. Just press Alt+F4 or F12 to put WordPerfect in Block mode and then press Ctrl+Home twice.

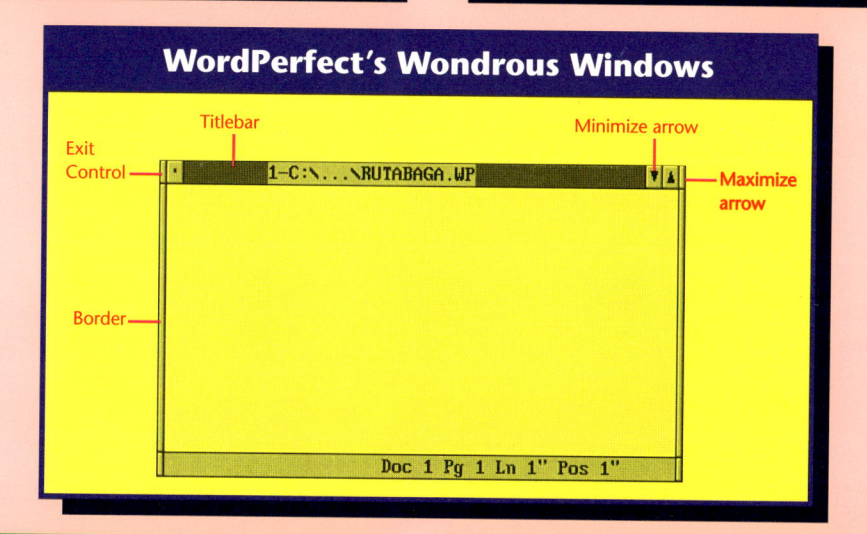

WordPerfect's Wondrous Windows

- Exit Control
- Titlebar
- Minimize arrow
- Maximize arrow
- Border

`1-C:\...\RUTABAGA.WP`

`Doc 1 Pg 1 Ln 1" Pos 1"`

Cool Tip #3

Version 6's new graphics mode lets you see most of your document formatting right on the screen without having to print (*and* you get cool 3-D dialog box buttons). Select Graphics Mode from the View menu.

Cool Tip #4

If you have a mouse, be sure to check out version 6's new Button Bar (select **B**utton Bar from the **V**iew menu). This gives you access to 15 of WordPerfect's most common tasks with the click of a mouse button.

The Un-Commands: Undo And Undelete

For those times when you zig instead of zag, WordPerfect includes an Undo feature that reverses your most recent action. Just select **U**ndo from the **E**dit menu or press Ctrl+Z.

If you've just deleted a crucial piece of text, remain calm and try not to panic. Slowly pull down the **E**dit menu and select the U**n**delete command (or just press Esc). WordPerfect displays the Undelete dialog box, adds the last deletion back into the text, and highlights it so you can see it clearly. If that's the text you want undeleted, select **R**estore. If it's not, select **P**revious Deletion until you see what you want and then select **R**estore. (If you use version 5.1, press F1 to select the Undelete command).

Cool Tip #5

If you're working with multiple documents, you can switch to a specific document number by pressing Home and then the number. If you're not sure of the number, press Home,0 to see a list.

alpha books

Caveat Dept.

Computers, being the temperamental beasts that they are, often seem to be just accidents waiting for a place to happen. Here are few tips to help keep you out of trouble:

- If you ever find yourself on some strange WordPerfect turf and you're starting to feel nervous about what may happen next, press Esc until you're back on more familiar ground. Esc is an all-purpose bailout key that should get you out of most sticky-wickets unscathed. (If you have version 5.1, use F1, instead.)
- Never shut off your computer while WordPerfect is still running. Doing so can lead to lost data, trashed files, and unsightly warts.
- You should save you work (by selecting the **S**ave command from the **F**ile menu) as often as you possibly can. You never know when a power outage or program crash may strike and blow away an afternoon's work.
- If you're trying to navigate with the numeric keypad, but all you get are numbers, press the Num Lock key.
- When you're using File Manager, only move or rename files that you've created yourself. Monkeying with any other files could cause WordPerfect to go on strike for better working conditions.
- Unless you have special "undelete" software, anything you delete in File Manager is gone for good, so you should be absolutely sure you can live without a file before getting rid of it.
- Speller and Grammatik are useful tools, but they're no substitute for either a flesh-and-blood dictionary or a thorough proofreading. Don't be lazy!
- Back up your documents regularly. If you don't have backup software, you can use File Manager's Copy command to back up your files to a floppy disk. There are *no* excuses!

The Ribbon: Formatting Made Easy

WordPerfect version 6 includes a fancy Ribbon tool that gives you easy access to some common formatting commands. To see it, select the Ribbon command from the View menu.

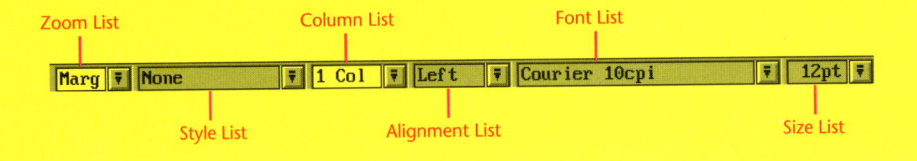

| Marg ▼ | None ▼ | 1 Col ▼ | Left ▼ | Courier 10cpi ▼ | 12pt ▼ |

Zoom List — Column List — Font List
Style List — Alignment List — Size List

Mouse Movements

Point Move the mouse pointer so that is rests on a specific screen location.

Click Quickly press and release the left mouse button.

Double-click Quickly press and release the left mouse button *twice* in succession.

Drag Press and hold down the left mouse button and then move the mouse.

Can You Repeat That?

You can use WordPerfect's Repeat command to save some legwork when navigating a document or deleting text. Just select **R**epeat from the **E**dit menu (or press Ctrl+R) to display the Repeat dialog box, then press whatever key you want repeated. If you press, say, the down arrow, WordPerfect moves down eight lines. Why eight? Well, that's the number that appears by default in the Repeat dialog box. If you'd like to use a different number, press Ctrl+R, type in the number, then press the key you want repeated. (In version 5.1, press Escape to activate the Repeat command.)

The Complete IDIOT'S Guide to WORDPERFECT® 6

by Paul McFedries

alpha
books

A Division of Prentice Hall Computer Publishing
11711 North College Avenue, Carmel, Indiana 46032 USA

To Karen: For those times when you need to give WordPerfect technical support to total strangers in Thai restaurants.

©1993 Alpha Books

All rights reserved. No part of this book shall be reproduced, stored in a retrieval system, or transmitted by any means, electronic, mechanical, photocopying, recording, or otherwise, without written permission from the publisher. No patent liability is assumed with respect to the use of the information contained herein. Although every precaution has been taken in the preparation of this book, the publisher and author assume no responsibility for errors or omissions. Neither is any liability assumed for damages resulting from the use of the information contained herein. For information, address Alpha Books, 11711 North College Avenue, Carmel, IN 46032.

International Standard Book Number:1-56761-187-7
Library of Congress Catalog Card Number: 93-70363

95 94 93   8 7 6 5 4 3 2 1

Interpretation of the printing code: the rightmost number of the first series of numbers is the year of the book's printing; the rightmost number of the second series of numbers is the number of the book's printing. For example, a printing code of 93-1 shows that the first printing of the book occurred in 1993.

Screen reproductions in this book were created by means of the program Collage Plus from Inner Media, Inc., Hollis, NH.

Printed in the United States of America

Publisher
Marie Butler-Knight

Associate Publisher
Lisa A. Bucki

Managing Editor
Elizabeth Keaffaber

Acquisitions Manager
Stephen R. Poland

Development Editor
Faithe Wempen

Manuscript Editor
Barry Childs-Helton

Cover Designer
Scott Cook

Designer
Roger Morgan

Indexer
Jeanne Clark

Production Team
*Diana Bigham, Katy Bodenmiller, Scott Cook,
Tim Cox, Mark Enochs, Linda Koopman, Tom Loveman,
Beth Rago, Joe Ramon, Carrie Roth, Greg Simsic*

Contents at a Glance

Part I: Day-to-Day Skills — **1**
- 1 The Least You Need to Know — 3
- 2 Word Processing: A Primer — 9
- 3 Diving In: Your First WordPerfect Session — 17
- 4 Keyboard and Mouse Basics — 29
- 5 WordPerfect the Easy Way: Using the Pull-Down Menus — 41
- 6 Talking to WordPerfect's Dialog Boxes — 49
- 7 Day-to-Day Drudgery I: Saving, Opening, and Closing — 61
- 8 Day-to-Day Drudgery II: Navigating Documents — 71

Part II: Getting It Right: Editing Stuff — **79**
- 9 Deleting Text (and Undeleting It, Too) — 81
- 10 Block Partying: Working with Blocks of Text — 89
- 11 Search and Ye Shall Replace — 99

Part III: Looking Good: Formatting Stuff — **109**
- 12 Making Your Characters Look Good — 111
- 13 Making Your Lines and Paragraphs Look Good — 121
- 14 Making Your Pages Look Good — 131
- 15 Other Ways to Look Good — 143

Part IV: Working with Documents — **153**
- 16 Getting It Down on Paper: Printing Documents — 155
- 17 Working with Multiple Documents — 167
- 18 Using WordPerfect's File Manager — 179

Part V: WordPerfect Tools — **189**
- 19 Cool Tools to Make Your Life Easier — 191
- 20 Using the Spell Checker and Thesaurus — 203
- 21 Painless Grammar Checking — 211

Speak Like a Geek Glossary — 221

Index — 229

Contents

Part I: Day-to-Day Skills — 1

1 The Least You Need to Know — 3
  1. Starting WordPerfect 3
  2. Entering Text 4
  3. Using Pull-Down Menus 4
  4. Opening a Document 5
  5. Saving a File 5
  6. Marking a Block of Text 6
  7. Formatting Characters 6
  8. Undoing a Mistake 6
  9. Printing a File 7
  10. Quitting WordPerfect 7

2 Word Processing: A Primer — 9
  What Is You-Know-What? 10
    Your Computer Is Not a Typewriter 10
    Editing: Getting It Right 10
    Formatting: Looking Good on Paper 11
    Printing: Getting Hard Copy 11
  Is Word Processing a Good Thing? 12
    Problem #1: Word Processors Encourage
      Sloppy Writing 12
    Problem #2: Word Processors Waste Time 13
    Problem #3: Word Processors Create Illiterates 14
  How Does WordPerfect Fit Into All This? 14

3 Diving In: Your First WordPerfect Session — 17
  Preflight Checklist 18
    Is your computer on? 18
    Is WordPerfect installed? 18
    Are you at the DOS prompt? 18
    Is the ambiance just right? 19
  The Two-Step Program for Starting WordPerfect 19
    Checking Out the WordPerfect Screen 19
    Explaining the Few Things You Can See 20

Now What? 22
Checking Out Graphics Mode 23
Getting Help 25
Exiting WordPerfect 26

4 Keyboard and Mouse Basics 29

The Keyboard: A Guided Tour 29
  Letters, Numbers, and Other Strangers 30
  Shift and Caps Lock 31
  Ctrl, Alt, and Those Bizarre WordPerfect
    Key Combinations 31
  The Esc Key 32
  The Cursor-Control Keys 32
  The Numeric Keypad 33
  The Function Keys 33
  A Note About Notebook Keyboards 34
WordPerfect Keyboarding for Non-Typists 34
  The Enter Key Redux 34
  Quick Fixes: Using Backspace and Delete 35
  Switching to Typeover Mode 35
  Key Combination Contortions 36
Mouse Machinations 36
  The Basic Mouse Technique 36
  The Hard Part: Controlling the Darn Thing! 38
  Mouse Actions 39

5 WordPerfect the Easy Way: Using the Pull-Down Menus 41

What the Heck Are Pull-Down Menus? 42
Why You Pull "Down" Instead of "Up" or "Out" 42
How to Use Pull-Down Menus with the Keyboard 43
How to Use Pull-Down Menus with a Mouse 44
More Fun Pull-Down Menu Stuff 45
  Underlined Characters: More Hot Keys 45
  Shortcut Keys: The Fast Way to Work 46
  Arrowheads (Menus, Menus, and More Menus) 46
  The Ellipsis (the Three-Dot Thing) 46

6 Talking to WordPerfect's Dialog Boxes 49

A Note to Users of Version 5.1 49
Where Do They Come From? 51
Dialog Box Basics 51
    Navigating Controls 52
Working with Radio Buttons 53
Working with Check Boxes 54
Working with Text Boxes 55
Working with Command Buttons 55
Working with Pop-Up Lists 56
Working with Drop-Down Lists 57
    Selecting Stuff From Drop-Down List Boxes 57
    A Brief Scroll Bar Primer 58
Dialog Box Commands 59

7 Day-to-Day Drudgery I: Saving, Opening, and Closing 61

Save Your Work, Save Your Life 61
    Saving an Existing Document 62
    What's Wrong with This Picture? 62
    Saving a New Document 63
    Sacred Filename Commandments 63
    What's Wrong with This Picture? 64
    Saving a Document When You Exit WordPerfect 65
    Saving a Document Under a New Name 66
Getting Documents: Opening Versus Retrieving 66
    How to Open a Document 67
    How to Retrieve a File 69
A Fresh Beginning: Starting a New Document 69
Closing a Document 69

8 Day-to-Day Drudgery II: Navigating Documents 71

Navigating with the Keyboard 72
    Navigating Characters and Words 72
    Navigating Lines and Paragraphs 72
    Navigating Screens, Pages, and Documents 73
    Navigating with the Go to Command 74
    How the Repeat Command Works 75

Navigating a File with the Mouse 75
  Scroll Whats? 77
  Where Am I? The Scroll Bar Knows 77
  Can I Get There From Here? Navigating
    with Scroll Bars 77

Part II: Getting It Right: Editing Stuff — 79

9 Deleting Text (and Undeleting It, Too) — 81

Deleting Characters 82
Deleting Words 82
Deleting Lines 83
Deleting Pages 84
Repeat Deleting 84
To Err Is Human, To Undelete Divine 85

10 Block Partying: Working with Blocks of Text — 89

Selecting a Block of Text 90
  Selecting Text With the Keyboard 90
  Selecting Text With the Mouse 91
  Using the Select Command 92
Copying a Block 92
  Copying with Two Commands 92
  Copying with One Command 93
Moving a Block 93
  Moving with Two Commands 93
  Moving with One Command 94
Saving a Block 94
Deleting a Block 94
Appending a Block to a File 95
The Life-Saving Undo Command 96

11 Search and Ye Shall Replace — 99

Searching for Text 100
  Searching Forward 100
  Searching Backward 100
  Continuing the Search 101
  Some Notes on Searching 101

Searching and Replacing Text 103
   Search and Replace: The Basic Steps 103
   Search and Replace Options 104

Part III: Looking Good: Formatting Stuff — 109

12 Making Your Characters Look Good — 111

Getting Graphic 112
Changing Character Attributes 112
Changing Character Size and Position 114
State Your Case: Converting Uppercase
   and Lowercase Letters 115
Working with Fonts 116
   Just What the Heck is a Font, Anyway? 116
   Selecting Different Fonts 117
Avoiding the "Ransom Note" Look 118
Adding Silly Symbols 119

13 Making Your Lines and Paragraphs Look Good — 121

Formatting Lines Versus Paragraphs 122
Working with Tab Stops 122
   Checking Out WordPerfect's Tab Types 123
   Setting Tabs 124
   Deleting Tabs 124
Justifying Your Text 124
Changing the Line Spacing 126
Indenting Text 126
Setting Paragraph Margins 127

14 Making Your Pages Look Good — 131

Adjusting Page Margins 132
Dealing with WordPerfect's Page Breaks 133
A Note About Page Mode 134
Adding Page Numbers 135
   Positioning the Page Numbers 135
   Setting the Page Number 136
Centering Text Between the Top and Bottom 138
Setting Up Headers and Footers 138

15 Other Ways to Look Good — 143

Inserting the Date and Time into a Document 144
Adding Footnotes and Endnotes 145
   Creating Footnotes and Endnotes 145
   Editing Footnotes and Endnotes 146
Adding Comments to a Document..............................146
Using Hyphenation to Clean Up Your Documents...........148
Working with Different Paper Sizes 150

Part IV: Working with Documents — 153

16 Getting It Down on Paper: Printing Documents — 155

Basic Printing 156
   Printing Multiple Pages 158
   What's Wrong with This Picture? 159
   Printing an Unopened Document 160
Canceling a Print Job 160
Using Print Preview 161
   Selecting Different Views 163
   Navigating Your Document 163
Selecting a Different Printer 164

17 Working with Multiple Documents — 167

Switching Among Multiple Documents 168
WordPerfect's Adjustable Windows 170
   Framing a Window 170
Anatomy of a Window 171
Adjusting Your Windows 172
   Sizing Up Your Windows 172
   Windows on the Move 173
   Letting WordPerfect Do the Work:
     Cascading and Tiling 174
   The Minimalist Approach: How to Minimize
     a Window 175
   Taking It to the Max: Maximizing a Window 176
   Closing a Window 176

Contents   xi

18 Using WordPerfect's File Manager 179

Starting File Manager 180
   Files and Directories: A Brief Primer 181
Anatomy of the File List..182
   Navigating the File List 183
What You Can Do with File Manager 184
   Opening and Retrieving Documents 184
   Looking at a Document..184
   Copying Files 185
   Moving and Renaming Files 186
   Deleting Files 187
   Selecting Multiple Files 187

Part V: WordPerfect Tools 189

19 Cool Tools to Make Your Life Easier 191

The Ribbon: Easy Formatting Access 192
   Working with the Ribbon 192
   The Zoom List 192
   The Style List 194
   The Columns List 194
   The Alignment List 195
   The Font List 195
   The Size List 195
The Button Bar: Easy Command Access 195
Have It Your Way: Customizing WordPerfect 196
   Customizing WordPerfect's Windows 196
   Customizing Your Mouse 198
   Doing WordPerfect's Colors 199

20 Using the Spell Checker and Thesaurus 203

Checking Out WordPerfect's Speller...204
   Cranking Up Speller 204
   Correcting Spelling Mistakes..205
   Editing Words..206
   Handling Weird Capitalizations 206

Handling Duplicate Words 207
Looking Up Words 207
Using the Splendiferous Thesaurus 208
Starting the Thesaurus 208
Displaying More Words 209

21 Painless Grammar Checking 211

Starting Grammatik 212
The Basic Interactive Check 212
Handling Grammatik's Errors 214
Quitting Interactive Check 215
A Word About Grammatik's Accuracy 216
Working with Writing Styles 216
Selecting a Different Style 217
Changing the Formality Level 218
Creating a Custom Style 218
Quitting Grammatik 219

Speak Like a Geek Glossary 221

Index 229

Introduction

If you've ever tried to have a conversation with a so-called computer "expert," then you know they have this uncanny ability to make the rest of us feel like complete idiots within five seconds. They prattle on in their techno-jargon, throwing in the odd "of course" and "obviously" to make it clear that any fool with half a brain ought to know this stuff. Nuts to them, I say! Not only are we *not* idiots, but we're smart enough to know a thing or two ourselves:

- We're smart enough to know that "cool" isn't defined by how many back issues of *Popular Mechanics* we keep in the bathroom. We simply don't need a lot of technical details (and we don't wear pocket protectors, either).

- We're smart enough to know that it doesn't make sense to learn absolutely *everything* about WordPerfect. We just need to know enough to get our work done, thank you.

- We're smart enough to know that life's too short to read five kazillion pages of arcane (and mostly useless) information. We have lives to lead, after all.

A Book for Smart WordPerfect Idiots

If you're no fool, but the computer gurus of the world make you feel like one, then welcome to *The Complete Idiot's Guide to WordPerfect*! This is a book for those of us who aren't (and don't even want to be) computer wizards. This is a book for those of us who have a job to do—a job that includes working with WordPerfect—and we just want to get it done as quickly and painlessly as possible. This *isn't* one of those absurdly serious, put-a-crease-in-your-brow-and-we'll-begin kinds of books. On the contrary, we'll even try to have—gasp!—a little fun as we go along.

You'll also be happy to know that this book doesn't assume you have any previous experience with WordPerfect. This means that we'll begin each topic at the beginning, and build your knowledge from there. But you won't find any long-winded discussions of boring technical details. With *The Complete Idiot's Guide to WordPerfect*, you get just the facts you *need* to know, not everything there *is* to know. All the information is presented in short, easy-to-digest chunks that you can easily skim through to find just the information you want.

How This Book is Set Up

I'm assuming you have a life away from your computer screen, so *The Complete Idiot's Guide to WordPerfect* is set up so that you don't have to read it cover to cover. If you want to know how to print, for example, just turn to the printing chapter. To make things easier to find, I've organized the book into five more or less sensible sections:

Part I—Day-to-Day Skills

WordPerfect follows the old 80-20 rule: you'll spend 80 percent of your time working with 20 percent of the program's features. The eight chapters in this section cover most of that 20 percent. You'll learn basic stuff such as starting WordPerfect (Chapter 3), using the keyboard and mouse (Chapter 4), and saving your work (Chapter 7).

Part II—Getting It Right: Editing Stuff

The benefits of a word processor over a typewriter are legion, but one of the biggest is being able to edit a document right on the screen. These three chapters show you how to delete—and undelete—text (Chapter 9), how to move chunks of text around (Chapter 10), and how to find stuff in your documents (Chapter 11).

Part III—Looking Good: Formatting Stuff

Because looking good is often as important as *being* good, WordPerfect gives you a fistful of ways to format your documents. The four chapters in Part III introduce you to these various options. You'll learn how to format individual characters (Chapter 12), lines and paragraphs (Chapter 13), pages (Chapter 14), and more.

Part IV—Working with Documents

The stuff you create in WordPerfect—your letters, memos, and mystery novels—are called *documents*. This section shows you how to print them (Chapter 16) and work with them on screen (Chapter 17). Chapter 18 also tells you about File Manager, WordPerfect's answer to the DOS command line.

Part V—WordPerfect Tools

The book ends with three chapters that take you through some of WordPerfect's collection of tools and utilities. Chapter 19 scopes out a few tools that'll make your life easier. Chapters 20 and 21 check out the spell checker, thesaurus, and grammar-checker that are built right into WordPerfect.

The Complete Idiot's Guide to WordPerfect also includes a glossary that'll help you make sense of all those bizarre computer terms as well as a handy tear-out reference card that gives you easy access to important (or just plain cool) WordPerfect stuff.

Features of This Book

The Complete Idiot's Guide to WordPerfect is designed so you can get the information you need fast and then get on with your life. If you ever need to type something (it comes up occasionally with word processors), it will appear like this:

type this

Also, look for the following icons that will help you learn just what you need to know:

> **By the Way . . .**
> These boxes contain notes about WordPerfect facts that are (hopefully!) interesting and useful.

SPEAK LIKE A GEEK

This icon defines geeky computer terms in plain English.

TECHNO NERD TEACHES

This icon gives you technical information you can use to impress your friends (and then forget five minutes later).

E-Z

There are always easier ways to do things on a computer, and the tips under this icon will tell you about them.

OOPS!

There are always dangerous ways to do things on a computer—and this icon will tell you how to avoid them.

5.1

WordPerfect made a lot of changes in the leap from version 5.1 to 6. Where there are differences, this icon points out the appropriate 5.1 instructions.

As if all this wasn't enough, you'll also get *Put It to Work* sections that give you real-life, hands-on, practical WordPerfect projects that you can try yourself. And to make sure you're paying attention (at least a little), you'll come across the odd *What's Wrong with This Picture* section that will give you totally unserious quizzes about what you've learned.

Acknowledgements (The Kudos and Huzzahs Dept.)

Ah, so many people to thank, so little time. Let's start with Acquisitions Editor Steve Poland: thanks for thinking of me. Development Editor Faithe Wempen: it was great being a team again; thanks for another job well done. Managing Editor Liz Keaffaber: thanks for keeping me in line (take a vacation!). Production Editor Annalise DiPaolo: always a pleasure (good luck in the future). Copy Editor Barry Childs-Helton and Tech Editor Kelly Oliver: thanks for making me look good.

Part I
Day-to-Day Skills

Let's face it, WordPerfect is one intimidating program: all those installation disks, the overstuffed manual bursting at the seams. The good news is that most of that stuff doesn't apply to the likes of you and me. All we really need are a few basic features that'll let us get our work done with a minimum of fuss and bother. In a sense, that's what this whole book is about, but the chapters here in Part I set the stage for everything else. You'll be learning basic stuff such as how to start WordPerfect, how to use your keyboard and mouse, and how to use things like the pull-down menus and dialog boxes to make your life easier. Believe me, if you can get through this stuff (and if you can dress yourself, you can handle any of this), then the rest will be a day at the beach.

Chapter 1
The Least You Need to Know

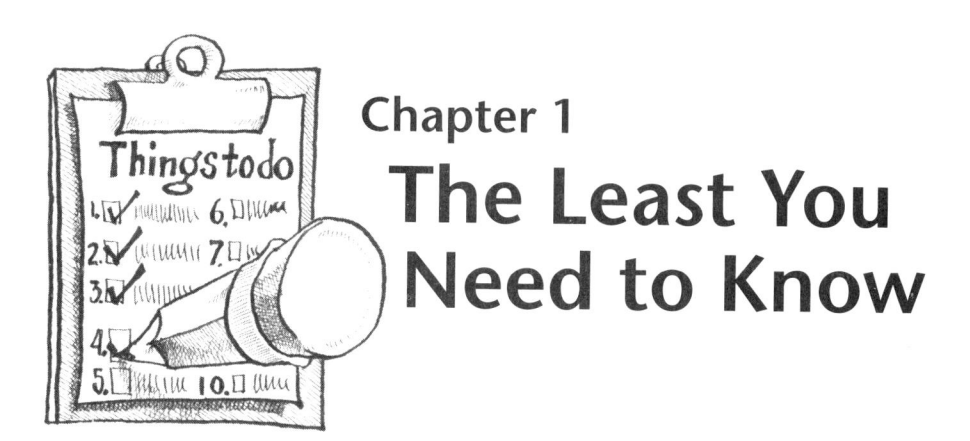

I know, I know. You can't wait to get started. What is it? A looming deadline? Unfettered curiosity? A type-A personality? Well, not to worry. This chapter gets you up to speed quickly by presenting a "just-the-facts" description of the 10 most important WordPerfect tasks. Of course, each of these items is discussed in more detail elsewhere in the book, so if you'd like to know more, I'll also point out the relevant chapters. If you're one of those people who likes to read ahead to the good bits, then this chapter's for you.

1. Starting WordPerfect

To start WordPerfect, you need to be at the DOS prompt. (The DOS prompt looks like C:\> or maybe just C>.) If your computer starts off in some kind of menu system, you need to exit the menu to get to DOS. Once you're in DOS, make sure you're logged onto the drive on which you installed WordPerfect. To do this, just type the drive letter followed by a colon (:), and then press **Enter**. For example, to change to drive C, type **C:** and press **Enter**. Now peck out **WP** on your keyboard, and press the **Enter** key. You'll know all is well if you see the WordPerfect logo on your screen.

See Chapter 3, "Diving In: Your First WordPerfect Session," for more information.

> **By the Way . . .**
>
> Whenever I ask you to type something, I'll show the appropriate text in capital letters. This is only to make the text easier to read, it doesn't mean you have to use capitals. Unless I tell you otherwise, you can enter most text in uppercase, lowercase, or any combination of the two that strikes your fancy.

2. Entering Text

Once WordPerfect is loaded, you can start typing right away. There are no complicated commands to run, and no messy formulas to remember. You don't even have to press Enter at the end of every line, the way you do with a typewriter (where the same key is called "Return"). WordPerfect wraps your prose onto the next line, free of charge. The only time you need to press **Enter** is when you want to start a new paragraph. If you make a mistake, just press the **Backspace** key to wipe it out.

Chapter 3, "Diving In: Your First WordPerfect Session," gives you a few more tips about entering text. For the lowdown on editing your documents, skim through Part II, "Getting It Right: Editing Stuff."

3. Using Pull-Down Menus

5.1 In version 5.1, press Alt+= to display the menu bar, look for the letter in the menu name that appears in a different color, then press the letter to pull down the menu.

Pull-down menus are hidden menus that list the various commands that are available for each WordPerfect task.

To pull down a menu with the keyboard, find the letter in the menu name that is underlined or appears in a different color. Then just hold down the **Alt** key and press the letter. Or, with a mouse, move the mouse pointer into the *menu bar* area (the horizontal strip along the top of the screen), and then click on the name of the menu you want to pull down. ("Click" means to press and release the left mouse button.)

Chapter 1 • *The Least You Need to Know*   **5**

Once you have your menu displayed, you then select a command. With your keyboard, you use the **up** and **down arrow keys** to highlight the command you want and then press **Enter**. With a mouse, you simply click on a command.

To learn more about pull-down menus, see Chapter 5, "WordPerfect the Easy Way: Using the Pull-Down Menus."

4. Opening a Document

When you start WordPerfect, you get a blank screen ready for your typing. If you'd prefer to work with an existing document, you need to open it. All you do is pull down the File menu and select the **O**pen command (or simply press **Shift+F10**) to display the Open Document dialog box. Now type the full name of the file into the **Filename** box. If the file is in a different drive or directory, be sure to include the drive letter and/or the directory name. When you're ready, select the **OK** button or just press **Enter**.

> **5.1**
> To open a file with version 5.1, press **Shift+F10**, type in the name of the file at the bottom of the screen, and then press **Enter**.

For more information on the **O**pen command, see Chapter 7, "Day-to-Day Drudgery I: Opening and Saving Documents." To learn more about dialog boxes, see Chapter 6, "Talking to WordPerfect's Dialog Boxes."

5. Saving a File

One of the most gut-wrenching experiences in computerdom is to work on a document for hours, and then lose everything because of a system crash or power failure. You can minimize this damage by saving your work regularly; just pull down WordPerfect's File menu and select the **S**ave command, or press **Ctrl+F12** key. If you're saving a new file, the Save Document dialog box will appear. Use the **Filename** box to give the file a name. When you're ready, select **OK**.

> **5.1**
> To save a new file in WordPerfect 5.1, press **F10**, then type in the name at the bottom of the screen and press **Enter**.

See Chapter 7, "Day-To-Day Drudgery I: Opening and Saving Documents," for more details about saving your work.

6. Marking a Block of Text

Much of what you do in WordPerfect—whether it's cutting, copying, formatting, or printing—involves highlighting a block of text beforehand. Here's how you do it:

- ☛ With the keyboard, position the cursor to the left of the first character in the block, and then select the **Block** command from the Edit menu (or just press **Alt+F4**). Now use the **arrow** keys (or **Page Up** and **Page Down** if you have a lot of ground to cover) to highlight the block.

- ☛ With a mouse, point at the first character in the block, and then drag the mouse to move the pointer over the block.

You'll find lots more block info in Chapter 10, "Working with Blocks of Text." To learn how to drag a mouse, see Chapter 4, "Keyboard and Mouse Basics."

7. Formatting Characters

To make your documents stand out from the crowd, use WordPerfect's *character formatting* commands. With these commands you can do simple formats like bold and italics, but you can also get into fancy stuff like different fonts, outlining, and shadowing. Just pull down the Font menu and select the appropriate command, or press **Ctrl+F8** and choose options from the dialog box that appears.

The full scoop on all this can be found in Chapter 12, "Formatting Characters."

8. Undoing a Mistake

The WordPerfect programmers thoughtfully included an **Undo** command you can use to reverse your most recent action. This is great if you've just made a formatting gaffe, or if you "cut" when you should have "copied."

To use the Undo feature, just pull down the **Edit** menu and select the **Undo** command (you can also simply press **Ctrl+Z**).

But wait, there's more. WordPerfect also has an Undelete feature that can get you out of trouble if you've just deleted your entire day's work. To use it, first select U**n**delete from the Edit menu (or press **Esc**). Your most recent deletion will appear highlighted in the text, and the Undelete dialog box will appear with two options: Restore and Previous Deletion. Select Restore to restore the highlighted text. Select **Previous Deletion** to take a look at text deleted previously (WordPerfect stores the last three deletions). When you have the text you want, select **Restore**.

> **5.1** Version 5.1 doesn't have an **Undo** command, but you can undelete text by pressing **F1**.

You'll learn about Undo in Chapter 10, "Working with Blocks of Text," and Undelete in Chapter 9, "Deleting Text (and Undeleting It, Too)."

9. Printing a File

Once you've finished working with a document, you'll want to print a copy to show to your friends and colleagues. To do this, pull down the **File** menu and select the **Print** command. The Print dialog box appears; it enables you to specify how much of the document to print, the number of copies, and various other settings. When you're ready to print, select the **Print** button.

For more printing particulars, take a look at Chapter 16, "Getting It Down on Paper: Printing Documents."

10. Quitting WordPerfect

When you've finished with WordPerfect, you can quit the program by pulling down the File menu and selecting the Exit WP command (or press **Home**, then **F7**). This displays the Exit WordPerfect dialog box, with a list of your open files. If necessary, select the documents you want to save, and

> **5.1** To quit version 5.1, press **F7** and respond to the prompts at the bottom of the screen.

then select the **Save and Exit** button. If you aren't saving any documents, select the **Exit** button.

See Chapter 3, "Diving In: Your First WordPerfect Session," for some additional stuff on quitting WordPerfect.

Chapter 2
Word Processing: A Primer

In This Chapter

- What is word processing?
- Is word processing a good thing?
- How does WordPerfect fit in?
- What's new with version 6?
- A short tirade about linguistics

Word processing. Personally, I've never liked the term. It sounds so cold and so, well, computer-like. I mean, processing words? What the heck does that mean? The bank processes checks, the IRS processes tax returns. Who processes words? We write them, play with them, misuse them, misspell them, forget them, but process them? No.

But the computer geeks of the world decided long ago that's what it should be called, so it looks like we're stuck with it. Despite these misgivings, this chapter takes a look at this whole word processing thing. What is it? What can you do with it? Why should you care?

What Is You-Know-What?

Well, in the most basic, watch-their-eyes-glaze-over terms, *word processing* is using a computer to write, edit, format, and print documents. Yeah, I know, it doesn't sound very glamorous, but it's not really supposed to be. I mean, think about it. Most of the writing we do is grunt work anyway: memos, letters, essays, diatribes, and harangues of one sort or another. All we really need is to get the words down, dot the i's and cross the t's, make it presentable, and then get some hard copy that we can ship out. Everything else—whether it's putting together a newsletter or writing a doctoral thesis—is just an extension of this basic stuff.

Your Computer Is Not a Typewriter

All word processors have some kind of work area that you use for writing. Generally speaking, you just start pecking away on the computer's keyboard and the characters appear like magic on the screen.

Works just like a typewriter, right? Wrong. Oh sure, the keyboard looks somewhat familiar: the letters and numbers are arranged more or less the same, the spacebar is where it should be, and your old friends the Shift and Tab keys are there. Things may look the same but, baby, this ain't no Selectric.

The biggest difference, of course, is that the word processor has the muscle of a full-fledged computer behind it. Computers may be a lot dumber than we are (and don't let anyone tell you otherwise), but even the cheapest PC clone is way smarter than the most highfalutin typewriter. For example, on a typewriter, a bell sounds to warn you when you near the end of a line. That's not bad, but the dumb beast still expects you to finish the line yourself and then press the Return key (or—gasp—crank the carriage return bar) to start a new line. A word processor, on the other hand, handles this chore for you. If you near the end of a line, you can blissfully continue typing, and the program will start a new line automatically. It'll even carry over any word you happen to be in the middle of.

Editing: Getting It Right

Word processors really begin to earn their stripes when it comes time to make changes in a document. With a typewriter, you can fix small mistakes, but you still have to fumble around with correction ribbons or (yuck) that ugly White-Out stuff. If you leave out a sentence or paragraph accidentally, forget about it. You've got to type the whole thing over.

Word processors, though, live to fix mistakes. Type the wrong character? Just press a button to delete it. Forget a paragraph? Just insert it where it needs to go. Want to move a section of text from the beginning of the document to the end? No problem: just "cut" it out and "paste" it in the appropriate place. Want to replace every instance of "affect" with "effect" (I can never remember which is which)? Most word processors have a "search and replace" command that'll do just that.

And this is just the tip of the iceberg. A full-featured program such as WordPerfect has all kinds of strange and wonderful ways (including, thank goodness, a spell checker!) to get the job done right.

Formatting: Looking Good on Paper

Writing and editing are important of course, but the area where word processors really shine is *formatting*. It's not enough, in these image-conscious times, merely to hand someone a piece of paper with a bunch of words on it. Documents today need impact to get their message across. The formatting options in most word processors can help.

You can use **bold** to make things stand out, or *italics* for emphasis. You can center text or set tabs with just a few keystrokes. Some of the better programs also allow you to organize your words into columns, or wrap them around a picture. In the really high-end word processors (WordPerfect is one), you can even add cool features such as footnotes and tables of contents without breaking a sweat. If you can picture it in your head, you can probably do it with a word processor.

Printing: Getting Hard Copy

Once you've finished changing a document, you'll need to print it out for others to see. This sounds like there wouldn't be much to it; just run some sort of "Print" command and the thing prints. But you can also choose to print only certain parts of a document (a single page or even a single paragraph, for example), or you can print multiple copies, or, if you have more than one printer, you can choose which one you want to use. Some programs even let you see a page-by-page preview of what the document will look like.

Is Word Processing a Good Thing?

This may sound like a silly question to ask after extolling the numerous virtues of word processing programs. And it may be moot in any case, because word processing is by far the most popular category of computer software. Some people do have concerns, however, about what word processing is doing to our minds—so we may as well tackle those before going any further.

Problem #1: Word Processors Encourage Sloppy Writing

This is the most common problem put forth by so-called "writing experts." You usually hear three kinds of complaints:

- If a section of text doesn't work for some reason, people using word processors don't rewrite the whole thing from scratch. Instead, trying to get their point across, they tend to insert more words and sentences. The usual result is bloated, overexplained thoughts that ramble incoherently.

- Most word-processor screens show only about a half a page at a time, so people tend to see the trees (words, sentences, and paragraphs) instead of the forest (the entire document). As a result, word processing documents tend to lack organization, and scatter separate pieces of the overall argument willy-nilly.

- The advent of the electronic thesaurus has made it easier to utilize cumbrous, orchidaceous words that serve only to obfuscate intendment and subjugate perspicuity.

My answer to these charges is that word processors don't write sloppily, *people* do. Forthwith, some suggestions you can use to avoid sloppiness in your own prose:

- Wherever possible, read your text out loud. If it doesn't flow off your tongue, it won't flow through someone's brain.

- If a sentence or paragraph doesn't feel right, try rewriting it from scratch instead of patching it up. If you can't bring yourself to delete it, at least move it off the screen where you can't see it (and so won't be influenced by it).

- A good word processor (such as WordPerfect) has outlining features that can help you organize large documents. This is a bit of an advanced topic, but it's worthwhile to learn before starting on that new novel.

- The best writing is clear and straightforward, without a lot of pretentious words that confuse more than they impress.

Problem #2: Word Processors Waste Time

You could see this one coming. Today's top-of-the-line word processors have so many bells and whistles that you can end up spending all your time fussing about with obscure fonts and complicated desktop publishing features. People often compound the problem by printing the document every time they make the slightest change. This just wastes paper and consumes valuable natural resources.

Again, these are behavioral problems, not word processor problems. On the one hand, it really is best to leave your work simple and uncluttered with fancy elements. This will keep your documents readable and your meaning clear. On the other hand, the best way to get familiar with any kind of software is to experiment with different features, and try out whatever looks interesting. You won't wreck anything, and most programs will warn you if you're about to do anything disastrous. And besides, you've got to have *some* fun.

> **SPEAK LIKE A GEEK**
>
> Programs that come fully loaded with complicated options are called *fritterware* because you end up frittering away your time playing around with the fun stuff instead of getting any work done.

Problem #3: Word Processors Create Illiterates

The same people who complained that calculators would turn our kids into math dropouts are now crying that computer spell checkers and grammar checkers will turn us all into illiterate slobs who wouldn't know a participle if it was dangled in front of us.

This one's easy to answer, folks: nuts to them, I say! If we can get our machines to handle the rote work of spelling and grammar, then I'm all for it. After all, meaning is what's most important. Why not take the time that would normally be spent with our noses in dusty dictionaries and use it to craft our concepts and polish our prose?

How Does WordPerfect Fit Into All This?

If word processing dominates the software industry, WordPerfect dominates the word processing industry, with something like 60% of the market. So what's the big deal? Well, it's hard to say, actually. Prior to version 6, the program was quirky—to say the least—and somewhat intimidating for beginners. (WordPerfect 6 changes all that, as you'll see shortly.)

All that aside, however, there's no doubt that WordPerfect has something for everyone. If all you need is basic editing features for things like letters and memos, WordPerfect will handle these chores with a few simple commands. If you need to put together large, complex documents, WordPerfect has features such as outlining, indexing, and footnotes that'll handle the biggest job without complaint. If your interests lie more toward desktop publishing (creating newsletters, brochures, and the like), WordPerfect can do page layout, columns of text, and graphics with the best of them. In other words, WordPerfect works they way you do, not the other way around.

Version 6 is a vastly changed product from its predecessors. It brings to the table a number of new features that put the program in line with some industry standards (such as pressing the **F1** key to get help) and make the program both easier to use and more powerful. Here's a quick summary of some of the new features:

- A "graphics mode" that lets you see on screen what your document will look like when it's printed.

- The ability to open up to nine, count 'em, nine documents at once. This makes it easy to compare two or more documents, and to move text from one document to another. (Learning how to juggle is optional.)

- An industry-standard interface that uses pull-down menus and dialog boxes (I'll explain what these things mean as we go along) to make your life easier.

- A new Ribbon and Button Bar; these give you easy access to the commands and features you use most often.

- A built-in grammar checker.

- Quick Finder, a new utility that lets you find your documents quickly.

- Improved printing functions such as Print Preview (that lets you view your document page-by-page before printing it out) and envelope printing.

This book covers most of these new version 6 features, but don't feel left out if you have an older incarnation of the program. Any major differences in version 5.1 are spelled out in separate sidebars for handy reference. (If you have 5.0, you can still get by with no problems, because it's not all that different from 5.1.)

> ### The Least You Need to Know
> This chapter took you on a quick tour of the shiny, happy world of word processing. Here's a recap of some of the sights we saw along the way:
>
> - Word processing is a dumb name for using a computer to write, edit, format, and print documents.
>
> *continues*

continued

- ☞ Your keyboard may look like a typewriter but, thanks to the computer in the box behind it, it's a lot smarter and a lot easier to use than a typewriter. Most editing and formatting commands are just a few keystrokes or mouse clicks away.

- ☞ Word processing is a good thing if you approach it the right way. Keep things simple, use the program's features to make your life easier, and don't be afraid to experiment.

- ☞ WordPerfect is the most popular word processor by far, because it works the way you do. Version 6 has all kinds of cool new features that'll keep you entertained for hours.

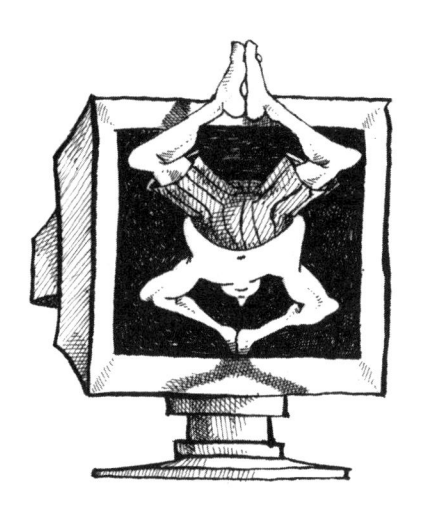

Chapter 3
Diving In: Your First WordPerfect Session

In This Chapter

- Starting WordPerfect
- Taking a tour around the screen
- Entering text
- Exiting WordPerfect
- A heartwarming story about skiing

The first time I ever went skiing, my friends (who, of course, were all experts and had little patience for a rank beginner) took me for a couple of token runs down the baby hill and then whisked me to the top of some huge mountain. (With friends like these . . . !)

In our travels down the mountain, we'd often come upon the steep, mogul-filled hills that my friends loved. These suckers scared the heck out of me, so I'd just follow everyone else, and I always made it down somehow. But I'd usually see groups of skiers standing at the top of these hills, fidgeting nervously, afraid to go down, but not able to turn back. In honor of these nervous-nellies, I developed my skiing motto: "Better a leg broken by boldness than a spirit broken by fear."

I tell you this story now, as we stand at the edge of WordPerfect Hill, to inspire you to, as the ads say, "just do it." Follow my lead and we'll get through without a hitch.

Preflight Checklist

Before starting WordPerfect, you should make sure you've got everything you need. Here's a quick checklist:

❏ Is your computer on?

This is, of course, important. Make sure not only that your computer is up and running, but that anything else you'll need (such as your monitor or printer) is also powered up.

❏ Is WordPerfect installed?

If the program hasn't yet been installed, you have two choices:

- ☞ Find the nearest computer guru and ask him or her to install the program for you. This is the easiest method (for you, anyway) and you'll find most gurus can be bribed with the appropriate junk food.

- ☞ If you can't find a guru or you'd like to give it a go yourself, you'll find WordPerfect's installation program to be friendlier than most. Just insert the disk labeled "Install 1" in the appropriate drive (usually A or B), type **A:INSTALL** (or **B:INSTALL**, depending on which drive the disk is in), and press **Enter**. Then just follow the prompts on the screen.

❏ Are you at the DOS prompt?

Before you can start WordPerfect, you need to be at the DOS prompt. (Ewww, DOS! Don't worry, we'll only be making a brief stop in bad old DOS-land before moving on.) The DOS prompt looks like C> or C:\> or some variation on this theme. If you don't see anything that looks like this, then you're likely in some other program. Here are some possibilities:

- The MS-DOS Shell program. If you see **MS-DOS Shell** at the top of your screen, hold down your keyboard's **Alt** key and press **F4** to return to DOS.

- Some kind of menu system. Your computer may be set up with a menu system that gives you a list of programs to run. If you're lucky, you may see a "WordPerfect" option. If so, great! Just select the option to start WordPerfect, and then skip to the section titled "Checking Out the WordPerfect Screen," later in this chapter. Otherwise, look for an option called "Exit to DOS," or "Quit," or something similar. You can also try pressing the **Esc** key.

❑ Is the ambiance just right?

Make sure your surroundings are comfortable and your favorite computer accessories are nearby (a good, strong cup of coffee, relaxing background music, a copy of *Feel the Fear and Do It Anyway*, etc.).

The Two-Step Program for Starting WordPerfect

Without further ado, here are the steps you need to follow to get WordPerfect up and running:

1. If necessary, change to the drive on which you installed WordPerfect by typing the drive letter, followed by a colon (:), followed by the **Enter** key. For example, to change to drive C, type **C:** and press **Enter**.
2. Type **WP** and press **Enter**. Yup, that's all there is to it: just peck out two lousy little letters and you're on your way. No complicated commands to remember, or snaggled syntax to scratch your head over. Ah, if only everything in life were so simple.

Checking Out the WordPerfect Screen

WordPerfect will take a few seconds to crank itself up to speed. When it finally does, you'll see the screen shown here.

The WordPerfect screen.

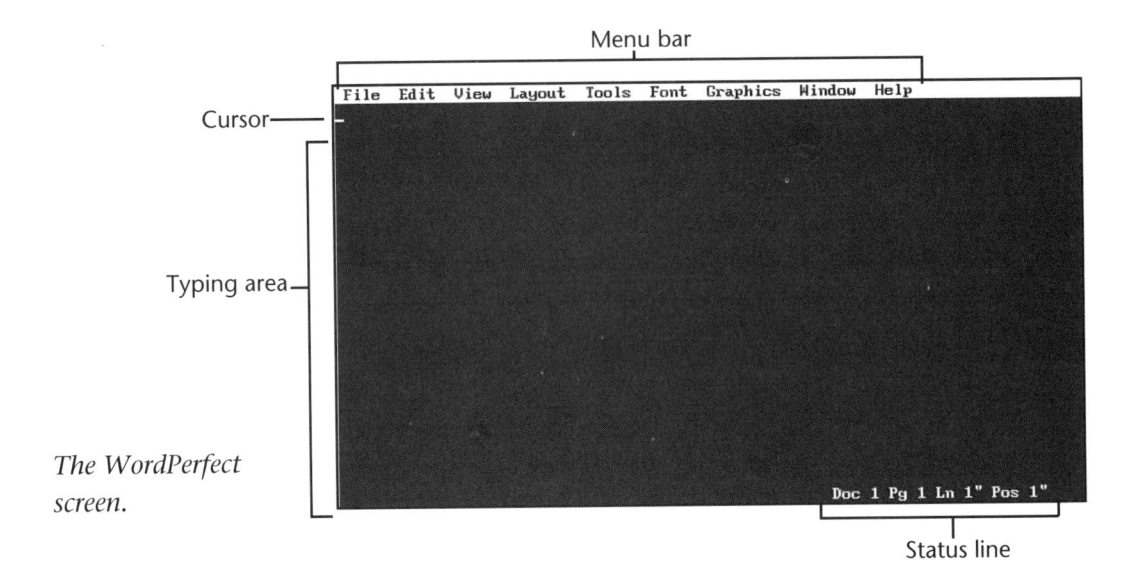

[Screen illustration labeled with: Menu bar (File, Edit, View, Layout, Tools, Font, Graphics, Window, Help), Cursor, Typing area, Status line (Doc 1 Pg 1 Ln 1" Pos 1")]

> **OOPS!**
>
> In DOS, however, things can always go wrong. After entering the **WP** command, you may see the following ominous message on your screen:
>
> **Bad command or file name**
>
> Yikes! Remain calm and take a deep breath. All you need to do is change to the directory where WordPerfect is installed. If you're using version 6, type **CD\WP60** and then press **Enter**; for version 5.1, type **CD\WP51** and press **Enter**. Try starting the program again.

There's not a lot to see, is there? It's almost disappointing, in a way. I mean, after loading all those disks this is all you get? Welcome to the WordPerfect philosophy: *hide as much stuff as possible, to maximize the amount of text that can be displayed on the screen.* This is a good idea for experienced word jockeys, but it can intimidate the heck out of beginners who haven't the faintest idea where to find what they need. This, then, will be our mission in this book: to seek out new WordPerfect life and new WordPerfect civilizations; to boldly go where you've never gone before. (Cue music.)

Explaining the Few Things You Can See

The WordPerfect screen may be stark, but it's not empty. Here's a quick rundown of what's there:

- **The typing area**   This is the large, blank expanse that covers everything but the top and bottom lines of the screen. This is where it all happens; everything you type will appear in this area. Think of it as the digital equivalent of a blank sheet of paper.

- **The cursor**   This small, blinking line has a single purpose in life: it tells you where the next character you type will appear. Go ahead and press a letter on your keyboard. See how it shows up on the screen right above where the cursor was? The cursor itself leaps ahead to tell you where your next character will appear. (Press **Backspace** to get rid of the character.)

- **The menu bar**   This is the top line of the screen. Although you'd never know to look at it, this innocuous-looking line is actually your gateway to every single WordPerfect feature. This prodigious feat is accomplished by the miracle of pull-down menus. You'll learn all about these magical beasts in Chapter 5, "WordPerfect the Easy Way: Using the Pull-Down Menus."

    > **5.1** If you're using version 5.1, you may not see the menu bar. Just hold down the **Alt** key on your keyboard and type an equals sign (=).

- **The status line**   This is the bottom line of the screen (although you only see stuff on the right side of the line at first, the rest of the line will, at different times, display other info). Looks pretty incomprehensible, doesn't it? The information is actually quite useful, although you probably won't appreciate it until you've used the program a bit. Here's a summary of what's there:

Info	What It Means
Doc 1	With WordPerfect 6.0, you can open as many as nine documents at once. (With version 5.1, you can open two at once.) This info helps keep things straight by telling you which one you're currently working on (Doc 1, Doc 2, etc.).
Pg 1	This is the page number you're on (Pg 1, Pg 2, and so on).

continues

Info	What It Means
Ln 1"	This tells you which line the cursor is on. The position is measured in inches—that's what the double-quote symbol (") means—from the top of the page. It starts at **1"** because you have a one-inch margin at the top of the page.
Pos 1"	This tells you which column the cursor is in. The position is measured in inches from the left edge of the page. Again, it starts at **1"** because there's a one-inch margin on the left side of the page.

Now What?

Okay, you've got this big-bucks word processor loaded, the cursor is blinking away insistently, the large, blank typing area seems to cry out to be filled with happy little characters. What else do you need to know before getting started? Well, in a word, nothing! That's right, just start pecking away on your keyboard, and your brilliance will be displayed for all to see. This is the beauty of WordPerfect (if beauty is the right term): the program gets out of your way so you can get down to the business of writing.

> **SPEAK LIKE A GEEK**
>
> **Margins** are the (usually) empty areas that surround your text on the page. WordPerfect's standard margins are one inch high on the top and bottom edges of the page, and one inch wide on the left and right edges. See Chapter 14, "Formatting Pages and Documents," to learn how to change margin sizes.

Here are a few things to watch for when typing:

- If you're used to typing with a typewriter, you may be tempted to press the Enter key when you approach the end of a line. Fortunately, you don't have to bother, because WordPerfect handles that chore for you. When you've filled up a line, WordPerfect moves the text onto the next line automatically. Even if you're smack in the middle of a word, the program will automatically truck the entire word onto the next line, no questions asked. The only time you need to press **Enter** is when you want to start a new paragraph.

- If you make a mistake, just press the **Backspace** key to wipe it out. (If you don't see any key with the word "Backspace" on it, look for a left-pointing arrow (←) on the right end of the row with all the numbers.)

> **SPEAK LIKE A GEEK**
> The feature that starts a new line automatically is called *word wrap*.

- As you type, some of the stuff on the status line will change. As you move across the screen, the column position (Pos) will increase, and as you move to a new line, the row position (Ln) will increase.

- If you're entering a lot of text, you may be startled to see a line suddenly appear across the screen. No, there's nothing wrong with your screen. It just means that you've moved to a second page, and to show you where one page ends and the next begins, WordPerfect displays a line. As proof that you're on a new page, check out the status line: WordPerfect bumps the page number (Pg) up to **2**, and resets the line position to **1"** (since you're at the top of a new page).

> **SPEAK LIKE A GEEK**
> This page-divider line is called a *page break*.

Checking Out Graphics Mode

One of the truly impressive new features you get with WordPerfect 6 is the ability to work with the program in *graphics mode* (as opposed to the normal *text mode*). This has two major advantages:

- When you format your documents (such as making characters bold or italic, or using different fonts), you can see the changes right on the screen, instead of having to wait for a printout. Here's an example of what I mean.

With WordPerfect's graphics mode, what you see on your screen is what you get when it's printed. This not only saves time when formatting and laying out your documents, but it also saves trees because you don't have to print out every little change to see if it looks right.

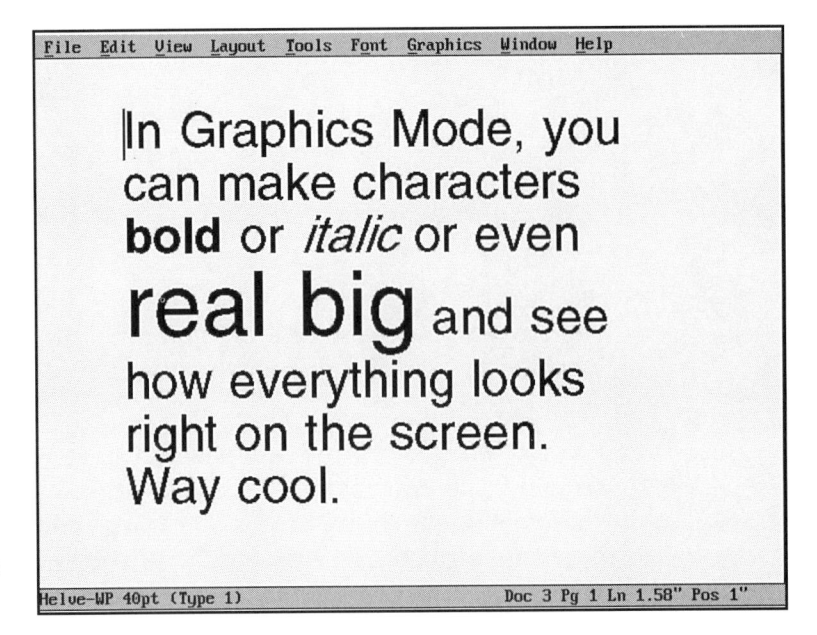

```
┌─────────────────────────────────────────────────┐
│ File  Edit  View  Layout  Tools  Font  Graphics  Window  Help │
│                                                 │
│       In Graphics Mode, you                     │
│       can make characters                       │
│       **bold** or *italic* or even              │
│       real big and see                          │
│       how everything looks                      │
│       right on the screen.                      │
│       Way cool.                                 │
│                                                 │
│ Helve-WP 40pt (Type 1)      Doc 3 Pg 1 Ln 1.58" Pos 1" │
└─────────────────────────────────────────────────┘
```

An example of a WordPerfect screen in graphics mode.

The ability to see on your computer screen what you end up getting from your printer is called **WYSIWYG** (What-You-See-Is-What-You-Get). It's pronounced—what for it—*wizzy wig*. (I swear I'm not making this up.)

- WordPerfect becomes a *graphical user interface*. This fancy term just means that the various WordPerfect elements—the pull-down menus and dialog boxes that you'll be learning about in the next few chapters—appear in cool 3-D formats. This is not only pretty, but it really makes it easier to use the program.

> **By the Way . . .**
> Are there any disadvantages to graphics mode? Well, only one: the program runs a little slower in graphics mode. But, to my mind, the speed penalty is greatly outweighed by the added conveniences.

I'll be using graphics mode for all the screen pictures you'll see in the rest of the book. To make it easier to follow along, you might want to switch to graphics mode yourself. It's easy: just hold down the **Alt** key on your keyboard, and tap the letter **V**. Release **Alt** and press the letter **G**. Your screen will go black for a second or two, and when it returns, you'll be in graphics mode.

> **By the Way . . .**
> When you switch to graphics mode, you won't notice many different elements right off the bat. The menu bar and status line appear in a different color, and the cursor becomes a vertical bar, but that's about it for now. The other differences will appear as we go along.

Getting Help

If you run into a problem with WordPerfect, or if you simply find yourself in a strange part of town, you want to get help fast before panic sets in. Thoughtfully, the WordPerfect programmers have provided you with a handy, on-line Help system. You start this system in one of two ways:

- Press **F1** to get help that is *context-sensitive*. This means the help screen that appears is related to whatever task you're in the middle of.

  > **5.1** In version 5.1, press **F3** to get context-sensitive help.

- Select a command from the Help menu. (You can display the Help menu by holding down **Alt** and pressing **H**. See Chapter 5, "WordPerfect the Easy Way: Using the Pull-Down Menus," for details.)

I won't go into the details of the Help system here. However, if you think you'll be using it regularly, read ahead to Chapter 6, "Talking to WordPerfect's Dialog Boxes," to learn how to navigate the Help system's dialog boxes. (By the way, to close a Help dialog box, just press **Esc**.)

Exiting WordPerfect

I know, I know, you're just starting to have fun, and here I am telling you how to exit the program. Well, you've gotta do it sometime, so you may as well know the drill:

> **By the Way . . .**
>
> These steps just tell you how to exit WordPerfect without saving your work. If you have a document that you want to save for posterity, skip ahead to Chapter 7, "Day-to-Day Drudgery I: Opening and Saving Documents," to learn the gory details.

1. Begin by pressing **Alt+F** (holding down the **Alt** key and pressing **F**, then releasing both). You'll suddenly see a big list of stuff appear on your screen. This is your first look at one of the pull-down menus that I mentioned earlier.

2. Ignore everything you see except the line at the bottom of the list that says Exit WP. There are a number of ways to select this command, but for now, the easiest is simply to press **X**. You'll see a box on your screen titled **Exit WordPerfect**.

> **By the Way . . .**
>
> In many places in this book, you'll see two keys separated by a plus sign, such as **Alt+F** in step 1. The plus sign means "hold down the first key, then press the second key, then release both keys."

3. You have three choices at this point:

   ☞ If you see a little rectangle inside the Exit WordPerfect box that simply says **Exit**, just press **Enter**.

   ☞ If you see a rectangle that says **Save and Exit**, press **M** (this tells the program that you don't want to save your work) and then press **Enter**.

Chapter 3 • Diving In: Your First WordPerfect Session — **27**

- If you change your mind and decide you don't want to exit after all, just press the **Escape** key.

E-Z

An easier way to display the Exit WordPerfect box is to press your keyboard's **Home** key and then press the **F7** key.

5.1

To quit version 5.1, first press **F7**. You'll see the following prompt in the status line:

Save document? No (Yes)

Press **N** to select No. Now you'll see another prompt:

Exit WP? No (Yes)

Press **Y** to select Yes and exit WordPerfect.

The Least You Need to Know

In this chapter, you made the big leap and learned how to start WordPerfect. The rest of the chapter wasn't terribly strenuous (I hope), but here's a quick summary anyway:

- To start WordPerfect, make sure you're in DOS, and then type **WP** and press **Enter**.

- The WordPerfect screen is mostly empty (this is the typing area), but it does include three other elements: the cursor, the menu bar, and the status line.

- To enter text, just start typing. Remember that you don't have to press Enter at the end of each line.

- WordPerfect 6 features an impressive new graphics mode. To switch to it, hold down **Alt**, press **V**, and then press **G**.

continues

continued

☞ To exit WordPerfect, hold down **Alt**, press **F**, and then press **X**. In the **Exit WordPerfect** box that appears, press **Enter** (if you see just the Exit button) or press **M** and **Enter** (if you see the Save and Exit button).

Chapter 4
Keyboard and Mouse Basics

In This Chapter

- A tour around the keyboard
- WordPerfect keyboarding basics
- The mouse made easy
- Musings on the ins and outs of garbage

"Garbage in, garbage out." That's an old expression computer geeks like to use to explain why things go haywire in software programs. Feed computers junk, and you get junk back because the dumb beasts just aren't smart enough to know the difference. In other words, input is everything.

When it comes to using WordPerfect, you have two ways to *input* stuff (that is, put stuff into your computer): the keyboard and the mouse. You don't have to become a keyboard connoisseur or a mouse maven to use WordPerfect, but to avoid the "garbage in" thing, it helps to digest a few basics. This chapter tells you all you need to know.

The Keyboard: A Guided Tour

Keyboards come in all shapes and sizes; like the proverbial snowflakes, it seems no two are alike. They all share a few common features, however, and most are laid out more or less the way you see here.

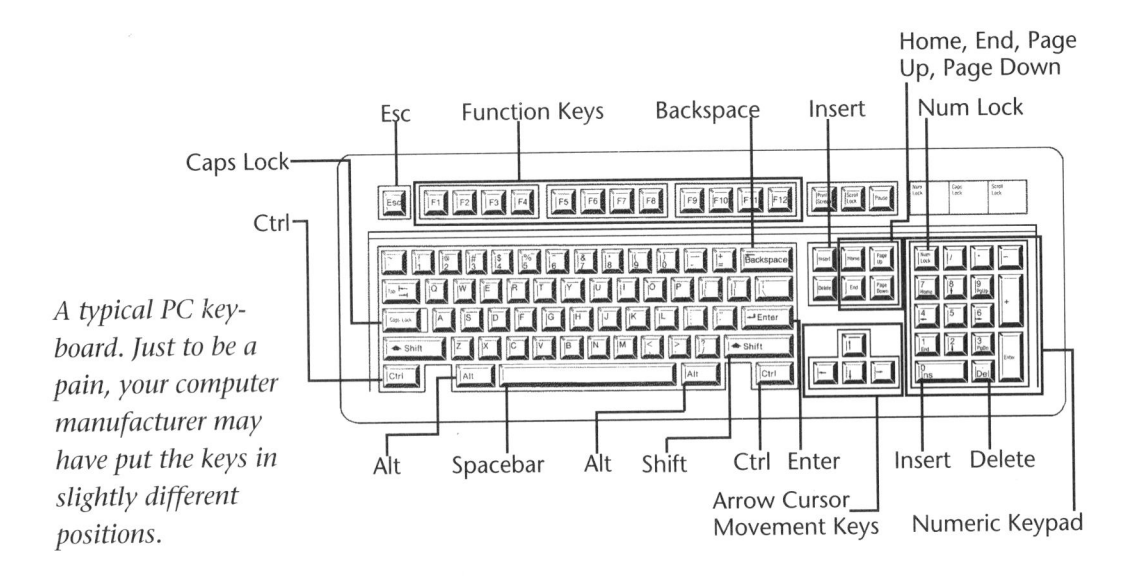

A typical PC keyboard. Just to be a pain, your computer manufacturer may have put the keys in slightly different positions.

Labels: Caps Lock, Ctrl, Esc, Function Keys, Backspace, Insert, Home, End, Page Up, Page Down, Num Lock, Alt, Spacebar, Alt, Shift, Ctrl, Enter, Arrow Cursor Movement Keys, Insert, Delete, Numeric Keypad

Letters, Numbers, and Other Strangers

The bulk of the keyboard is taken up by the basic letters, numbers, punctuation marks, and other special characters that you'll be using most often (and some, like ~ and ^, that you may never use).

> **By the Way . . .**
>
> Typing teachers always suggest limbering up your fingers before getting down to heavy typing. One of the best ways to do this is to type out *pangrams*—sentences that use all 26 letters of the alphabet. The standard pangram that everybody (sort of) knows is *The quick brown fox jumps over the lazy dog.* This is fine, but it's a bit dull. Try some of these on for size:
>
> Pack my box with five dozen liquor jugs.
> The five boxing wizards jump quickly.
> Sexy zebras just prowl and vie for quick, hot matings.
> Judges vomit; few quiz pharynx block.

Shift and Caps Lock

Just like on a typewriter, you use the Shift key to get capital letters. For keys with two symbols (except the ones on the numeric keypad; I'll talk about those later), hold down **Shift** to get the upper symbol. If you want to type nothing but capital letters for a stretch, it's better to press the **Caps Lock** key (similar to a typewriter's Shift Lock key). This only works for letters; to get the other symbols (such as **$** and **+**), you still need to use **Shift**. When you want to switch back to normal letters, just press **Caps Lock** again.

> **SPEAK LIKE A GEEK**
>
> The area of the keyboard that contains the letters, numbers, and punctuation keys is called the *alphanumeric keypad*.

> **By the Way . . .**
>
> When Caps Lock is on, the Caps Lock indicator on your keyboard lights up, and in WordPerfect's status line, Pos changes to **POS**.

Ctrl, Alt, and Those Bizarre WordPerfect Key Combinations

If you press **Ctrl** (it's pronounced "control") or **Alt**, nothing much happens, but that's okay because nothing much is supposed to happen. You don't use these keys by themselves, but as part of *key combinations* (the Shift key often gets into the act as well).

Let's try an example so you can see what I mean. Hold down the **Ctrl** key with one hand, use the other to tap **W** on your keyboard, then release **Ctrl**. Like magic, you'll see a box titled **WordPerfect Characters** appear on your screen. The point of this exercise isn't to do anything with this box (which you can get rid of by pressing the **Esc** key twice; or turn to Chapter 12 to figure out what it does), but to

> **TECHNO NERD TEACHES**
>
> The keyboard shown above is called an Enhanced Keyboard. Most older computers come with lesser keyboards that have only 10 function keys and the cursor-control keys are mixed in with the numeric-keypad keys. While these aren't crucial problems, they can be inconvenient because WordPerfect does use function keys F11 and F12, and separate cursor keys are much easier to use. If you're thinking of buying a new keyboard, though, be careful. Some older machines can't handle the Enhanced Keyboard.

show you that you can get WordPerfect's attention simply by entering certain combinations of keys. Using the **Ctrl** and **W** combo is like saying, "Hey, I wanna see the WordPerfect Characters box on the screen!"

> **By the Way . . .**
>
> WordPerfect has all kinds of these strange-but-useful key combinations, so we need some kind of shorthand for verbose instructions such as "Hold down the **Ctrl** key, tap **W**, and then release **Ctrl**." From now on, instead of this mouthful, I'll just say "Press **Ctrl+W**."
>
> Just to make things confusing, WordPerfect has a second kind of key combination where you press and release one key (say, **Home**) and then press and release another (say, **1**). For these, I'll say something like "Press **Home,1**."

The Esc Key

If you find yourself in some strange WordPerfect neighborhood, and you're not sure what to do next, you can usually get back to Kansas not by clicking your ruby slippers, but by pressing the **Esc** key until things look more familiar. If you're in the Edit screen, however, Esc activates WordPerfect's Undelete feature (see Chapter 9 for the scoop on Undelete).

The Cursor-Control Keys

One of the principal differences between a word processor and a typewriter is that the word processor lets you leap around to any place in the document to fix blunders or just to check things out. You do this with the *cursor-control* keys, which you'll find either on a separate keypad or mixed in among the numeric-keypad keys. You'll be learning all kinds of fun navigation stuff in Chapter 8, but for now, here's a quick summary of some basic cursor-control techniques:

Press	To move the cursor
←	Left one character
→	Right one character
↑	Up one line
↓	Down one line
PageUp	To the top of the previous page
PageDown	To the top of the next page

The Numeric Keypad

On each type of keyboard, the numeric keypad serves two functions. When the Num Lock key is on, you can use the numeric keypad to enter numbers. If Num Lock is off, the keypad cursor keys are enabled, and you can use them to navigate a document. Some keyboards (called *extended keyboards*) have a separate cursor keypad so you can keep Num Lock on all the time.

> **By the Way . . .**
>
> You usually have two ways to tell when Num Lock is on. On your keyboard, look for a light under the Num Lock indicator. In WordPerfect itself, watch Pos in the status line. If Num Lock is on, Pos will either be highlighted (if you have version 6.0 and you're in text mode), or it'll be blinking (in version 5.1).

The Function Keys

The *function keys* are located either to the left of the alphanumeric keypad, or across the top of the keyboard. There are usually 10 function keys (although some keyboards have 12), and they're labeled F1, F2, and so on. In WordPerfect, you use these keys either by themselves or as part of key combinations. For example, the **Home,F7** key combination is a quick way to exit WordPerfect (press just **F7** in version 5.1).

> **OOPS!**
> If you press a key in the numeric keypad and, instead of getting a number, you go racing off to another part of the document, you probably have Num Lock turned off. Just tap the **Num Lock** key to enable the numbers.

A Note About Notebook Keyboards

If you're ever forced to type for an extended period on a notebook or laptop keyboard, then you have my deepest sympathies. These suckers are not only cramped, but they have all the feel of a piece of cement. To make things even worse, there's usually no separate numeric keypad, so the cursor control keys are scattered about willy-nilly. On some notebooks, the cursor keys are hidden among the letters, and you have to hold down a special key (usually labeled "Fn") to get at them. Yuck!

So what's my point? Well, just that you need to be a little more careful when using a notebook keyboard. Fingers that would normally fly (relatively speaking) on a regular keyboard will be bumping into each other in the cramped confines of the notebook layout. One solution that many notebooks offer is the capability of hooking up a separate numeric keypad—or even a full-fledged keyboard. You should check into this; it's definitely worth it.

WordPerfect Keyboarding for Non-Typists

As I've said, getting the most out of WordPerfect doesn't mean you have to become some kind of touch-typing, thousand-words-per-minute keyboard demon. Heck, I've been using computer keyboards for years, and I wouldn't know what touch-typing was if it bit me in the face. In this section, we'll just go through a few things that should make your life at the keyboard easier.

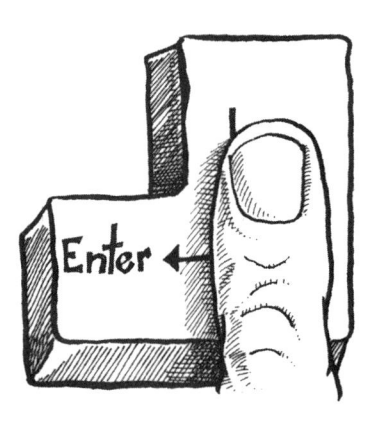

The Enter Key Redux

When you use a typewriter, a little bell goes off as you near the end of each line. This sound warns you to finish off the current word (or to add only a couple of small ones) and then press Return to start a new line. WordPerfect frees you from this old-fashioned drudgery; it starts new lines for you automatically. If you're smack in the middle of a word, this feature will even transport the whole word to the next line. So even though you ex-typewriter types may be sorely tempted to do so, *don't* press Enter as you near the end of a line. Just keep typing—WordPerfect will handle all the hard stuff. (You'll probably find you miss the little bell. Oh, well.)

You can press **Enter** when you need to start a new paragraph. WordPerfect creates a new, blank line, and moves the cursor to the beginning of it.

> **SPEAK LIKE A GEEK**
>
> The feature that starts a new line automatically is called *word wrap*.

You can also use Enter to insert blank lines in your text. Just position the cursor at the beginning of a line, and press **Enter**. The new line appears above the current line.

Quick Fixes: Using Backspace and Delete

You'll be learning all kinds of fancy techniques for editing your documents in Part II. For now, though, you can use the Backspace and Delete keys to get rid of small typos. Just use the **arrow** keys to position the cursor appropriately, and then use these keys as follows:

Backspace—Use this key to delete the character immediately to the left of the cursor.

Delete—Use this key to delete the character immediately above the cursor.

Switching to Typeover Mode

If you position the cursor in the middle of some text, anything you type gets inserted between the existing characters. If you're redoing a few words, you could delete them first and then retype, but usually it's easier to just type over them. To do this, you need to put WordPerfect in *typeover mode* by pressing the **Insert** key. (I know, I know, that doesn't make sense, but bear with me.) You'll see the

> **OOPS!**
>
> The problem with typeover mode is that, one of these days, you'll forget to turn it off, and you'll end up wiping out all kinds of important prose. When this happens, press **Ctrl+Z** to undo the typeover, and then press **insert** to return to Insert mode.

word **Typeover** appear in the bottom left corner of the screen, and when you type now, the new characters replace the existing ones. To resume normal operations, just press **Insert** again.

Key Combination Contortions

WordPerfect has a key combination for just about anything you'd ever want to do with the program, and I'll be letting you in on some of them as we go through this book.

Most people find it faster to use one hand for these key combinations, but I'll warn you now to expect some real contortions. This is especially true for key combos that use either Ctrl or Alt and the function keys. Some of these nasty devils can be quite a stretch for all but the biggest hands. (Although things are made easier by some thoughtful computer companies that put Ctrl and Alt keys on both sides of the spacebar.) My advice? Don't strain yourself unnecessarily. Use two hands if you have to.

Mouse Machinations

Learning how to use a mouse is by no means an essential WordPerfect survival skill. You'll find, however, that it makes many everyday tasks just plain faster and easier. The good news is that using a mouse takes no extraordinary physical skills. If you can use a fork without poking yourself in the eye, then you'll have no trouble wielding a mouse.

The Basic Mouse Technique

A mouse is a marvelous little mechanical miracle that can seem incomprehensible to the uninitiated. The basic idea, though, is simple: you move the mouse on its pad or on your desk, and a small arrow moves correspondingly on the screen. By positioning the arrow on strategic screen areas, you can select text, operate the pull-down menus, and choose all kinds of WordPerfect options. Not bad for a rodent!

SPEAK LIKE A GEEK
The arrow (or block) that moves on your screen when you move the mouse is called the **mouse pointer**.

> **By the Way . . .**
>
> If you're using version 5.1, or if you're not in version 6's graphics mode, you'll see a small block instead of an arrow. If you'd like to try graphics mode, slip back to Chapter 3, "Diving In: Your First WordPerfect Session," to get the details.

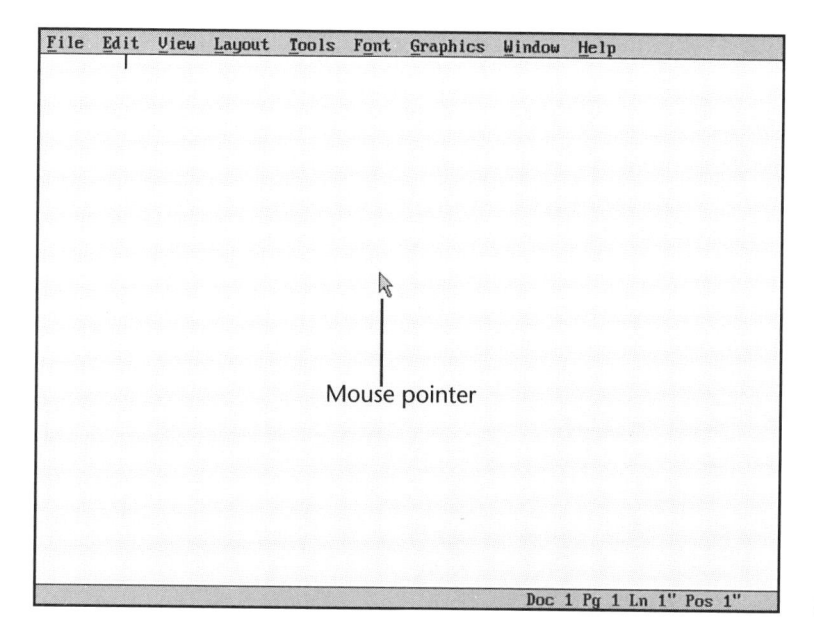

The WordPerfect mouse pointer.

> **By the Way . . .**
>
> If you don't see the mouse pointer on your screen, but you know you have a mouse installed, just wiggle the mouse a bit and the pointer should appear. WordPerfect always hides the pointer whenever you type something.

Using a mouse is straightforward, but it does take some getting used to. Here's the basic technique:

1. Turn the mouse so that its cable extends away from you.
2. Place your hand over the mouse in such a way that:
    - ☞ the part of the mouse nearest you nestles snugly in the palm of your hand;
    - ☞ your index and middle fingers rest lightly on the two mouse buttons (if your mouse has three buttons, rest your fingers on the two outside buttons; leave the middle one alone for now);
    - ☞ your thumb and ring finger hold the mouse gently on either side.
3. Move the mouse around on its pad or on your desk. Notice how the mouse pointer on the screen moves in the same direction as the mouse itself.

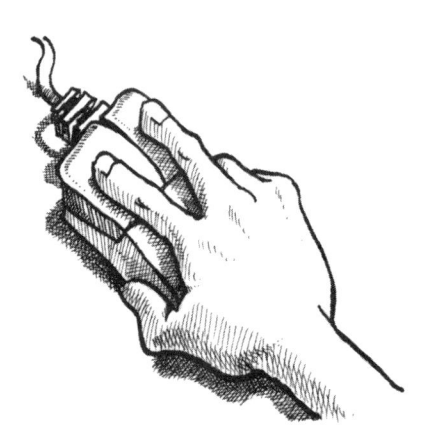

The proper way to hold a mouse.

The Hard Part: Controlling the Darn Thing!

While moving the mouse pointer is simple enough, controlling the pesky little thing is another matter. Most new mouse users complain that the pointer seems to move erratically, or that they move to one part of the screen and run out of room to maneuver. To help out, here are a few tips that will get you well on your way to becoming a mouse expert:

☞ Don't grab the mouse as if you were going to throw it across the room. (On occasion you may be tempted to actually throw it, but try to resist.) A light touch is all that's needed.

☞ The distance the mouse pointer travels on the screen depends on how quickly you move the mouse. If you move the mouse very slowly for about an inch, the pointer moves about the same distance (a little more, actually). However, if you move the mouse very fast for about an inch, the pointer leaps across the screen.

☞ If you find yourself at the edge of the mouse pad but the pointer isn't where you want it to be, simply pick up the mouse and move it to the middle of the pad. This doesn't affect the position of the pointer, but it does allow you to continue on your way.

Mouse Actions

Here's a list of the kinds of actions you can perform with a mouse:

Point—This means that you move the mouse pointer so that it rests on a specific screen location.

Click—This means that you press and release the left mouse button once, quickly.

Double-click—As you might expect, double-clicking means that you quickly press and release the left mouse button twice in succession.

Drag—This has nothing to do with dressing funny. It simply means that you press and hold down the left mouse button, and then move the mouse.

> ### The Least You Need to Know
> This chapter gave you the lowdown on using the keyboard and mouse in WordPerfect. Here are a few highlights:
>
> ☞ Most of your typing time will be spent pecking out letters, numbers, and punctuation in the alphanumeric keypad.
>
> *continues*

continued

- You use the **Ctrl** and **Alt** keys (and sometimes **Shift**) in combination with other keys to access WordPerfect's commands.

- The cursor control keys help you move around in a document. They appear in a separate keypad, or mixed in with the numeric keypad (in which case, you have to turn Num Lock off to get at them).

- Use the numeric keypad to enter numbers into your documents quickly. Make sure **Num Lock** is turned on before using these keys.

- The function keys are the 10 (or sometimes 12) keys labeled F1, F2, and so on. In WordPerfect, you use these either by themselves or combined with other keys to run certain commands.

- A mouse can make WordPerfect easier to use, but it does take some getting used to.

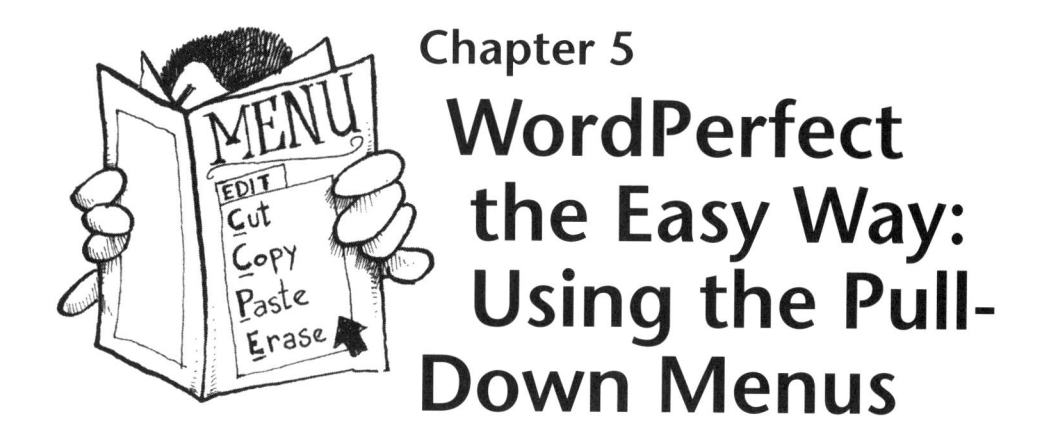

Chapter 5
WordPerfect the Easy Way: Using the Pull-Down Menus

In This Chapter

- What are pull-down menus?
- How to use pull-down menus with the keyboard
- How to use pull-down menus with a mouse
- Rambling ruminations on desks, drawers, and the Dead Sea Scrolls

As I've said before, the WordPerfect philosophy is to get out of your way by presenting you with a clean and uncluttered screen. However, you (or your company) didn't shell out the big bucks just so you could type all day. To get the most out of your WordPerfect investment, you need to use the program's other features.

How do you access those features? Well, if you read the last chapter, then you know that one way is through the use of key combinations. But key combinations, while often quicker, have two major drawbacks:

- You either have to memorize them (shudder) or you have to interpret WordPerfect's arcane templates (a task akin to deciphering the Dead Sea Scrolls).

☞ They can be physically brutal unless you have basketball-player-sized hands.

Fortunately, there's an easier alternative: *pull-down menus*. They group commands in logical chunks, they're a snap to use (you can even use a mouse!), and you still maintain access to every WordPerfect feature. Sound good? Then read on, and I'll show you how they work.

What the Heck Are Pull-Down Menus?

Take a good look at the desk you're sitting at. (If you're not sitting at a desk, picturing one in your head will do.) You've probably got an area where you do your work, surrounded by various tools (pens, pencils, and so on) and things that keep you informed (such as a clock and calendar). Probably you also see a few drawers, from which you get your work and in which you store your desk tools.

The WordPerfect screen is also a lot like a desk. You have the typing area, of course, and you have the status line to keep you informed. And you also have pull-down menus that work, in fact, just like desk drawers. When you need to get more work (i.e., open a document) or access a WordPerfect command, you simply open the appropriate menu and select the menu option that runs the command.

> **SPEAK LIKE A GEEK**
>
> The choices you see in a pull-down menu are called *commands*. You use these commands to tell WordPerfect what you want it to do next.

Why You Pull "Down" Instead of "Up" or "Out"

Why are they called "pull-down" menus? Well, because they're hidden inside the menu bar at the top of the screen. Selecting any one of the nine menu bar options (**File**, **Edit**, **View**, etc.) displays a menu of choices, such as the File menu shown here.

The effect, you'll note, is as though you pulled the menu down from the menu bar. See, sometimes this stuff actually makes sense!

Chapter 5 • *WordPerfect the Easy Way: Using the Pull-Down Menus*   **43**

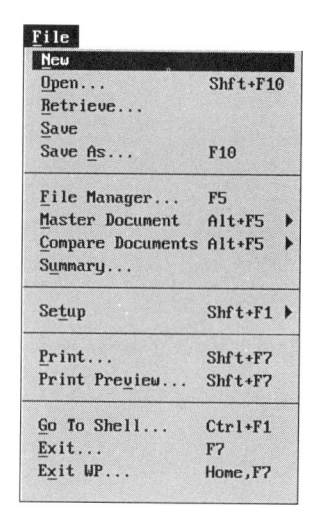

```
┌─────────────────────────────────┐
│ File                            │
│ New                             │
│ Open...              Shft+F10   │
│ Retrieve...                     │
│ Save                            │
│ Save As...           F10        │
│                                 │
│ File Manager...      F5         │
│ Master Document      Alt+F5  ▶  │
│ Compare Documents    Alt+F5  ▶  │
│ Summary...                      │
│                                 │
│ Setup                Shft+F1 ▶  │
│                                 │
│ Print...             Shft+F7    │
│ Print Preview...     Shft+F7    │
│                                 │
│ Go To Shell...       Ctrl+F1    │
│ Exit...              F7         │
│ Exit WP...           Home,F7    │
└─────────────────────────────────┘
```

WordPerfect's File pull-down menu.

How to Use Pull-Down Menus with the Keyboard

The secret to using pull-down menus from the keyboard is to look for the underlined letter in each menu bar option. (If you're not in graphics mode, look for the different colored letter in each option.) For example, look at the "F" in File, the "E" in Edit, and so on. These underlined letters are the menu option's *hot keys*. How do they work? Simple: you just hold down **Alt**, and press the hot key on your keyboard. For example, to pull down the File menu, use the **Alt+F** key combination.

> **5.1**
>
> To pull down a menu in version 5.1, first display the menu bar by pressing **Alt+=**. You'll see the File option highlighted. Then either press the highlighted letter of the menu, or use the **left** and **right arrow** keys to highlight the option you want, and then press **Enter**.

Once you have a menu displayed, you need to select one of the commands. This is simple enough. You just use the **up** and **down arrow** keys to highlight the command you want, and then press **Enter**.

> **OOPS!**
>
> While you're getting the hang of all this, occasionally you may find that you pull down a menu and discover you don't want to select any of its commands. Don't panic. You can remove the menu by simply pressing **Esc** twice (yes, it has to be twice). If you find that you've pulled down the wrong menu, just use the **left** or **right arrow** keys to cycle through the other menus.

> **5.1**
>
> If you have version 5.1, and you don't see the menu bar on your screen, just click the right mouse button to display it.

> **OOPS!**
>
> What do you do if you pull down a menu and discover you don't want to select a command? No problem. You can remove the menu by either clicking on any empty part of the screen, or by just pulling down a different menu.

Depending on which one you select, one of three things will happen:

- The command will execute.
- Another menu will appear. In this case, use the **arrow** keys to select the command you want from the new menu, and then press **Enter**.
- A dialog box will appear, asking you for more information. See Chapter 6, "Talking to WordPerfect's Dialog Boxes," for details on using dialog boxes.

How to Use Pull-Down Menus with a Mouse

If you have a mouse, using pull-down menus is a breeze. All you do is move the mouse pointer into the menu bar area, and then click on the name of the menu you want to pull down. For example, clicking on File in the menu bar pulls down the File menu.

Once you have your menu displayed, you then simply click on the command you want to execute. As I explained in the keyboard section, one of three things will happen, depending on the option you select:

- The command will execute.
- Another menu will appear. In this case, just click on the command you want to execute from the new menu.
- A dialog box will appear, to get further info from you.

More Fun Pull-Down Menu Stuff

If you've been pulling down some menus, you may have noticed a few strange things. For example, did you notice that some commands have a triangle on the right-hand side of the menu? Or that some are followed by three ominous-looking dots? Or that others also list a key (or key combination)? These are just a few of the normal features found in all pull-down menus, and you can take advantage of them to make your life easier. The rest of this section summarizes these features. I'll be using the File menu (shown here) as an example, so you might want to pull it down now to follow along.

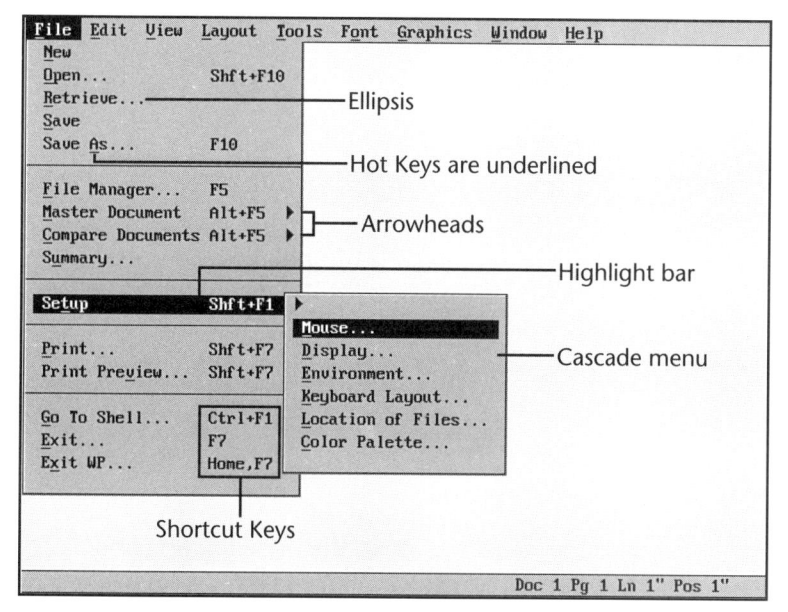

WordPerfect pull-down menu features.

Underlined Characters: More Hot Keys

Every command in a version 6 pull-down menu has one underlined character (or a character that appears in a different color, if you're not in graphics mode). This is the command's hot key; it means that when the menu is displayed, you can select that option by simply pressing the underlined letter on your keyboard. For example, in the File menu, you could select, say, the Exit WP command simply by pressing X.

Shortcut Keys: The Fast Way to Work

Some menu commands also show a key or key combination on the right-hand side of the menu. These are called *shortcut keys*; they allow you to bypass the menus altogether, and activate a command quickly from your keyboard. For example, you can select the File menu's **Open** command simply by pressing **Shift+F10**. (If you try this, press **Esc** twice to remove the box that appears. To learn about opening WordPerfect files, see Chapter 7, "Day-to-Day Drudgery I: Opening and Saving Documents.")

> **SPEAK LIKE A GEEK**
>
> When a command displays another menu, the new menu is called a *cascade* menu.

Once you've worked with WordPerfect for a while, you may find it faster to use these shortcut keys for some of the commands you use most often.

Arrowheads (Menus, Menus, and More Menus)

With some commands, you'll see an arrowhead [▶] on the right side of the menu. This tells you that yet another menu will appear when you select this command. For example, select the Setup command from the File menu to see a menu of setup commands. (Press **Esc** to remove the new menu.)

The Ellipsis (the Three-Dot Thing)

An *ellipsis* (...) after a command name indicates that a dialog box will appear when you select the option. WordPerfect uses dialog boxes to ask you for more information, or to confirm a command you requested. For example, if you select the File menu's **Open** command, a dialog box appears to ask you for the name of the file you want to open. (Press **Esc** twice to remove this dialog box.) See Chapter 6, "Talking to WordPerfect's Dialog Boxes," for more dialog box details.

The Least You Need to Know

This chapter explained WordPerfect's pull-down menus, and showed you how to use them with both a mouse and keyboard. Here's a summary of what you now know:

- Pull-down menus are a lot like desk drawers, because they "store" tools (commands) that you use with WordPerfect.

- To pull down a menu with the keyboard, look for the menu's hot key and then, while holding down **Alt**, press the key on your keyboard.

- To pull down a menu with the mouse, simply click on the menu name in the menu bar.

- Once a pull-down menu is displayed, you can select a command by using your keyboard's **up** and **down arrow** keys to highlight the command, and then pressing **Enter**. If you have a mouse, just click on the command you want.

Chapter 6
Talking to WordPerfect's Dialog Boxes

In This Chapter

- What is a dialog box?
- Getting around in dialog boxes
- Learning about dialog box buttons, boxes, and lists
- Odd dialog box details that you might never have thought to ask about

As you work with WordPerfect, little boxes will appear incessantly on your screen to prompt you for more information (and generally just confuse the heck out of things). These are called *dialog boxes*, and they're WordPerfect's way of saying "Talk to me!" This chapter looks at these chatty little beasts, and offers some helpful tips for surviving their relentless onslaught.

A Note to Users of Version 5.1

If you're using WordPerfect 5.1, the good news is that you don't have to learn about dialog boxes—because there aren't any! (They were introduced in version 6.) The bad news is that you have something even worse: menus. Menus are sort of like dialog boxes (they're boxes that ask you for more information), but they're pretty stark and unappealing (and they lack the cool 3-D effects you get in version 6's graphics mode). However, you need to know how to use them to get through the program, so here's a quick course:

Menu choices will appear in one of two forms. The first is a simple list of options, like so:

Print
1 - **Full Document**
2 - **Page**
3 - **Document on Disk**
4 - **Control Printer**
5 - **Multiple Pages**

To select the option you want, just press the number (or, in some cases, letter) listed on the left. In this example, you'd press, say, **1** to select the **Full Document** option. If you use a mouse, you can just click on the option you'd like.

The second kind of menu displays a bunch of information, and then lists your options at the bottom of the menu, like this:

1 Move; 2 Copy; 3 Delete; 4 Append

Again, to select one of these choices, just press the appropriate number or click on the option with your mouse.

In simpler situations, WordPerfect doesn't display a menu at all. Instead, you'll see a prompt on the status line that will either look something like this

Exit WP? No (Yes)

or like this

Document to be saved:

In the first case, you answer the question by pressing **Y** (for Yes) or **N** (for No), or by clicking on the appropriate answer. In the second case, WordPerfect wants you to type something (such as the name of a document). Type your response and then press **Enter**.

Where Do They Come From?

Dialog boxes may sometimes seem to appear out of nowhere, but they generally show up after you select certain options from WordPerfect's pull-down menus or press certain key combinations. Whether or not a dialog box appears depends on whether or not the program needs more information from you. For example, if you select the File menu's Open command, WordPerfect displays the Open Document dialog box (shown here) to ask you the name of the document you want to open.

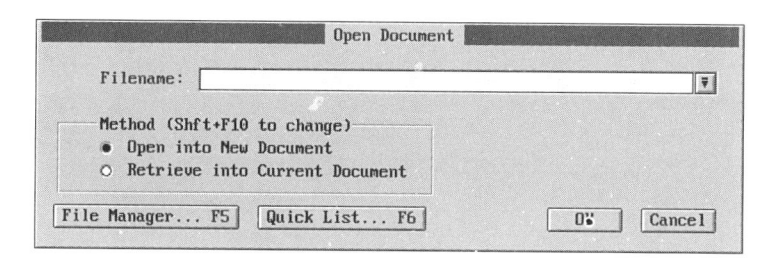

If you select the Open command, WordPerfect asks you for the name of the file you want to open.

> **By the Way . . .**
> You can always tell when a command will generate a dialog box by looking for three dots (...) after the command name. These three dots (they're known as an *ellipsis*) tell you that some kind of dialog box will appear if you select the option. This gives you time to prepare yourself mentally for the ordeal to come.

Dialog Box Basics

Before we can talk any more about dialog boxes, we need to get a specimen on the screen. If you pull down the File menu and select the Print command, you'll see the Print dialog box shown here. This one should serve us nicely (don't worry, you won't actually have to print anything).

Before getting started, here are a few points about dialog boxes to keep in mind:

☞ Dialog boxes always have a title at the top of the box. This lets you know if you selected the right command.

☞ Dialog boxes like to monopolize your attention. When one is on the screen, you can't do other things such as enter text in the typing area or select a pull-down menu. Deal with the dialog first, then you can do other things.

☞ The various objects you see inside a dialog box are called *controls* because you use them to control the way the dialog box works.

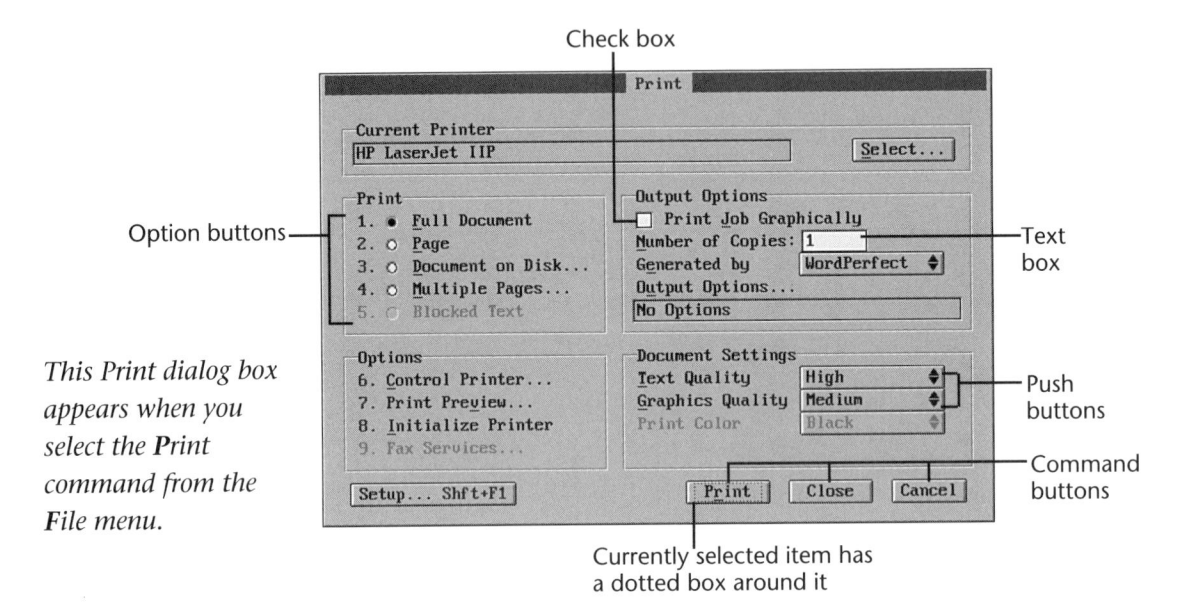

*This Print dialog box appears when you select the **P**rint command from the **F**ile menu.*

Navigating Controls

Before you learn how these controls operate, you need to be able to move among them. (This section applies only to keyboard users. Mouse users select a control merely by clicking on it.)

The first thing you need to be able to figure out is which control is currently selected. (This can be easy or hard depending on how many controls the dialog box has.) You need to look for the control that has its name surrounded by a dotted outline (or, in text mode, look for the control that is highlighted). Think of this as a "You are here" sign on a map. When you first display the Print dialog box, for example, the **P**rint button at the bottom of the box has the dotted outline, so it's currently selected.

Once you know where you are, you can move around by pressing **Tab** (to move, more or less, left to right and top to bottom through the controls) or **Shift+Tab** (to move right to left or bottom to top). Go ahead and try some experiments in the Print dialog box. Each time you press Tab (or Shift+Tab), make sure you can find the selected control before moving on.

> **E-Z**
> If you see a number or letter beside a control, then you can select it simply by pressing the letter or number on your keyboard. For example, in the Print dialog box you'd select the **Page** control by just pressing **2**.

Most WordPerfect dialog boxes organize related controls into groups and surround them with a box. The Print dialog box, for example, has five such groups (Current Printer, Print, Output Options, Options, and Document Settings). When you're inside one of these groups, you can usually select another control in the group simply by pressing the underlined letter in the control. For example, if you're in the Output Options group, you could select the Number of Copies control by pressing **N**.

Working with Radio Buttons

Radio buttons are WordPerfect's equivalent of the old multiple-choice questions you had to struggle with in school. You're given two or more choices, and you're only allowed to pick one. In the Print dialog box, the Print group contains five radio buttons.

> **By the Way . . .**
> Why are they called *radio buttons*? Well, they're named for those old car radios where you had to push a button to select a station; this would release the currently selected station. The radio buttons in our dialog box work the same way.

As you can see, a radio button consists of a small circle with a label beside it that tells you what the option is. Remember that the purpose of a dialog box is to get more information from you. When you selected the **Print** command from the **File** menu earlier, you told WordPerfect that you wanted to print something. These radio buttons are WordPerfect's way of asking "What, exactly, do you want to print?" Your mission (should you decide to accept it) would be to activate one of these options and then move on.

> **By the Way . . .**
> Don't worry too much about what the various options mean. I'll explain all in Chapter 16, "Getting It Down on Paper: Printing Documents."

How do you activate a radio button? From the keyboard, you need to press **Tab** until the radio button you want is selected (its name is surrounded by a dotted outline) and then press either the **Spacebar** or **Enter**. Notice how a black dot appears inside the circle when you activate one of the buttons.

> **OOPS!**
> If your mouse or keyboard skills aren't quite up to snuff yet, you may select the wrong radio button. No problemo. Just select the correct one, and WordPerfect will deactivate the incorrect one automatically.

If you have a mouse, simply click on the option you want (you can either click on the button itself or on the name).

Working with Check Boxes

The real world is constantly presenting us with a series of either/or choices. You're either watching Oprah or you're not; you're either eating Heavenly Hash or you're not. That kind of thing. WordPerfect handles these sorts of yes-or-no, on-or-off decisions with a control called a *check box*. The check box presents you with an option that you can either activate (check) or not.

In the Print dialog box, for example, the Print Job Graphically control is a check box. This control is on when an "X" appears in the square and it's off when the square is empty. (Call me crazy, but wouldn't it make more sense if an activated check box actually had a check mark in it instead of an X? Just thought I'd ask.)

To activate a check box from the keyboard, press **Tab** until the check box you want is selected and then press the **Spacebar**. To deactivate the check box, press the **Spacebar** again.

To activate a check box with a mouse, click on the box or on its name. To deactivate the box (remove the "X"), just click on the box again.

Working with Text Boxes

A *text box* is a screen area you use to type in text information such as a description or a file name. When you select one, you'll either see a blinking, horizontal cursor inside the box (if it's empty) or highlighted text (if it's not). The Print dialog box has a single text box: the Number of Copies control.

To use a text box from your keyboard, press **Tab** until you see either the cursor in the box or until you see the text in the box highlighted, and then begin typing. To use a text box with a mouse, click anywhere inside the box and then type in your text.

> **By the Way . . .**
> When the text in a text box is highlighted, it means that it'll get replaced by whatever you type. If you don't want to replace the entire text, just press either the **left** or **right arrow** key to remove the highlight, and then position the cursor appropriately.

Working with Command Buttons

The Print dialog box also includes a number of controls called *command buttons* (for example,

> **OOPS!**
> If you make a typing mistake, press the **Backspace** key until the offending letters are deleted.

there are four along the bottom: Setup, Print, Close and Cancel). When you select a command button, you're telling WordPerfect to execute the command written on the face of the button.

To select a command button from the keyboard, press **Tab** until the command button you want is selected and then press **Enter**. To select a command button with a mouse, you just click on the button.

> ### By the Way . . .
> WordPerfect uses command buttons for all kinds of things, but two are particularly common: OK and Cancel. You use the **OK** button (the Print dialog box doesn't have one) when you've finished with the dialog box and you want to put all your selections into effect. This is the "Make it so" button. Use the **Cancel** button when you panic and realize that you're looking at the wrong dialog box or if you've made a mess of your selections. This is the "Delay that last order" button.

Working with Pop-Up Lists

Pop-up lists are controls that let you select from a list of choices. The button face always shows the current selection. In the Print dialog box, each of the controls in the Document Settings group is a pop-up list.

To work with a pop-up list from the keyboard, use **Tab** to select the button name and then press **Enter** to display the list of available choices (the current selection has a star beside it). Use the **up** and **down arrow** keys to highlight the choice you want and then press **Enter**.

With a mouse, place the pointer over the appropriate pop-up list and then press and hold down the left mouse button. In the list that appears, keep the mouse button pressed and move the mouse up and down until the selection you want is highlighted, then release the button.

Chapter 6 • Talking to WordPerfect's Dialog Boxes **57**

Working with Drop-Down Lists

At this point, the Print dialog box has outlived its usefulness. Select the **Cancel** button to remove it from the screen, then select the Font command from the Font pull-down menu. This displays (surprise, surprise) the Font dialog box, which I'll use to explain what drop-down lists are.

A *drop-down list* is like a combination of a text box and a pull-down menu. You can type in the option you want or you can select it from a list that drops down (hence the name) when you select it. Drop-down list boxes usually contain lists of related items such as font names or document files. The Font dialog box has two drop-down list boxes: **Font** and **Size**. Here's what things look like when the Font list is dropped down.

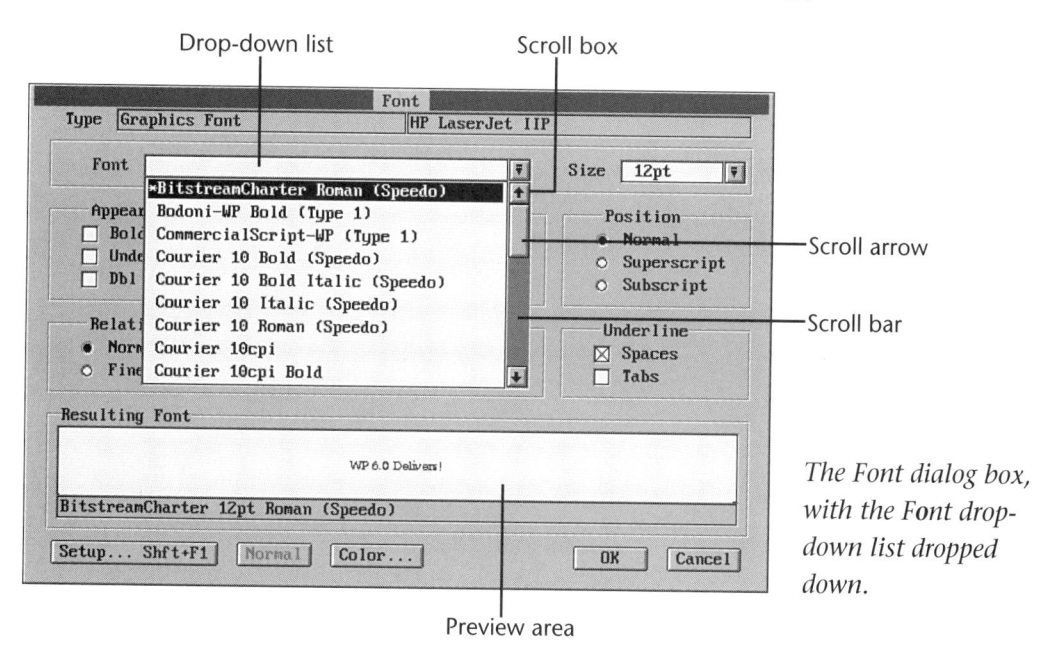

The Font dialog box, with the Font drop-down list dropped down.

Selecting Stuff From Drop-Down List Boxes

To use your keyboard to select an item from a drop-down list, follow these steps:

1. Press **Tab** until the name of the drop-down list is selected.
2. Press **Enter** to open the list.

3. Type in your selection or use the **up** and **down arrow** keys to highlight the item you want.

4. Press **Enter**.

To use a mouse to select an item from a drop-down list, follow these steps:

1. Click on the downward-pointing arrow on the right side of the control. This opens the list to display its options.

2. Click on the item you want. If you don't see the item you want, use the scroll bar to view more of the list. (If you're not sure how a scroll bar works, see the next section.)

A Brief Scroll Bar Primer

You'll be learning more about scroll bars in Chapter 8, but I'll give you a brief introduction here so you'll be able to use the drop-down lists.

Some lists contain too many items to fit inside the box. In this case, a scroll bar appears on the right hand side of the box to make it easier to navigate the list. The box inside the scroll bar (called, appropriately enough, the *scroll box*) tells you where you are in the list. For example, if the scroll box is halfway between the top and the bottom of the scroll bar, then you're approximately halfway down the list.

To navigate a list with the scroll bar, use the following mouse techniques:

> Here's a neato tip that can save you oodles of time. Once the drop-down list is open, press the first letter of the item you want. WordPerfect leaps down the list and highlights the first item in the list that begins with the letter you pressed. If you keep typing, WordPerfect tries to find any item that matches the letters you've entered.

- To scroll through the list one item at a time, click on either of the arrows at the top and bottom of the scroll bar.

- To jump quickly through the list, click inside the scroll bar between the scroll box and the top (to move up) or between the scroll box and the bottom (to move down).

- To move to a specific part of the list, drag the scroll box up or down.

Dialog Box Commands

Many dialog boxes also include simple commands that work much like the commands in a pull-down menu. In the Print dialog box, for example, each of the items in the Options group (Control Printer, Print Preview, Initialize Printer, and Fax Services) is a command.

To select a command with your keyboard, press **Tab** until the command is selected and then press **Enter**. With a mouse, just click on the command.

> ### The Least You Need to Know
>
> This chapter showed you the ins and outs of using dialog boxes to communicate with WordPerfect. We covered a lot of ground and you learned all kinds of new things. If it's not all clear in your head right now, don't worry about it because, believe me, you'll be getting plenty of practice. In the meantime, here's some important stuff to remember:
>
> - WordPerfect uses dialog boxes to ask you for more information or to confirm that the command you've selected is what you really want to do.
>
> - Keyboard jockeys use the **Tab** key (or **Shift+Tab**) to move through the dialog box controls.
>
> - Some controls display a number or letter to the left. You can select these controls simply by pressing the number or letter on your keyboard.
>
> - Many controls have underlined letters. When you're in a group, you can select these controls by pressing the letter on your keyboard.

Chapter 7
Day-to-Day Drudgery I: Saving, Opening, and Closing

In This Chapter

- Saving a document
- Saving a document under a different name
- Opening and retrieving a document
- Closing a document
- Cat waxing and other handy skills

WordPerfect, especially version 6, is jam-packed with powerful features that let you do everything but wax the cat. But even with all that power at your fingertips, you still need to take care of mundane drudgery such as opening and saving documents (the subject of this chapter) and navigating your way through large files (which I'll save for Chapter 8).

Save Your Work, Save Your Life

Most people learn about saving documents the hard way. For me, it was a power failure that wiped out an entire day's writing. Believe me, that kind of thing can make you old before your time.

Why is saving necessary? Well, when you open a document, WordPerfect copies it from its safe haven on your hard disk to the volatile confines of your computer's memory. When you shut off your computer (or if a power failure forces it off), everything in memory is wiped out. If you haven't saved your document to your hard disk, you'll lose all the changes you made.

Saving an Existing Document

Fortunately, WordPerfect makes saving your work as easy as shooting fish in a barrel. In fact, I can tell you the whole thing in a single sentence: To save the document you're working on, pull down the File menu and select the **S**ave command. That's it!

> **E-Z**
> To make saving even easier, there's a handy shortcut key you can use: **Ctrl+F12**.

What's Wrong with This Picture?

Saving your work is vital, but few people do it often enough. How often is "often enough"? Here's a quiz you can take to see if you know:

You should save your work if:

(a) You have a delay while you think of what to say next (a common occurrence for many of us).

(b) You've just entered a long passage.

(c) You've just formatted a large section of text.

(d) You've just rearranged a bunch of stuff.

(e) You've just retrieved another document into the current one.

(f) All of the above.

The answer, of course, is (f), All of the above. Saving is so easy that you really should do it as often as you can. Use (a) through (e) as a guideline when deciding if it's time to save.

> **5.1**
> Version 5.1 isn't quite so simple. After selecting the **S**ave command, you'll see the following prompt:
>
> **Document to be saved:**
>
> The name of the file will appear as well. Press **Enter**—and WordPerfect, as though it didn't believe you, now prompts you with this:
>
> **Replace filename? No (Yes)**
>
> Press **Y** to select Yes.

Chapter 7 • Day-to-Day Drudgery 1: Saving, Opening, and Closing   63

Saving a New Document

Well, actually, there's a little more to this saving business than I've let on. If you're saving a new document, WordPerfect will need to know the name you want to use, so you'll see the Save Document dialog box shown here.

Type a name in the **Filename** text box (before you do, however, you should read the "Techno Nerd Teaches" note about filenames) and then select the **OK** button.

If you give the document the name of a file that already exists, WordPerfect will warn you, and ask if you want to replace the existing file. Replacing the file will mean it's gone for good—and no amount of hocus-pocus will get it back. So, unless you're sure you won't ever need the other file, select **No** and try again.

TECHNO NERD TEACHES

Many new WordPerfect users (and some of us old-timers) wonder why, if we're working with documents all day, we have to deal with a "File" menu instead of a "Document" menu? Well, I suppose the only answer is tradition: 99.9% of all pull-down menus ever created have a File menu, and the WordPerfect programmers didn't want to buck the trend. And besides, documents are files (although document sounds more impressive). You'll be learning more about what files are in Chapter 18, "Using the File Manager."

When you save a new document, WordPerfect displays the Save Document dialog box so you can name the file.

Sacred Filename Commandments

Filenames usually contain a period flanked by a *primary name* on the left and an *extension* on the right. When naming your documents, make sure you observe the sacred Filename Commandments handed down by the great DOS Nerd Gods:

5.1

When you save a new file in 5.1, you'll see this prompt:

Document to be saved:

Just type in a name and press **Enter**.

I   Thou shalt not use more than eight characters for the file's primary name.

II Thou shalt not use more than three characters for the file's extension.

III Thou shalt separate the primary name and the extension with a period.

IV Thou shalt not use a space or any of the other forbidden characters:
    + = \ | [ ] ; : , . < > ? /

V   Thou shalt not take the name of an existing file.

What's Wrong with This Picture?

Here's a list of filenames, some of which violate the sacred Filename Commandments. Take a look through the list—write down which commandment the name blasphemes (if any), and the reason.

1. COWABUNGA.TXT

    Commandment violated:

    Reason:

2. WHATTHE.HECK

    Commandment violated:

    Reason:

3. NO_FRUIT.SIR

    Commandment violated:

    Reason:

4. IS THIS.OK?

    Commandment violated:

    Reason:

5. THISISIT

    Commandment violated:

    Reason:

6. DUH,SAID.HE

    Commandment violated:

    Reason:

OOPS!

If you do enter an illegal name, WordPerfect will display a dialog box that says "Invalid drive/path specification." Don't let the techspeak faze you. Just select **OK** and try again.

Answers:

1. Incorrect: This name violates Commandment I because the primary name is nine characters long.

2. Incorrect: Commandment II is violated because this name uses a four-character extension.

3. Correct: The underscore character (_) is legal, and it's useful for making filenames more legible.

Chapter 7 • Day-to-Day Drudgery 1: Saving, Opening, and Closing **65**

4. Incorrect: This name actually has two mistakes. The space in the primary name and the question mark in the extension both violate Commandment IV.

5. Correct: The extension is optional. (Notice that when there's no extension, you don't need the period.)

6. Incorrect: The comma in the primary name violates Commandment IV. The two-character extension is okay, though.

By the Way . . .

Even though extensions are optional, most people use them anyway because they're handy for identifying what type of file you're dealing with. For your WordPerfect documents, for example, use something like **WP** or **DOC**.

5.1

You exit version 5.1 by selecting **Exit** from the **File** menu. WordPerfect then asks if you want to save the current document:

Save Document

If you don't want to save it, press **N**; otherwise, press **Y**. If you're saving a new document, you'll be prompted for a filename. Enter the name and press **Enter**. Another prompt will appear (this is the last one, I promise), asking you if you want to exit WordPerfect. Select **Yes**.

Saving a Document When You Exit WordPerfect

To exit WordPerfect, you'll recall, you select the Exit WP command from the File menu. To let you save the current file, if necessary, the Exit WordPerfect dialog box (shown below) appears.

When you exit WordPerfect, the program gives you an opportunity to save your work.

> To select the Save As command quickly, press **F10**.

> Version 5.1 has no Save As command. To save the current document under a different name, select **S**ave from the **F**ile menu. Then, when WordPerfect prompts you for the name of the document to be saved, delete the displayed name (using the **Backspace** key), enter the new name, and then press **Enter**.

Here are your options:

- If you've saved the document before, its name will appear in the Filename text box. Select the **Save and Exit** button to save the document and exit.
- If the document is new, enter a filename in the **Filename** text box, and then select the **Save and Exit** button.
- If you don't want to save your changes, turn off the **Save** check box and then select the **Exit** button.

Saving a Document Under a New Name

The File menu also includes a Save As command. This command is a lot like **S**ave, except that you can save the file to a new name or a new location. This is useful for creating a new file that is very similar (but not identical) to an existing file. Instead of creating the new file from scratch, just open the existing file, make the changes, and then use the Save As command to save your changes to the new file. The old file remains as it was.

Getting Documents: Opening Versus Retrieving

Each time you start WordPerfect, you see a blank *typing area* waiting patiently for you to type something. Most of the time, though, you'll want to work with an existing document you've saved

Chapter 7 • Day-to-Day Drudgery 1: Saving, Opening, and Closing   **67**

sometime in the past. WordPerfect gives you two ways to do this: you can *open* a document or you can *retrieve* one. Here's a summary of the difference:

- When you open a document, WordPerfect sets up a fresh typing area, displays the document, and positions the cursor at the beginning of the file.

- When you retrieve a document, WordPerfect adds it to the current file at the cursor position. This is a handy way of reusing material in another document.

SPEAK LIKE A GEEK

Text that you reuse over and over is called *boilerplate*. It's the word processing equivalent of the old maxim, "Don't reinvent the wheel."

E-Z

To display the Open Document dialog box quickly, press **Shift+F10**.

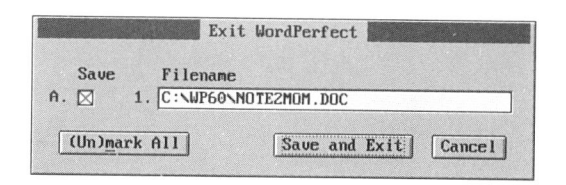

Selecting the Open command from the File menu displays the Open Document dialog box.

How to Open a Document

To open a document pull down the File menu and select the Open command. You'll see the Open Document dialog box shown here.

If you know the name of the document, enter it in the **Filename** text box and then select **OK**. For reference, WordPerfect displays the name of the file in the status line.

OOPS!

If you enter a filename that WordPerfect can't find, it'll display a message telling you so. Select **OK** to return to the **Open Document** dialog box and try again.

> You can go to the Specify File Manager List dialog box quickly by pressing **F5**.

> **5.1**
> To open a file in version 5.1, first close the current file (as described later in this chapter). Then select **R**etrieve from the **F**ile menu, and you'll see the following prompt in the status line:
>
> **Document to be retrieved:**
>
> Enter the name of the document, and press **Enter**.

> Once you have either the Open Document or Retrieve Document dialog box open, you can toggle between them by pressing **Shift+F10**.

> **By the Way . . .**
> Did you know that you can tell WordPerfect to display a document automatically when you start the program? Sure! All you do is add a space after the **WP** and then type the name of the document. For example, to open a document called STARTME.DOC, you'd enter the following:
>
> **WP STARTME.DOC**
>
> Press **Enter** and, a few seconds later, WordPerfect loads and displays the file.

If you're not sure about the name, you can tell WordPerfect to display a list of files by following these steps:

1. In the **Open Document** dialog box, select the **File Manager** button. You'll see another dialog box called Specify File Manager List.

2. WordPerfect is asking you to specify which directory you want displayed. If you have no idea what a directory is, just select **OK** (I'll be giving you the lowdown on weird DOS things like directories in Chapter 18). If you're familiar with directories, make whatever changes are necessary in the **Directory** text box, and then select **OK**. The File Manager appears on the screen.

3. Yikes! Pretty scary-looking, huh? Luckily, you can safely ignore most of the gobbledygook you see. Just use the **up** and **down arrow** keys to highlight the file you want to open, and then press **Enter** or click on the Open into New Document command.

How to Retrieve a File

When you want to retrieve a file, first position the cursor at the point where you want the new text to appear. Then select the **Retrieve** command from the File menu to display the Retrieve Document dialog. Enter the name of the document in the **Filename** text box, or use the File Manager as described in the previous section.

A Fresh Beginning: Starting a New Document

As I mentioned earlier, WordPerfect displays a new document when you first start the program. However, you can start a fresh file anytime you want. All you do is pull down the File menu and select the New command.

Closing a Document

When you're done with a document, you should close it to make room for other files. All you do is pull down the File menu and select the Close command.

5.1

To retrieve a file in version 5.1, first position the cursor appropriately and then select **Retrieve** from the **File** menu. When prompted for a document, enter the name and press **Enter**.

5.1

To start a new document in 5.1, just close the current document (as described later in the next section).

5.1

In 5.1, you close a document by selecting **Exit** from the **File** menu. When prompted to save the document, select **Yes**, and then press **Enter** when WordPerfect displays the filename. (Unless, of course, you want to save the file under a different name. In this case, just change the displayed name, and then press **Enter**.) WordPerfect asks if you want to replace the file. Select **Yes**. WordPerfect, ever relentless with the questions, now asks if you want to exit the program. Select **No**.

The Least You Need to Know

Now that was a chapter! WordPerfect sure seems to like complicating simple tasks such as saving and opening documents. Here's a summary of what you need to know:

- ☞ You should save your documents as often as you can to avoid losing any work. All you have to do is select the **S**ave command from the **F**ile menu.

- ☞ When saving a new document, WordPerfect will ask you to enter a name for the file. Be sure to follow DOS's arcane file-naming rules or you'll get an error.

- ☞ If you want to save a document under a different name, use the **F**ile menu's Save **A**s command.

- ☞ To open a document, select **O**pen from the **F**ile menu, and enter the name of the file in the **Open Document** dialog box.

- ☞ To retrieve a file, select **R**etrieve from the **F**ile menu.

- ☞ To close a document, use the **F**ile menu's **C**lose command.

Chapter 8
Day-to-Day Drudgery II: Navigating Documents

In This Chapter

- Navigating a document with the keyboard
- Using WordPerfect's Go to command
- Navigating a document with a mouse
- Using scroll bars
- Tales of a thousand-and-one key combos

A lot of what you do in WordPerfect will be short little letters and memos that'll fit right on screen. But you'll also be creating longer documents, and what you see in the typing area will only be a small chunk of the entire file. To see the rest of the document, you'll need to learn a few *navigational* skills. Now, I'm not talking about navigating the Baja 500 or anything, but just a few simple skills to help you get around. With this chapter riding shotgun, you'll get through just fine.

> **By the Way . . .**
> To get the most out of this chapter, you should follow along and try each of the techniques as I present them. For best results, open (or create) a document that's larger than the screen.

Navigating with the Keyboard

WordPerfect has a fistful of ways to navigate your documents from the keyboard. In this section, we'll work our way up from short hops between characters and words to great leaps between screens and pages.

Navigating Characters and Words

The simplest move you can make in a document is to use the **left** and **right arrow** keys to move left or right one character at a time. If you've got a bit of ground to cover, try holding down the key. After a slight delay, the cursor will start racing through each line. (Notice that when it hits the end of one line, it starts over at the beginning of the next.)

If you need to jump over a couple of words, hold down the **Ctrl** key and then use the **left** or **right arrow** keys to move one word at a time.

Navigating Lines and Paragraphs

If you need to move up or down one line at a time, use the **up** or **down arrow** key. If you're at the bottom of the screen and you press the down arrow, the text will move up so you can see the next line. (The line that used to be at the top of the screen heads off into oblivion, but don't worry: WordPerfect keeps track of everything). A similar thing happens if you're at the top of the screen (unless you're at the top of the document): if you press the up arrow, the text moves down to make room for the next line.

TECHNO NERD TEACHES

When you hold down an arrow key, the speed at which the cursor moves is governed by two factors: the *delay* after the first movement, and the *repeat rate* (the rate at which the keyboard repeats the key). For the fastest possible keyboard (the shortest delay and the quickest repeat rate), type **mode con delay=1 rate=32** at the DOS prompt and press **Enter**. Now start WordPerfect, and your cursor keys will whizz your cursor around the screen.

E-Z

If you're in the middle of a long word such as "pseudo-antidisestablishmentarianism," use **Ctrl+left arrow** to move quickly to the beginning of the word.

SPEAK LIKE A GEEK

Moving text up or down is called *scrolling* through the document.

To move to the beginning of the current line, press **Home** and then press the **left arrow** key. To move to the end of the current line, press **Home,right arrow**.

If you need to jump around a paragraph at a time, use **Ctrl+up arrow** (to move up one paragraph) or **Ctrl+down arrow** (to move down one paragraph).

> **E-Z**
>
> A faster way to get to the end of a line is just to press the **End** key.

Navigating Screens, Pages, and Documents

For really big documents, you need to know how to cover a lot of ground in a hurry. WordPerfect, of course, is up to the task.

To move to the top of the screen, press the minus key (−) on your keyboard's numeric keypad. (You can also press **Home,up arrow**.) To move to the bottom of the screen, press the numeric keypad's plus key (+). (The **Home,down arrow** combination also works.) Keep pressing these keys to navigate the document one screenful at a time.

> **OOPS!**
>
> If pressing plus or minus on your numeric keypad only produces plus or minus signs in your text, turn **Num Lock** off, or else try holding down the **Shift** key, as well.

For multi-page documents, use **Page Up** to move to the beginning of the previous page, and **Page Down** to move to the beginning of the next page.

> **By the Way . . .**
>
> Once you start hopping madly through a file, get your bearings by keeping your eyes on the status line's data. The **Pg** setting will tell you which page you're on, and the **Ln** setting tells you where you are in the current page.

For truly large leaps, press **Home**, **Home**, **up arrow** (yes, you press **Home** twice) to move to the beginning of the document, or **Home**, **Home**, **down arrow** to move to the end of the document.

Navigating with the Go to Command

> **E-Z**
> To select the **Go** to command quickly, press **Ctrl+Home**.

No document jockey's arsenal of navigation tricks would be complete without WordPerfect's **Go to** command. If you select **Go to** from the Edit menu, you'll see the Go to dialog box shown here.

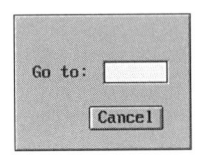

Use the Go to command to jump strategically through a document.

```
Go to: [      ]
       [Cancel]
```

Go to lets you jump to specific parts of a document at warp speed. Here's a summary of what you can do once the Go to dialog box is displayed:

- Press the **up arrow** to go to the top of the current page.
- Press the **down arrow** to go to the bottom of the current page.
- Type a number and press **Enter** to move to the top of that page number.
- Type a character and press **Enter** to move to the next occurrence of the character. (This only works if the character isn't too far away.)

> **By the Way . . .**
> With all these key combinations, you may find occasionally that you jump somewhere you didn't intend. If this happens, press **Ctrl+Home** to start the **Go to** command, and then press **Ctrl+Home** again. This takes you back to your original position.

How the Repeat Command Works

You can use the **Repeat** command to save some legwork. Just press **Ctrl+R** (or select **Repeat** from the **Edit** menu) to display the Repeat dialog box, then press whatever key you want repeated. If you press, say, the down arrow, WordPerfect moves down eight lines.

Why eight? Well, that's the number that appears by default in the Repeat dialog box. If you'd like to use a different number, press **Ctrl+R**, type in the number, then press the key you want repeated.

> **5.1** In version 5.1, press **Escape** to activate the **Repeat** command.

Navigating a File with the Mouse

Keyboard users, of course, can't have *all* the fun. If you like using a mouse, you can still navigate a document. Here are the basic techniques:

- ☞ To move the cursor to any spot on the screen, just click on it.
- ☞ To scroll the text down, position the pointer at the bottom of the typing area, hold down the right mouse button, and then drag the pointer down into the status line.
- ☞ Scrolling text up is similar: position the pointer at the top of the typing area, hold down the right button, and then drag the pointer up towards the menu bar.

These techniques are fine, but to really get around with a mouse, you have to learn about scroll bars. Before you can use 'em, though, you need to display 'em. Just pull down the **View** menu, select the **Vertical Scroll Bar** command, and you'll see a scroll bar on the right side of the screen, as shown here.

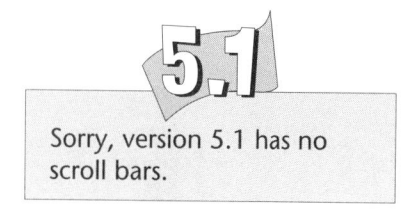

> **5.1** Sorry, version 5.1 has no scroll bars.

Here are a few things to note before we move on:

- ☞ The size of the scroll box depends on how big your document is. The bigger the document, the smaller the scroll box.

- ☛ You might have noticed that the **View** menu also has a **Horizontal Scroll Bar** command. You can use this to scroll left and right in documents that are too wide to fit on the screen.

- ☛ The **Vertical Scroll Bar** command displays the scroll bar only temporarily. It'll be gone the next time you start WordPerfect. Chapter 19, "Cool Tools to Make Your Life Easier," will show you how to display them permanently.

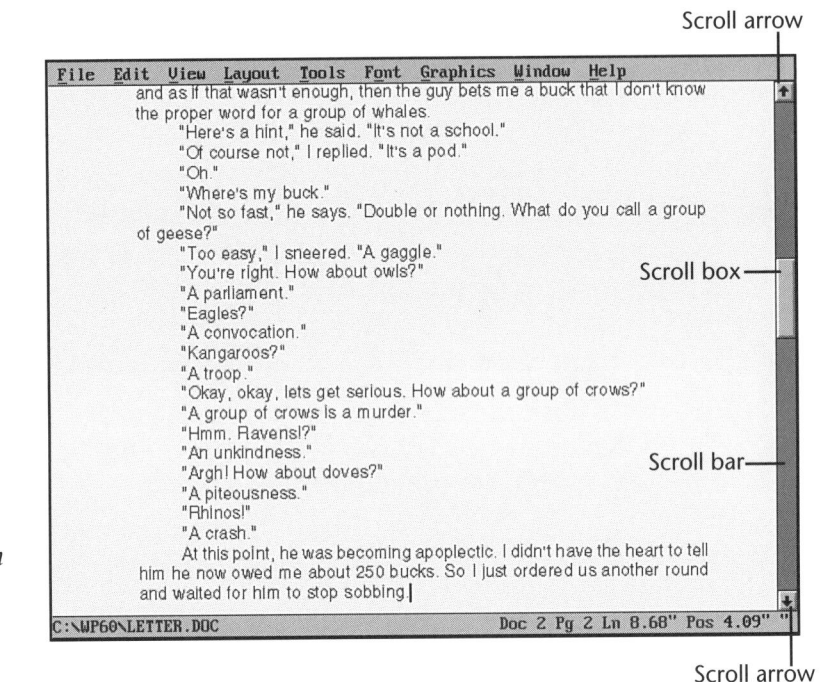

A WordPerfect screen with a vertical scroll bar.

By the Way . . .

If you're using graphics mode, you may be wondering why my typing area extends all the way over to the right edge of the screen when yours doesn't. Simple: I cheated. I just selected **Z**oom from the **V**iew menu and then, in the cascade menu that appeared, I selected Page **W**idth. See Chapter 17, "Working with Document Windows," for more Zoom info.

Scroll Whats?

Scroll bars are a lot like elevators. They sort of look like elevator shafts—and, like your favorite Otis device, they serve a dual purpose: they can tell you where you are, and they can take you somewhere else.

Where Am I? The Scroll Bar Knows

Thanks to my innately lousy sense of direction, I always seem to get lost in any document longer than a couple of pages. Fortunately, I have scroll bars to bail me out. The idea is simple: the position of the scroll box tells me my relative position in the document. So, for example, if the scroll box is about halfway down, then I know I'm somewhere near the middle of the file. They're just like the floor indicators on an elevator.

Can I Get There From Here? Navigating with Scroll Bars

The real scroll bar fun begins when you use them to move around in your documents. There are three basic techniques:

- ☛ To scroll vertically through a document one line at a time, click on the scroll bar's **Up** or **Down scroll arrows**.

- ☛ To leap through the document one screen at a time, click inside the scroll bar between the scroll box and the scroll arrows. For example, to move down one screenful, click inside the scroll bar between the scroll box and the Down scroll arrow.

- ☛ To move to a specific part of a document, drag the vertical scroll box up or down to the appropriate position. For example, to move to the beginning of a document, drag the scroll box to the top.

The Least You Need to Know

This chapter concluded our look at document drudgery by examining a few easy navigation techniques. Here's the lowdown:

- Use the **left** and **right arrow** to keys move left and right one character at a time.

- Use **Ctrl+left arrow** or **Ctrl+right arrow** to jump left or right one word at a time.

- The **up arrow** and **down arrow** keys move you up or down one line at a time.

- **Ctrl+up arrow** moves you up one paragraph and **Ctrl+down arrow** moves you down one paragraph.

- Press minus (–) or plus (+) on the numeric keypad to move to the top or bottom of the screen.

- **Page Up** moves you to the beginning of the previous page, while **Page Down** moves you to the top of the next page.

- The **G**o to command (**Ctrl+Home**) gives you more control over your document-leaping.

- When navigating with a mouse, just click to move to a spot you can see, or use the scroll bars to navigate the entire document.

Part II
Getting It Right: Editing Stuff

If, as they say, the essence of good writing is rewriting, then word processors ought to make us all better writers because rewriting—or editing—is what they do best. WordPerfect, in particular, has an impressive array of editing tools (some might say too impressive). The chapters in this section give you the basics of editing your prose in WordPerfect. You'll learn everything from simple deleting (and, thankfully, undeleting) to shuffling great hunks of text to new locations. I don't know if it'll make you a better writer, but it'll sure make you a heck of a rewriter.

Chapter 9
Deleting Text (and Undeleting It, Too)

In This Chapter

- Deleting one character at a time
- Deleting one word at a time
- Deleting entire pages
- Using the Repeat and Undelete features
- A small slice of the author's life

I moved recently, and it only took me five minutes of packing to realize something: I'm a hoarder (I said *hoarder*). I never throw anything away: Old gum wrappers; ticket stubs from every baseball, football, hockey, and basketball game I've ever attended; an ancient (and British!?) version of Monopoly. And books! Don't get me started with books!

I have the same trouble throwing things away when I'm writing. As my editor will tell you, I have a hard time deleting *anything*. (I think I just get too attached.) However, that's not WordPerfect's fault, because it gives you all kinds of ways to nix troublesome text. This chapter will show you how.

Deleting Characters

Did you spell *potato* with an *e* again? Or perhaps you've just seen the Queen on TV, and have been using words like *colour* and *cheque*. Well, not to worry; WordPerfect makes it easy to expunge individual characters. You have two options:

> Before going on any kind of deletion rampage, you should know that there's a section at the end of this chapter called "To Err Is Human, To Undelete Divine." If you wipe out anything you shouldn't have, read ahead to this section to see how to make everything okay again.

- Press the **Delete** key to delete the character to the right of the cursor (or, if you're in text mode, the character above the cursor).
- Press **Backspace** to delete the character to the left of the cursor.

If you'd like to delete several characters in a row, hold down **Delete** or **Backspace** until all the riffraff is eliminated. (Be careful, though: the cursor really picks up speed if you hold it down for more than a second or two.) You can also switch to typeover mode, and simply overwrite the text you want deleted. Just press **Insert** and you'll see the word **Typeover** in the status line. To return to insert mode, press **Insert** again.

> **SPEAK LIKE A GEEK**
> In *typeover mode*, your typing replaces existing characters. With *insert mode*, your typing is inserted between existing characters.

Deleting Words

To handle any stray words that creep into your documents, WordPerfect lets you delete entire words with a single stroke. Just position the cursor anywhere inside the word you want to blow away, and press **Ctrl+Backspace**.

> **By the Way . . .**
> If you place the cursor in between two words and press **Ctrl+Backspace**, WordPerfect deletes the word to the *left* of the cursor.

For real fine-tuned deleting, you can even delete portions of a word. Here's how:

- To delete from the cursor to the end of a word, press **Home,Delete**.
- To delete from the cursor to the beginning of a word, press **Home,Backspace**.

> **By the Way . . .**
> Here's how I remember whether to use Home,Backspace or Home,Delete: the word *end* ends with *d*, so you use Home,*Delete* to delete to the end of a word; the word *beginning* begins with *b*, so you use Home,*Backspace* to delete to the beginning of a word. Clearer? No? Well, I tried.

Deleting Lines

WordPerfect lets you delete a portion of a line, or even (with just a little extra work) an entire line. For starters, if you just need to delete text from the cursor to the end of the line, press **Ctrl+End**.

Deleting an entire line takes an extra step: first place the cursor at the beginning of the line (by pressing **Home,left arrow** or by clicking to the left of the line) and *then* press **Ctrl+End**.

> **By the Way . . .**
> To learn how to delete entire sentences and paragraphs, see Chapter 10, "Block Partying: Working with Blocks of Text."

Deleting Pages

If you've really made a mess of things, you may need to obliterate great chunks of text. One handy way to do this is to delete everything from the cursor to the end of the page. You do this by pressing **Ctrl+Page Down**. Since this is such a destructive command, WordPerfect asks if you're sure you want to go through with it, as shown here.

*When you press **Ctrl+Page Down** to delete from the cursor to the end of the page, WordPerfect—ever cautious—asks you to confirm.*

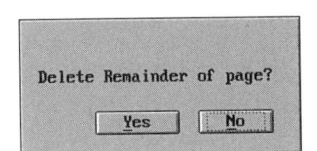

Just select **Yes** to continue (or, of course, **No** to cancel).

> **By the Way . . .**
> Recall that WordPerfect places a line across the screen to show you where one page ends and another begins. Just to be safe, you should scroll down to the bottom of the page before using **Ctrl+Page Down** to make sure you're not going to wipe out anything important.

Repeat Deleting

5.1 Press **Ctrl+R** to display the Repeat dialog box quickly.

5.1 In version 5.1, press **Esc** to select the Repeat command.

The Repeat command is a handy way to speed up your deletion chores. Just select **R**epeat from the Edit menu and then press the appropriate deletion key or key combination. The default repeat value is 8 (which means that if you press, say, Delete, WordPerfect will delete eight characters), but you can use whatever value you need. Just type the number you want in the Repeat dialog box. Unfortunately, **R**epeat doesn't work with the Backspace key.

To Err Is Human, To Undelete Divine

Lets face facts: *everybody* deletes stuff accidentally, and one day *you'll* do it, too. It's one of those reality things (like nose hair and paying taxes) that we just can't avoid. The good people at WordPerfect know this, and the gurus in their programming department came up with a way to ease the pain: the U**n**delete command. This command, as its name implies, miraculously reverses any of your three most recent deletions. (Which, believe me, has saved *my* bacon on more than one occasion.)

Here are the steps to follow to undelete something:

1. Get whatever cursing, fuming, and gesticulating you normally do when you've just deleted your last three hours' work out of the way first. You need a clear head for what's to come.

2. Select U**n**delete from the Edit menu. As you can see here, WordPerfect displays the Undelete dialog box, adds the last deletion back into the text, and highlights it so you can see it clearly.

3. If that's the text you want undeleted, select **Restore**. If it's not, select **Previous Deletion** until you see what you want and then select **Restore**. (Remember that WordPerfect only stores the last three things you deleted.)

E-Z

Pressing **Esc** is the fastest way to select the Undelete command.

5.1

Press **F1** to crank up the Undelete command in version 5.1. You'll see the following prompt at the bottom of the screen:

Undelete: 1 Restore; 2 Previous Deletion: 0

Press **R** (or **1**) to restore a deletion. Press **P** (or **2**) to see the other deletions.

TECHNO NERD TEACHES

How does Undelete perform its magic? Well, each time you delete something, it might appear as though it has gone off to some la-la land of deleted text, but that's not quite the case. WordPerfect sneakily saves each of the last three deletions in a special file called a *buffer* that stores not only the text itself, but its original location. Undeleting, then, is a simple matter of restoring the text from the buffer.

WordPerfect adds your last deletion back into the text.

When you select the Undelete command, WordPerfect adds the last deletion back into the text, and displays the Undelete dialog box.

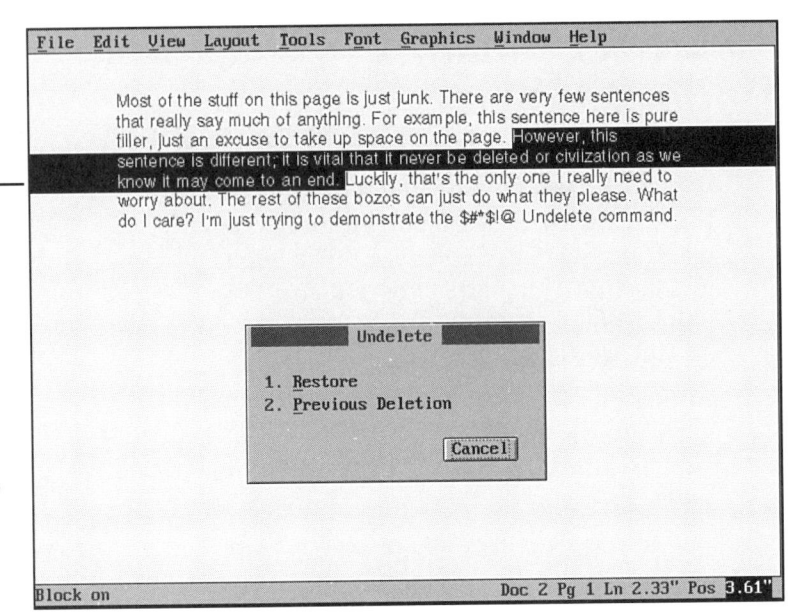

The Least You Need to Know

This compact little chapter gave you the scoop on deleting text (and undeleting it too, just in case). Here are few pointers to take with you on your travels:

- ☞ To delete individual characters, use the **Delete** key (to delete whatever is to the right of the cursor or, if you use text mode, whatever is above the cursor), or the **Backspace** key (to delete whatever is to the left of the cursor).

- ☞ To delete a word, put the cursor inside the word and press **Ctrl+Backspace**.

- ☞ Press **Ctrl+End** to delete from the current cursor position to the end of the line.

- ☞ To delete from the current cursor position to the end of the page, press **Ctrl+Page Down**.

- ☞ You can speed up your deleting by using the **Repeat** command. Just press **Ctrl+R** to display the Repeat dialog box, enter a different number, if needed, and then press the appropriate deletion key or key combo.

- ☞ If you delete something by accident, immediately select **U**ndelete from the **E**dit menu (or press **Esc**). Select **R**estore to undelete the highlighted text, or select **P**revious Deletion to see other deleted text.

Chapter 10
Block Partying: Working with Blocks of Text

In This Chapter

- How to select a block of text
- Making copies of text blocks
- Moving text blocks to different locations within a document
- Reversing errors with the Undo command
- Pleasurable prose chock-a-block with practical WordPerfect stuff

Blocs (as in the "Eastern bloc") may be out, but *blocks* are definitely in. I mean, we have block parents, block parties, block captains. Why even the old *Gumby and Pokey* show (which featured the villainous Blockheads, of course) has made a bizarre comeback of sorts.

WordPerfect uses blocks, too. In this case, though, a *block* is just a section of text. It could be a word, a sentence, two-and-half paragraphs, or 57 pages. Whatever you need. The key is that WordPerfect treats a block as a single entity; a unit. And what does one do with these units? Well, you name it: you can

> **SPEAK LIKE A GEEK**
>
> A *block* is a section of text of any length.

> Pressing either **F12** or **Alt+F4** is the quick way to select the **Block** command.

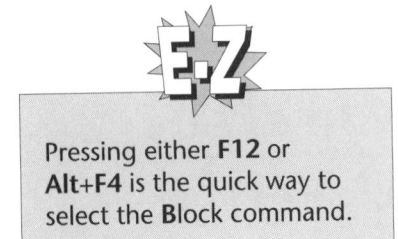

copy, move, delete, print, format, spell-check, take them to lunch, whatever. This chapter shows you not only how to select a block, but it also takes you through a few of these block tasks.

Selecting a Block of Text

WordPerfect, bless its electronic heart, gives you no less than three ways to select a block of text: you can use your keyboard, your mouse, or the handy **Select** command.

Selecting Text With the Keyboard

To select some text with your keyboard, begin by positioning the cursor at the beginning of the text. Now select **Block** from the Edit menu. You'll see a **Block on** message in the status line. (The next step is optional: make a fist with your right hand, raise it over your head, and say "Block on, man!")

Once **Block** is on, you can use the **arrow** keys to move through the text you want to select. As you do, the characters you're selecting become highlighted (i.e., they appear white on a black background), as you can see here.

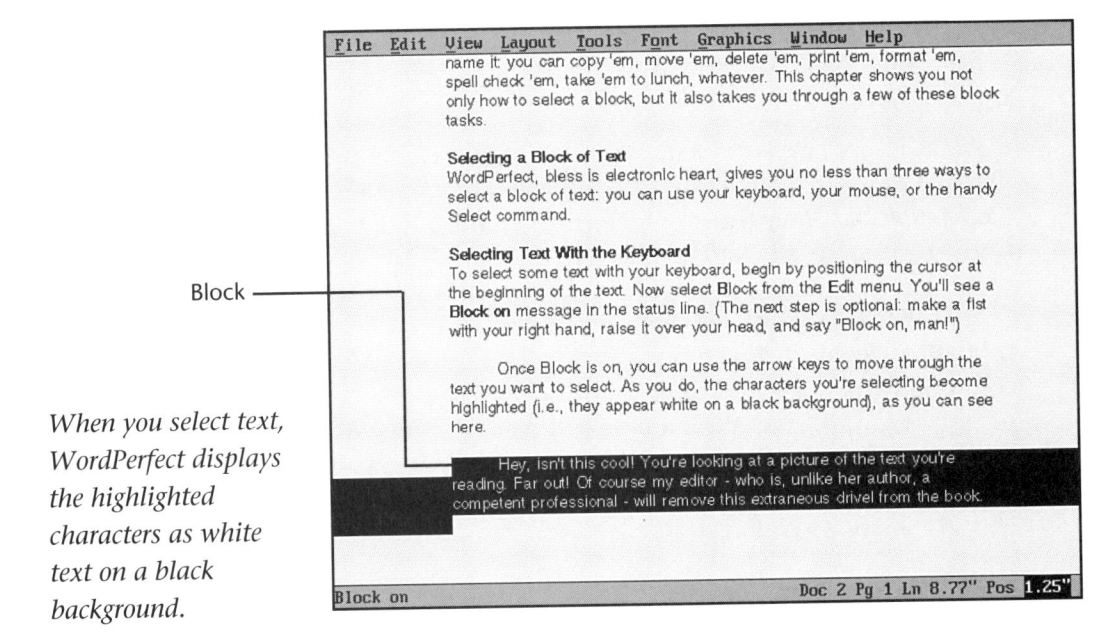

When you select text, WordPerfect displays the highlighted characters as white text on a black background.

Block

For more fine-tuned selecting, Table 10.1 presents some key combos you can use while **Block** is on.

Table 10.1   Key combinations to use while selecting text.

Press	To select text to
Ctrl+right arrow	The next word
Ctrl+left arrow	The previous word
Home, right arrow	The end of the line
Home, left arrow	The beginning of the line
Ctrl+down arrow	The end of the paragraph
Ctrl+up arrow	The beginning of the paragraph
Home, down arrow	The bottom of the screen
Home, up arrow	The top of the screen
Page Down	The beginning of the next page
Page Up	The beginning of the previous page

By the Way . . .

The sharp-eyed will have noticed that the key combinations in Table 10.1 bear a remarkable resemblance to the navigation keys you struggled through back in Chapter 8. Hey, you get an extra dessert tonight—because, yes, they're exactly the same! In fact, you can use any of the stuff from that chapter (including **Ctrl+Home**—the handy **G**o to command) to select text.

Selecting Text With the Mouse

Mouse users, forget the keyboard—because selecting text with the little rodent guy is *way* easier. All you have to do is position the pointer at the beginning of the block, press and hold down the left button, and then drag the mouse over the text you want to select. That's it! No unsightly key combinations!

OOPS!

If you decide you don't want to select a block after all, just press **Esc** (version 6) or **F1** (in version 5.1).

Using the Select Command

WordPerfect's Select command makes it easier to select single sentences, paragraphs, and pages. Just position the cursor in the sentence, paragraph, or page you want to select, and then run the Select command from the Edit menu. You'll see a cascade menu appear with three entries: Sentence, Paragraph, or Page. Just select the appropriate command, and WordPerfect does the rest.

> **OOPS!** Need to cancel your block selection? That's easy too: just click anywhere in the typing area.

> **E-Z** Once Block is on, just press any character and WordPerfect will extend the selection down to the next instance of the character. Cool, huh? In particular, press period (.) to select to the end of the sentence, and press Enter to select to the end of the paragraph.

Copying a Block

One of the secrets of computer productivity is a simple maxim: "Don't reinvent the wheel." In other words, if you've got something that works, and you need something similar, don't start from scratch. Instead, make a copy of the original, and then make whatever changes are necessary to the copy.

Happily, WordPerfect makes it easy to copy stuff. In fact (if you have version 6), you get not one but *two* copy methods: the regular two-command method (first Copy, then Paste) and the new one-command method (Copy and Paste).

Copying with Two Commands

With this method, once you've selected what you want to copy, just pull down the Edit menu and select the Copy command. You then position the cursor where you want to place the copy and then select Paste from the Edit menu. A perfect copy of your selection appears instantly. If you need to make other copies, just position the cursor appropriately, and select the Paste command again.

> **E-Z** The shortcut key for the Copy command is **Ctrl+C**. For Paste, press **Ctrl+V**.

Copying with One Command

If you need to make only a single copy, version 6's new Copy and Paste command will do the job. To use it, just select your text, and then choose Copy and Paste from the Edit menu. Now position the cursor where you want the copy to appear, and then press **Enter**.

> **5.1**
> In version 5.1, after you select **Paste** from the **Edit** menu, select **Block** in the status line prompt.

Moving a Block

One of the all-time handiest word processor features is the ability to move stuff from one part of a document to another. This is perfect for rearranging everything from single sentences to humongous chunks of text.

> **E-Z**
> The Copy and Paste command's shortcut key is **Ctrl+Insert**.
>
> The easiest way to choose the Cut command is to press **Ctrl+X**.

Now, you might think you'd do this by making a copy, pasting it, and then going back and deleting the original. Well, you *could* do it that way, but your friends would almost certainly laugh at you. Why? Because there's an easier way. WordPerfect lets you *cut* a selection right out of a document, and then paste it somewhere else. And version 6 gives you (as with copying) two methods.

Moving with Two Commands

Once you've selected what you want to move, pull down the Edit menu and select the Cut command. Your selection will disappear from the screen, but don't panic; WordPerfect is saving it for you in a secret location. Now

> **OOPS!**
> To cancel the **Copy** command, press **Esc**.

position the cursor where you want to move the selection and then choose Paste from the Edit menu. Your stuff miraculously reappears in the new location. If you need to make further copies of the selection, just reposition the cursor and select Paste again.

> The Cut and Paste shortcut key combo is **Ctrl+Del**.

If you cut a selection accidentally, immediately select **U**ndo from the **E**dit menu. For more **U**ndo info, see the section titled "The Life-Saving Undo Command" later in this chapter.

Moving with One Command

For quick text moves, you can't beat version 6's new Cut and Past**e** command. Select your text, pull down the **E**dit menu, and then choose Cut and Past**e**. Again, WordPerfect plucks the text from the screen (but stores it in the secret location). Now position the cursor where you want the text moved, and press **Enter**.

Saving a Block

If you've just written some particularly breathtaking prose, you might want to save it in a file all its own. No sweat. Just select it, pull down the **F**ile menu, and choose the Save **A**s command. WordPerfect displays the Save Block dialog box, shown here.

Use the Save Block dialog box to save a highlighted block to a file.

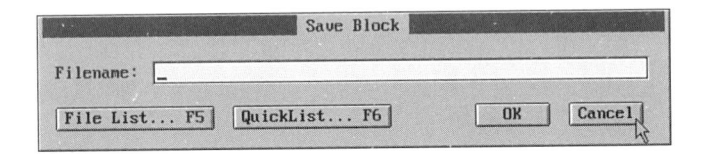

Enter a name for the file in the **Filename** text box, and then select **OK**.

> In version 5.1, enter a name for the file in the status line's **Block name** prompt, and then press **Enter**.

Deleting a Block

Deleting a block of text is a no-brainer. Just make your selection, and then press either **Delete** or **Backspace**. Remember that if you delete anything accidentally, you can always fall back on

WordPerfect's Undelete command. See Chapter 9, "Deleting Text (and Undeleting It, Too)," for the skinny on Undelete.

Appending a Block to a File

WordPerfect also has the strange Append command that few people seem to know about. The idea behind it is that you might be working in one document and then suddenly decide that the sentence (paragraph, whatever) you just wrote *must* be included in yesterday's memo. Append lets you tack it on to that document without having to go through the whole rigmarole of opening it.

> **5.1**
> Version 5.1 displays a **Delete Block?** prompt in the status line after you press Delete or Backspace. Select **Y**es to continue with the deletion or **N**o to cancel.

To use this feature, all you do it select the appropriate block, choose **A**ppend from the **E**dit menu, and then choose To File from the cascade menu that appears. In the Append To dialog box, enter the name of the file, and then select **OK**.

> **Put It to Work**
>
> The **A**ppend command lets you take the idea of boilerplate text to new heights. Since **A**ppend lets you easily add text to a document, why not create a separate file to hold all your boilerplate phrases and passages? (You could call it BLRPLATE.WP, or something.) Any time you come across some new text that you want to add to the file, just select it, run the **A**ppend To **F**ile command, and enter the name of the boilerplate file in the Append To dialog box. You'll need to open the boilerplate document when you need to use something from it. To learn how to work with multiple open documents, check out Chapter 17, "Working with Document Windows."

The Life-Saving Undo Command

OOPS!

Make sure you select the **Undo** command *immediately* after making your mistake. WordPerfect can only reverse your last action, so if you do anything else in the meantime, you may not be able to recover.

Every WordPerfect user—from the rawest novice to the nerdiest expert—ends up at some time or other doing something downright silly. It may be cutting when you should have been copying, or just pasting a chunk of text in some absurd location.

Fortunately, WordPerfect has an Undo feature to get you out of these jams. The Undo command restores everything to the way it was before you made your blunder. (I've had some relationships where an Undo command would have come in *real* handy.) All you have to do is pull down the Edit menu and select Undo.

When I make mistakes (which is embarrassingly often, I have to tell you), I like to invoke the Undo command as quickly as I can. So, instead of the menus, I just use the **Ctrl+Z** key combination.

The Least You Need to Know

This chapter led you through the basics of working with WordPerfect's text blocks. We really only scratched the surface here, because there's plenty more you can do with blocks. However, I'll save all that rot for the chapters to come. For now, here's a rehash of what just happened:

- A block is just a selection of text that you can work with as a whole.

- To select text with the keyboard, first choose **Block** from the **Edit** menu (or press **F12** or **Alt+F4**), then use WordPerfect's navigation keys to highlight the text you want.

- Selecting text with a mouse is even easier. Position the pointer at the beginning of the text, and then drag the mouse over the selection you need.

- To copy a block, select **C**opy from the **E**dit menu, position the cursor, and then select **P**aste. Alternatively, select **C**opy and **P**aste, position the cursor, and then press **Enter**.

- To move a block, pull down the **E**dit menu and select **C**ut, position the cursor, then select **P**aste from the **E**dit menu. Or select Cut and Past**e**, position the cursor, then press **Enter**.

- To delete a block, just press **Delete** or **Backspace**.

- To reverse a blunder, immediately select **U**ndo from the **E**dit menu.

Chapter 11
Search and Ye Shall Replace

In This Chapter

- Searching for text, forwards
- Searching for text, backwards
- Search strategies
- Searching for and replacing text
- A sad little song, sure to bring a tear to your eye

Oh where, oh where has my little text gone?
Oh where, oh where can it be?

If you've ever found yourself lamenting a long-lost word adrift in some humongous mega-document, the folks at WordPerfect can sympathize (probably because it has happened to *them* a time or two). In fact, they were even kind enough to build a special Search feature into WordPerfect to help you find missing text. And that's not all: you can also use this feature to seek out and *replace* every instance of one word with another. Sound like fun? Well, okay, but it *is* handy, so you might want to read this chapter anyway.

> **E-Z**
> The fast way to display the Search dialog box is simply to press **F2**.

Searching for Text

If you need to find a certain word or phrase in a short document, it's usually easiest just to scroll through the text. But if you're dealing with more than a couple of pages, don't waste your time rummaging through the whole file. WordPerfect's Search feature lets you search forward (i.e., toward the end of the document) or backward (toward the beginning) to find what you need.

Searching Forward

Here are the steps you need to follow to search for a piece of text, from the current cursor position to the end of the document:

1. Pull down the **Edit** menu and select the **Search** command. The Search dialog box appears, as shown here.

2. In the **Search** For text box, type the text you want to find (you can enter up to 80 characters).

Fill in the Search dialog box to hunt for text in a document.

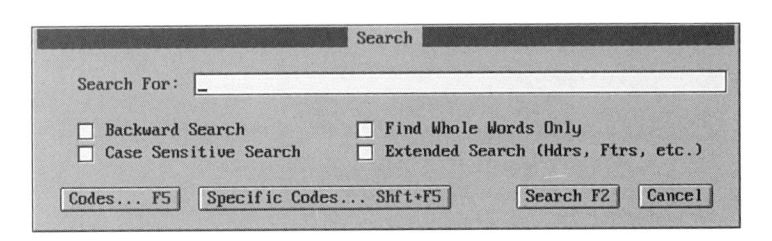

3. Select the Search button. If WordPerfect finds a match, it places the cursor to the left of the text. If no match was found, WordPerfect displays a message to that effect (which you can remove from the screen by selecting **OK**).

> **E-Z**
> Once you've filled in the Search For text box, just press **F2** to get the search under way.

Searching Backward

If you do a forward search and WordPerfect doesn't find a match, the darn program just bails out at the end of the document. If it was up to me, I'd make it wrap around and start checking from the beginning. However, they never asked for my opinion, so we're stuck with having to search *backward*, instead. Here are the steps to follow:

1. Pull down the Edit menu and select the Searc**h** command to display the Search dialog box.
2. In the Search For text box, type the text you want to find.
3. Select the **B**ackward Search check box.
4. Select the Search button to start searching.

> **5.1**
> To search forward for text in version 5.1, pull down the Search menu and select Forward. Type the search text (up to 80 characters) at the ←**Srch** prompt, and then press **F2**.

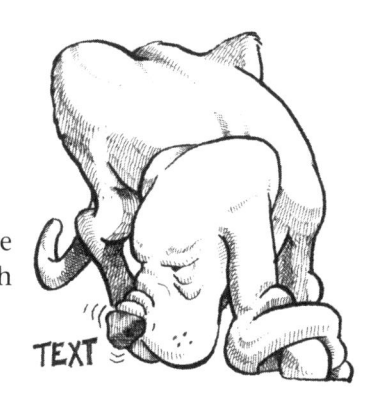

Continuing the Search

Sometimes the text that WordPerfect finds is not the particular instance you want. To continue the search in the same direction, simply repeat the steps just mentioned. Note, however, that WordPerfect is smart enough to remember your last search text, and displays it automatically. So once the Search dialog box is displayed, select the Search button to find the next example of the text.

> **E-Z**
> To display the Search dialog box with the **B**ackward Search check box already selected, press **Shift+F2**.

Some Notes on Searching

Searching for text is a pretty straightforward affair, but it wouldn't be WordPerfect if there weren't five thousand other ways to confuse the heck out of us. To makes things easier, here are a few plain-English notes that'll help you get the most out of the Searc**h** feature:

☛ For best results, don't try to match entire sentences. A word or two is all you really need.

> **5.1**
> In 5.1, you search backward for text by pulling down the Search menu and selecting Backward. Then type the search text at the →**Srch** prompt and press **F2**.

> **5.1**
>
> Version 5.1's Search menu contains two other commands—**N**ext and **P**revious—that you can use to continue the search.
>
> In WordPerfect 5.1, if you type everything in lowercase, Sear**c**h finds all occurrences of a word, regardless of case. If you add uppercase letters, Sear**c**h will find only words that match the uppercase.
>
> To find whole words in 5.1, put a space on either side of the word in the search text.

> **E-Z**
>
> Press **F2** twice to move to the next occurrence of the same word.

☞ If you're not sure how to spell a word, just use a piece of it. WordPerfect will still find *egregious* if you search for *egre* (although it'll also find words like *regret* and *degree*).

☞ To find only words that *begin* with your search text, add a space before the text.

☞ Rather than fumbling around with searching both forward and backward, you can make sure you search the entire document by first positioning the cursor at the beginning (by pressing **Home,Home,up arrow**) and then searching forward.

☞ When your search is complete, you can return to your original position by pressing **Ctrl+Home** (to display the **G**o to dialog box), and then pressing **Ctrl+Home** again.

☞ If you need to differentiate between, say, *Bobby* (some guy) and *bobby* (as in a *bobby* pin or an English *bobby*), select the **C**ase Sensitive Search check box in the Search dialog box. This tells WordPerfect to match not only the letters, but also whatever uppercase and lowercase format you use.

☞ If you search for, say, *gorge*, WordPerfect may find not only the word *gorge*, but also *gorged*, *gorgeous*, and *disgorge* as well. If all you want is *gorge*, select the Find Whole **W**ords Only option in the Search dialog box.

☞ Select the Search dialog box's Extended Search option to tell WordPerfect to search inside things like document headers, footers, and footnotes.

Searching and Replacing Text

If you do a lot of writing, one of the features you'll come to rely on the most is *search and replace*. This means that WordPerfect seeks out a particular bit of text and then replaces it with something else. This may not seem like a big deal for a word or two, but if you need to change a couple of dozen instances of *irregardless* to *regardless*, it can be a real time-saver.

> **5.1**
> To run an extended search in version 5.1, press **Home,F2** (to search forward) or **Home,Shift+F2** (to search backward).

Search and Replace: The Basic Steps

Searching and replacing is, as you might imagine, not all that different from plain old searching. Here's how it works:

> **E-Z**
> The shortcut key for the Replace command is **Alt+F2**.

1. Select the Replace command from the Edit menu. You'll see the Search and Replace dialog box shown here.

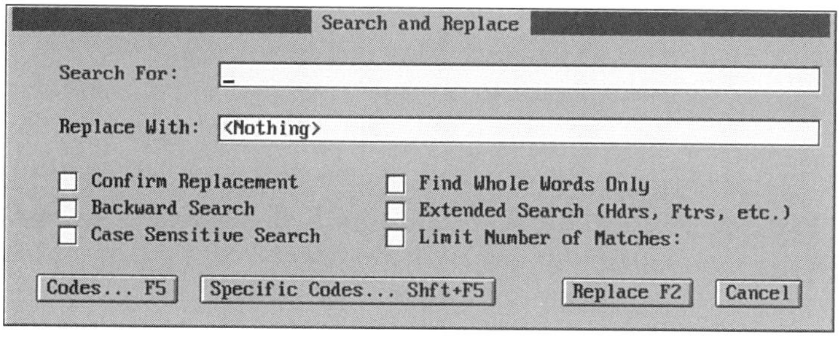

Use the Search and Replace dialog box to search for text and then replace it with something else.

2. In the **Search** For text box, enter the text you want to find (you can enter up to 80 characters).

3. In the **Replace** With text box, enter the text you want to use as a replacement. (Again, you have an 80-character limit.)

4. Select the **Replace** button. WordPerfect races through the document, searching and replacing as it goes. When it's done, it displays a report on-screen of how many occurrences of the searched text it found, and how many it replaced. (Select **OK** to get rid of the report.)

> **By the Way . . .**
>
> To keep your search-and-replace operations focused, you can first select a block (glance back at Chapter 10 "Block Partying: Working with Text Blocks," if you need to learn block basics). This tells WordPerfect to search and replace *only* within the block. (Sorry, this doesn't work for plain searches.)

> **TECHNO NERD TEACHES**
>
> WordPerfect litters your documents with bizarre, hidden things called *formatting codes*. These codes are just WordPerfect's notes to itself about things like fonts and page layout. (If you're curious, you can see them by selecting Reveal **C**odes from the **V**iew menu, or by pressing **Alt+F3**; personally, these things give me the willies, so I prefer to keep 'em hidden. To send them back from whence they came, press **Alt+F3** again.) The Search dialog box's **C**odes and Specific **C**odes buttons let you search for these formatting codes if you have the stomach for such things.

Search and Replace Options

To get the most out of the powerful search-and-replace stuff, you'll probably want to test-drive a few options. Here's what's available in the Search and Replace dialog box:

- Many of the Search and Replace dialog box options are identical to those in the Search dialog box. In particular, you can search backward, perform case sensitive searches, find whole words only, and extend the search into headers, footers, and so on.

- Normally, WordPerfect just goes on a rampage through the document, replacing everything it finds. If you'd like a little more control over the process, select the Con**f**irm Replacement option. When you start searching, each time WordPerfect finds a match, it displays the text as highlighted, and you'll see the Confirm Replacement dialog box shown here.

- To replace the highlighted text, select **Y**es; to move on without replacing, select **N**o. If you get tired of the constant confirmations, you can either select **R**eplace All to let WordPerfect go crazy, or **Cancel** to bail out of the operation altogether.

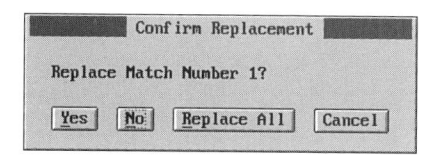

With the Confirm Replacement option selected, WordPerfect asks you for confirmation each time it's about to replace the search text.

☞ Sometimes you want to replace only the first few occurrences of a piece of text. In this case, select the Limit Number of Matches check box and enter the number of replacements you want in the text box that appears.

☞ If you want to search and *delete* text, just keep the Replace With text box blank and proceed normally (although, in this case, it's probably a good idea to turn on the Confirm Replacement option).

Put It to Work:

Search and replace is one of those features for which you'll find endless uses. But perhaps one of the best is to weed out words used improperly. For example, you might need to replace some instances of *affect* with *effect* (one of my own personal bugaboos). Here's a list of some of the most commonly confused words you might want to check for (in most cases you can reverse the *Search for* and *Replace with* terms, depending on which usage is correct):

Search for	Replace with
affect (to influence)	effect (a result)
already (action has happened)	all ready (entirely ready)
alright (no such word)	all right
all together (as one)	altogether (entirely)
any body (any human form)	anybody (any person)

continues

continued

Search for	Replace with
averse (disinclined)	adverse (opposed)
breath (inhalation)	breathe (to inhale)
capitol (govt. building)	capital (seat of govt.)
censure (to blame)	censor (to expurgate)
continual (frequently recurring)	continuous (uninterrupted)
different than (improper)	different from
hanged (refers to a person)	hung (refers to an object)
irregardless (improper)	regardless
momento (wrong)	memento
regretful (improper)	regrettable
seasonable (timely)	seasonal (periodical)

The Least You Need to Know

This chapter introduced you to WordPerfect's handy Search and Search and Replace features. Here's a fond look back:

- To search forward for some text, select Searc**h** from the **E**dit menu (or press **F2**), enter the search text, and then select the Searc**h** button (or press **F2** again).

- To search backward, select the **E**dit menu's Searc**h** command, enter the search text, activate the **B**ackward Search check box, and then select the Search button.

- If you're searching for proper names and other things where case matters, make sure you activate the **C**ase Sensitive Search option in the Search dialog box.

- The Search and Replace feature is a great way to replace every instance of a word or phrase quickly. To use it, select **R**eplace from the **E**dit menu (or press **Alt+F2**), enter your text in the **S**earch For and **R**eplace With boxes, and then select the **R**eplace button.

- Normally, WordPerfect doesn't ask you to confirm replacements in a Search and Replace operation. If you'd like the added safety of a confirmation, be sure to activate the Confirm Replacement check box before starting the Replace.

Part III
Looking Good: Formatting Stuff

"The least you can do is look respectable." That's what my mother always used to tell me when I was a kid. This advice holds up especially well in these image-conscious times. If you don't look good up front (or if your work doesn't look good), then you'll often be written off without a second thought.

When it comes to looking good—whether you're writing up a memo, slicking up a report, or polishing up your resumé—WordPerfect gives you a veritable cornucopia (I've always wanted to use that phrase) of formatting options. The chapters in this part give you the skinny on these various options, including lots of hints about how best to use them.

Chapter 12
Making Your Characters Look Good

In This Chapter

- Applying character attributes such as bold and italics
- Using different character sizes
- Converting letters between uppercase and lowercase
- Working with different fonts
- Adding WordPerfect's symbols to your documents
- Frighteningly fun formatting frolics

The first step on our road to looking good is the lowly character. I know, I know, you want to try out some really *big* stuff, but don't forget all that blather about the longest journey beginning with a single step. Besides, working with characters *can* make a big difference. Why, just a little bit of bolding here, a couple of italics there, throw in a font or two, and suddenly that humdrum, boring memo is turned into a dynamic, exciting thing of beauty. People from all over will be clamoring to read your stuff. You will be, in short, a star.

Getting Graphic

The first order of business (for those of you who have version 6, anyway; 5.1 users are out of luck) is to remind you about that *graphics mode* thing. Graphics mode is a *very* cool new feature that lets WordPerfect users actually see what they're doing. In normal *text mode*, WordPerfect can't show things like italics or large characters; you just have to trust that everything is okay and wait until you get a printout to see how things look—or (shudder) try to decipher the bizarre colors WordPerfect uses for different formats.

Graphics mode changes all that, because you can see everything right on the screen. Sure, it slows things down a tad, but it more than makes up for the time you'd otherwise spend printing out 57 copies until you get things just right. And it's real easy, too: just pull down the View menu and select the Graphics Mode command.

Changing Character Attributes

My *Concise Oxford Dictionary* defines an *attribute* as a "characteristic quality." So this means that a *character attribute* would be a "characteristic character quality." Hmm. In any case, WordPerfect lets you alter the attributes of your document characters to get things like bold, underlining (single and double), and italics, as you can see on the next page.

The good news is that WordPerfect makes it real easy to mess around with these attributes. You begin by selecting the block of text you want to change (by pressing **Alt+F4** and using the arrow keys, or by dragging the mouse over the text; see

---

TECHNO NERD TEACHES

For the curious, here's the difference between text mode and graphics mode: Text mode (it's also called *character-based mode*) operates by dividing your screen into 25 rows, with 80 columns in each row. Each of the resulting 2,000 screen positions can display only a single character from a predefined set of 254 so-called *ASCII* (American Standard Code for Information Interchange) characters. There's no room for bizarre things like italics or letters that are larger or smaller than the standard size. Graphics mode, on the other hand, divides your screen into tiny pinpoints of light called *pixels*. A basic graphics mode might have 480 rows divided into 640 columns, resulting in a whopping total of 307,200 pixels! This makes it easy to show different fonts and character attributes right on screen.

E-Z

Three of the attributes have shortcut keys: for **Bold**, press **F6**; for **Underline**, press **F8**; for Italics, press **Ctrl+I**.

Chapter 10, "Block Partying: Working with Text Blocks," for more info). Then just pull down the Font menu and select the attribute you want.

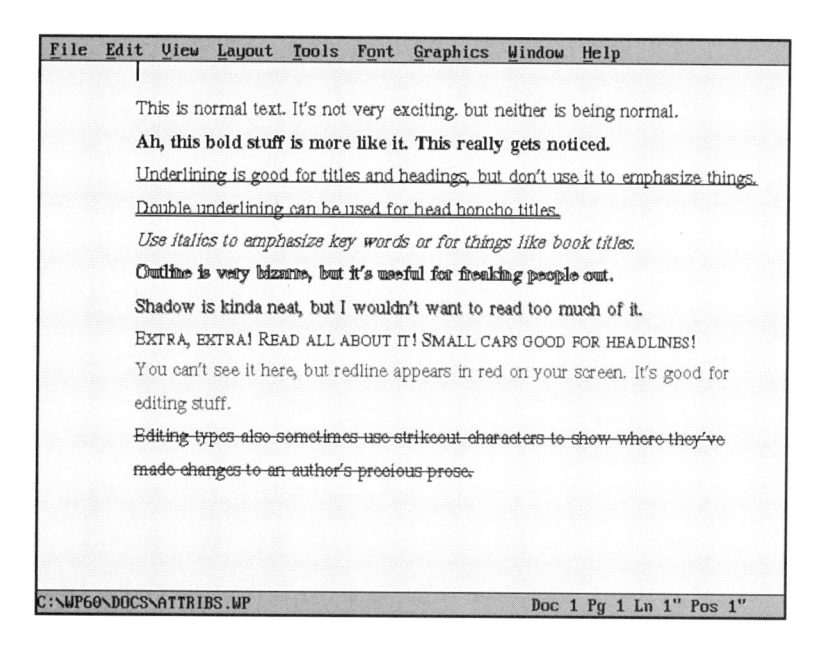

Some of the character attributes you can play with.

Instead of changing existing text, you might prefer to have any *new* text you type appear with a certain attribute. This is even easier; just select the attribute from the Font menu and start typing. WordPerfect displays subsequent characters with the attribute you chose. To turn off the formatting, just reselect it from the menu.

For even more formatting fun, you can *combine* attributes to get, say, **bold italic** text or double-underlined strikeout characters. All you do is rehighlight the block, and select whatever you need from the Font menu. To get rid of multiple formats, you can either reselect the options from the Font menu or select the Normal command.

> **OOPS!**
> In order to use graphics mode, you need to have a monitor and something called a *video card* that can handle it. If WordPerfect won't switch to graphics mode, then you know you don't have the proper equipment.

> **5.1** In version 5.1, select the **Appearance** command from the **Font** menu, and then select the attribute from the cascade menu that appears. In most cases, you won't see the attribute on the screen (you *will* see bold, and—if you have a monochrome monitor—underlining). Instead, WordPerfect uses all the colors of the rainbow to represent the formatting.

An even easier way to apply multiple attributes is to use the Font dialog box. See the section, "Working with Fonts," later in this chapter.

Changing Character Size and Position

You can also format the size of your characters. You can make characters really big to scare the heck out of people, or really small so that no one can read them. You can even change the relative *position* of characters to get superscripts (slightly higher than normal) or subscripts (slightly lower than normal), as shown here.

```
File  Edit  View  Layout  Tools  Font  Graphics  Window  Help

   You can be reading quietly, minding your own beeswax,
   when suddenly you get a superscript floating up there above
   the text. Whoa! And just when you've recovered from
   that, along comes a subscript to really mess with your head!

   I suppose they're useful, though. I mean, if you plan to
   use equations like x² + y³ = 25 in your documents (hey,
   it could happen), then you've just gotta use superscripts.

   And subscripts are great for symbols like H₂O.

C:\WP60\DOCS\POSITION.WP              Doc 1 Pg 1 Ln 4" Pos 1"
```

WordPerfect lets you change the relative position of characters to get superscripts and subscripts.

> **E-Z** To select the **Normal** command quickly, press **Ctrl+N**.

To change the size or position of existing text, first select the block you want to work with. Then pull down the Font menu, and select the Size/Position command; in the cascade menu that appears, select the command you need.

Chapter 12 • Making Your Characters Look Good **115**

> **Put It to Work**
>
> Using different character sizes and attributes is an easy way to fool people into thinking you're a competent professional. For example, you can make your titles and section headings stand out by using bold characters that are larger than your regular text. Italic is good for things like company names and book titles, and you can also use it for emphasizing important words or phrases.

State Your Case: Converting Uppercase and Lowercase Letters

On most keyboards, the Caps Lock key is just above the Shift key. Inevitably, in the heat of battle, I end up hitting Caps Lock by mistake a few times a day. The result: anything from a few words to a few lines all in uppercase! Fortunately, WordPerfect lets me off the hook easily with its case-conversion feature. You can change uppercase to lowercase, lowercase to uppercase, and you can even get it to convert only the initial letter in each word to uppercase (to change *alphonse* to *Alphonse*, for example).

To convert case, select the appropriate block, pull down the Edit menu, and then select the Convert Case command. In the cascade menu that appears, select Uppercase, Lowercase, or Initial Caps.

> **E-Z**
>
> Rehighlighting a block can be a pain, but here's a nifty trick that makes it easy. Once you've added some formatting, press **Alt+F4** (or **F12**) to turn **B**lock mode back on. Press **Ctrl+Home** *twice*. Voilà! Your block is rehighlighted instantly!

> **5.1**
>
> In 5.1, the various size and position commands are on the Font menu.

> **5.1**
>
> Sorry, but version 5.1 doesn't have the Initial Caps command.

Working with Fonts

Until now, you may not have given much thought to the individual characters that make up your writings. After all, an *a* is an *a*, isn't it? Oh, sure, you can (as you've just learned) make it bold or italic or big or small, but it still looks more or less the same. However, when you start working with different *fonts*, you'll see that not all *a*'s are the same (or *b*'s or *c*'s for that matter).

Just What the Heck is a Font, Anyway?

Fonts are to characters what architecture is to buildings. In architecture, you look at certain features and patterns; if you can tell a geodesic dome from a flying buttress, you can tell whether the building is Gothic or Art Deco or whatever. Fonts, too, are distinguished by a set of unique design characteristics that can make them wildly different, as you can see here.

As these examples show, fonts can be very different.

Chapter 12 • Making Your Characters Look Good **117**

Fonts come in three flavors: *serif, sans-serif,* or *decorative*. A serif font contains fine cross-strokes—typographic technoids call them *feet*—at the extremities of each character. These subtle appendages give the font a traditional, classy look. ITC Bookman is a common example of a serif font.

A sans-serif font doesn't contain these cross-strokes. As a result, serif fonts usually have a cleaner, more modern look (check out Helvetica in the figure below).

Decorative fonts are usually special designs used to convey a particular effect. So, for example, the Commercial Script font shown above would be ideal for fancy-shmancy invitations or certificates, but you wouldn't want to use it for a novel.

Selecting Different Fonts

Okay, enough theory. Let's get down to business and see how you go about selecting different fonts for your documents. To begin with, pull down the Font menu and select the Font command. You'll see the Font dialog box, shown here.

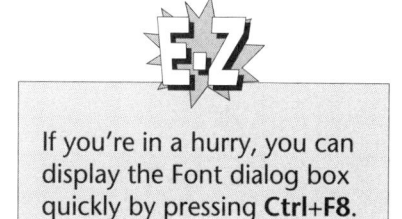

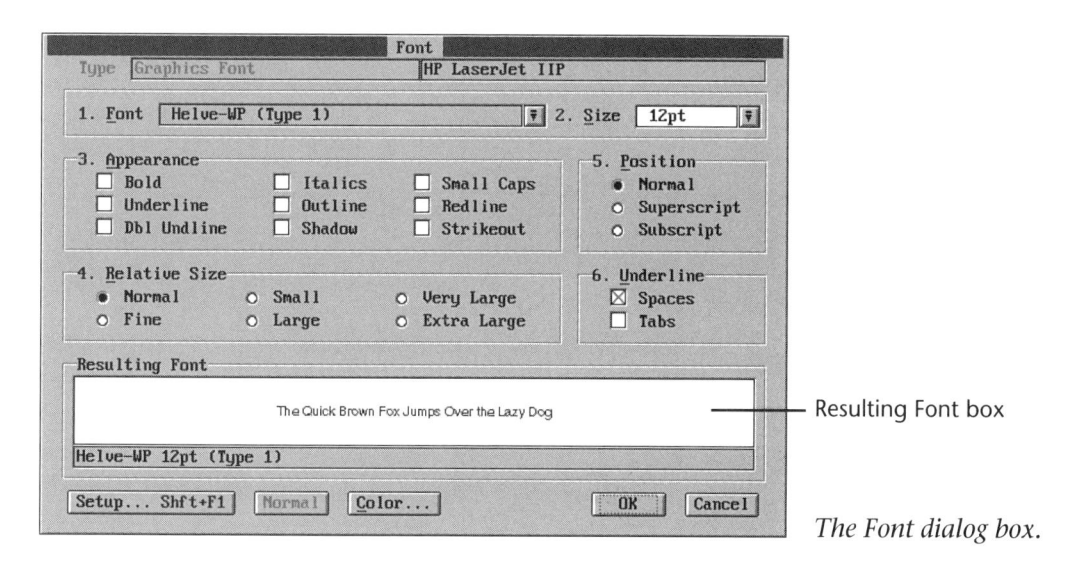

> **E-Z**
> If you're in a hurry, you can display the Font dialog box quickly by pressing **Ctrl+F8**.

The Font dialog box.

From here, selecting the font you want is easy: just open the **Font** drop-down list (by selecting **Font** and pressing **Enter**, or by clicking on the downward-pointing arrow) and then select the one you want. While you're here, you can also pick out any other character attributes you want to set. Just activate the appropriate check boxes or radio buttons, or use the **Size** drop-down list to set the character size. When you're done, select **OK** to return to the document.

> **By the Way . . .**
> As you're selecting your formatting options, keep your eyes on the **Resulting Font** box. It'll give you an idea of what your font will look like.

Avoiding the "Ransom Note" Look

> **TECHNO NERD TEACHES**
> The various radio buttons in the **R**elative Size group are equivalent to the sizing options on the **F**ont menu. These just change the character size *relative to* the normal size (or *base font*, as it's called). Use the **S**ize list when you want an explicit type size. The numbers you see are measured in *points*, where there are 72 points in an inch.

The downside to WordPerfect's easy-to-use character attributes and fonts is that they can sometimes be *too* easy to use. Flushed with your newfound knowledge, you start throwing every formatting option in sight at your documents. This can turn even the most profound and well-written documents into a real dog's breakfast. (It's known in the trade as the "ransom note" look.) Here are some tips to avoid overdoing your formatting:

- Never use more than a couple of fonts in a single document. Anything more looks amateurish, and will only confuse the reader.
- If you need to emphasize something, bold or italicize it in the *same* font as the surrounding text. Avoid using underlining for emphasis.
- Use larger sizes only for titles and headings.

☞ Avoid bizarre decorative fonts for large sections of text. Most of those suckers are hard on the eyes after a half dozen words or so. Serif fonts are usually very readable, so they're a good choice for long passages. The clean look of sans serif fonts makes them a good choice for headlines and titles.

Adding Silly Symbols

Were you stumped the last time you wanted to write "Dag Hammarskjöld" because you didn't know how to get one of those ö thingamajigs? I thought so. Well, you'll be happy to know that your documents aren't restricted to just the letters, numbers, and punctuation marks that you can eyeball on your keyboard. In fact, WordPerfect comes with all kinds of built-in characters that will supply you not only an ö, but a whole universe of weirdo symbols.

> **E-Z**
> Press **Ctrl+W** to get the WordPerfect Characters dialog box on the screen lickety-split.

> **SPEAK LIKE A GEEK**
> A *character set* is just a collection of related characters.

To start, position the cursor where you want to insert the symbol (at this point, it doesn't matter all that much where you put the cursor). Now pull down the Font menu, and select the WP C**h**aracters command. A dialog box called **WordPerfect Characters** will appear on the screen.

The layout is pretty simple: the squares in the Characters area show you all the symbols available for whatever character set is selected in the **Set** box. If you select a different character set, a whole new set of symbols is displayed.

To use a symbol from a character set, move into the Characters area, use the **arrow** keys to highlight a symbol, and then press **Enter**. If you have a mouse, just double-click on the symbol.

The Least You Need to Know

This chapter was the first stop on our journey toward looking good on paper. You learned how to format characters by making them bold or italic, giving them larger or smaller sizes, or using different fonts. Here's the condensed version of what happened:

- ☞ If you have version 6 (and you have a system that can handle it), select the **G**raphics Mode command from the **V**iew menu. Graphics mode lets you see your formatting right on the screen instead of having to wait for it to be printed.

- ☞ To alter the attributes of your characters, select the block you want to work with and then choose the appropriate command from the **F**ont menu.

- ☞ Select the **F**ont menu's Size/Position command to get a menu of sizing and position choices.

- ☞ If you need to convert a block of text from upper- to lowercase (or vice versa), select Convert Case from the **E**dit menu, and choose the appropriate command.

- ☞ Fonts are distinctive character designs. To select a different font, choose **F**onts from the **F**ont menu and pick out what you need from the Fonts dialog box.

- ☞ WordPerfect comes with various character sets built-in. These sets can give you international characters, scientific symbols, and more. Select the WP **C**haracters command from the **F**ont menu.

Chapter 13
Making Your Lines and Paragraphs Look Good

In This Chapter

- Setting and deleting tab stops in a paragraph
- Left-justifying, centering, and right-justifying text
- Adjusting the line spacing
- Indenting paragraph text
- Working with paragraph margins
- The usual motley collection of trenchant tips and topical tirades

The last chapter showed you how to format characters, so now we'll bump things up a notch, and look at formatting lines and paragraphs. How will this help you look good on paper? Well, all the character formatting in the world won't do you much good if your lines are all scrunched together, and if the various pieces of text aren't lined up like boot-camp recruits. Documents like these look cramped and uninviting, and will often get tossed in the old "circular file" without a second look. This chapter will help you avoid this sorry fate.

If things somehow go haywire and your document ends up all askew, you need to do two things. First, start chanting the following mantra in your head: "This is not my fault, this is WordPerfect's fault. This is not my fault . . . ." Second, select **Undo** from the **Edit** menu (or press **Ctrl+Z**) to reverse the mayhem.

Formatting Lines Versus Paragraphs

The way WordPerfect formats lines and paragraphs can be hopelessly confusing, even for experienced word processing hacks. So, to soften the blow a little, here are some things to keep in mind when working with this chapter's formatting options:

- If you select a format option *without* selecting a block, WordPerfect formats everything from the current paragraph to the end of the document.

- If you select a block (even just a single character), WordPerfect formats only the paragraph that contains the block.

Working with Tab Stops

Documents look much better if they're properly indented, and if their various parts line up nicely. The best way to do this is to use tabs instead of spaces whenever you need to create some room in a line. Why? Well, a single space can take up different amounts of room, depending on the font and size of the characters you're using. So your document can end up looking pretty ragged if you try to use spaces to indent your text. Tabs, on the other hand, are fastidiously precise. When you press the **Tab** key, the insertion point moves ahead exactly to the next tab stop, no more, no less.

To begin, pull down the Layout menu and select the Tab Set command. This displays the Tab Set dialog box. The ruler across the top of this dialog box shows you where the current tabs are set. (0" represents the left edge of the page.) Each **L** you see represents a tab stop (the "L" indicates that it's a *left* tab; I'll explain what this means in a second).

By the Way . . .

It's often best to start with a clean slate and just set your own tabs. See the section titled "Deleting Tabs," later on in the chapter.

Checking Out WordPerfect's Tab Types

As you can see, WordPerfect has a tab for your every mood. Here's a quickie summary of the available types:

Left   Text lines up with the tab on the left.

Right   Text lines up with the tab on the right.

Center   Text is centered on the tab.

Decimal   Numbers line up with the tab at their decimal places.

Dot Leader   The tab is preceded by a bunch of dots.

> **5.1**
>
> In version 5.1, select **Line** from the **Layout** menu and then select the **Tab Set** option. This displays the tab set ruler at the bottom of the screen.

Here's a picture that illustrates each of these tab types.

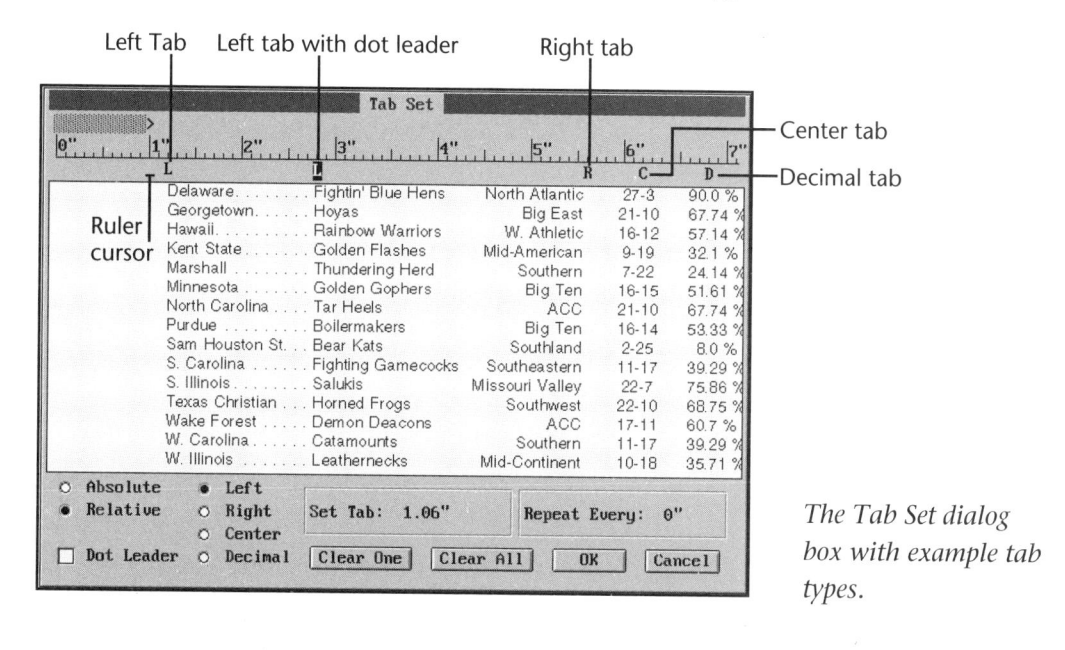

The Tab Set dialog box with example tab types.

Setting Tabs

Once you've displayed the Tab Set dialog box, WordPerfect gives you umpteen different ways to actually set the little beasts. Here are the easiest ones:

- Move the ruler's cursor to the position you want and then press either **L** (for a left tab), **R** (for right), **C** (for center), or **D** (for decimal).

- With a mouse, click on the tab type, and then double-click on the ruler position you want.

- To move an existing tab, place the cursor under the tab, hold down **Ctrl**, and use the **left** or **right arrow** keys to move it. When you've got it positioned just right, let go of Ctrl and press **Enter**.

- To set a bunch of tabs at a regular interval, select the R**e**peat Every text box, enter a number for the interval (in inches), and then press **Enter**.

Deleting Tabs

If you'd like to get rid of a tab or two, just position the ruler's cursor under the tab stop and either press Delete or click on the Clear One button. If you'd like a fresh start, select the Clear All button.

Justifying Your Text

Justifying your text has nothing to do with defending your ideas (luckily for some of us!). Rather, it has to do with lining up your paragraphs so they look all prim and proper. Here's an example document, showing the various justification options.

TECHNO NERD TEACHES

You can also make your tab stops *absolute* or *relative*. Absolute tab stops are measured from the left edge of the page. They're rock-solid; they wouldn't change position in a hurricane. Relative tab stops are more laid back. They're measured from the left margin, so if you change the margin position (which I'll show you how to do in the next chapter), they're happy to move right along. In general, it's best to stick with relative tab stops.

5.1

To set tabs in version 5.1, select **L**ine from the **L**ayout menu and then choose **T**ab **S**et from the menu that appears. A ruler with the current tab stops appears at the bottom of the screen. Move the cursor to the tab position you want. Then select **L**eft, **R**ight, **C**enter, or **D**ecimal. Press period (.) to add a dot leader. When you're done, press **F7** twice.

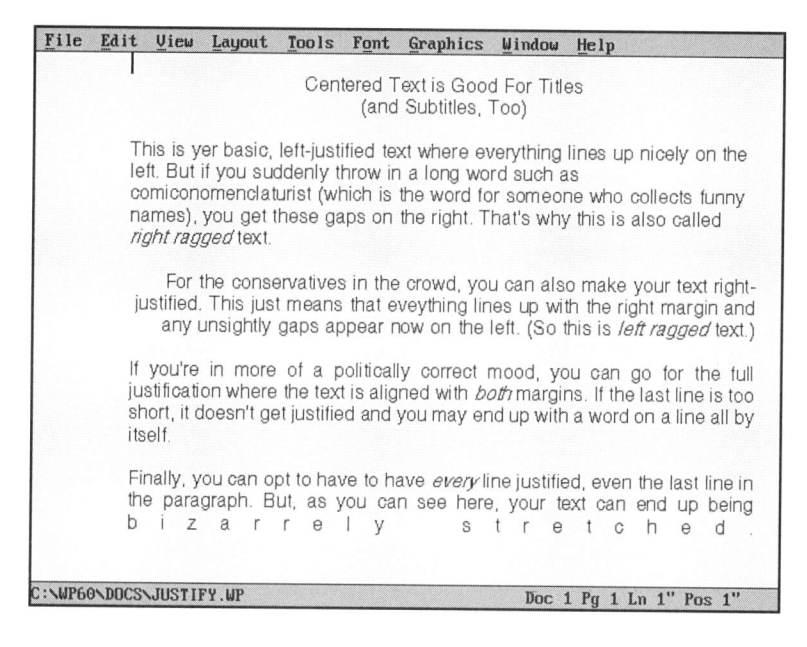

Chapter 13 • Making Your Lines and Paragraphs Look Good **125**

Some text justification examples.

You get five options for your justification fun:

Left   Justifies each line on the left margin.

Center   Centers each line between both margins.

Right   Justifies each line on the right margin.

Full   Justifies each line on both margins. Ignores the last line in a paragraph if it's too small.

Full, All Lines   Justifies every line in a paragraph on both margins.

> **5.1**
> With the tab ruler displayed, you delete a tab in version 5.1 by positioning the cursor under the tab and pressing **Delete** or **Backspace**. To delete all tabs, move the cursor to the beginning of the ruler and press **Ctrl+End**.

If you try to do any of this stuff on a typewriter, you just end up adding to your stomach's ever-growing ulcer population. On a computer, though, it's a walk in the park. All you do is pull down the Layout menu, select Justification, and then choose the command you want from the cascade menu that appears.

Part III • Looking Good: Formatting Stuff

> **SPEAK LIKE A GEEK**
> Left justified text is said to be *right ragged* because the right side of each line doesn't line up. Similarly, right-justified text is called *left ragged*.

Just to make things confusing, WordPerfect also gives you a way to justify individual lines. To check this out, place the cursor anywhere in the line, and select Alignment from the Layout menu. If you want to center the line, select the Center command from the cascade menu. To right justify the line, select the Flush Right command.

Changing the Line Spacing

Typewriters have little levers or buttons you can maneuver to alter the line spacing. Well anything a typewriter can do, WordPerfect can do better. So, while a typewriter usually only lets you set up double- or triple-spacing, WordPerfect can handle just about any number of spaces—and even takes things to two decimal places! (Anybody need *four-point-two-five*-ple-spacing?)

> **E-Z**
> To format tabs and justification at the same time, select the Layout menu's Line command and use the options in the Line Format dialog box.

To set your line spacing, pull down the Layout menu, and select the Line command. Now get into the Line Spacing text box and enter the number of spaces you want. When you're ready, select **OK**.

> **By the Way . . .**
> The maximum value you can use for line spacing is 65,516. Just thought you might like to know.

Indenting Text

> **5.1**
> In version 5.1, select the Layout menu's Line command, and then select Justification from the menu that appears. In the status line prompt, select the justification option you want, and then press **F7**.

If you need to indent a whole paragraph from the margin, don't do it with tab stops. Instead, WordPerfect will indent an entire paragraph for you. Just place the cursor at the beginning of the paragraph (you don't need to select a block this time—didn't I tell you this was confusing?), select

Alignment from the Layout menu, and then select the Indent → command from the cascade menu. WordPerfect indents each line in the paragraph to the first tab stop.

> **By the Way . . .**
> If you want to indent only the first line, see the next section.

If you need to indent a paragraph from *both* margins, place the cursor at the beginning of the paragraph, select Alignment from the Layout menu again, but this time choose the Indent →← command.

> **Put It to Work:**
> Indented paragraphs are best used to separate a section of text from the rest of a document. A good example is when you need to quote a large passage. "If you only need to quote a sentence or two, like I'm doing here, just include it in the normal flow of the text." But if it's longer, use a separate, indented paragraph and lead into it with a colon:
>
>> See? By moving the quote out of the regular text, you do two things: you avoid cluttering your prose with a long, rambling quotation such as this, and you also give the quote more prominence (whether it deserves it or not). Notice, too, that you don't need quotation marks. It's understood from the context that this is someone talking.
>
> Whether you indent just from the left or on both sides is a matter of personal choice. Personally, I like using both sides, because it creates a greater sense of separation from the rest of the text. End of style lesson.

Setting Paragraph Margins

Every page in a document has a margin around each side. I'll show you how to work with these in the next chapter, but as a warmup, let's see how

> The shortcut for centering a line is **Shift+F6**. For right-justifying a line, press **Alt+F6**.

> If you have a mouse, you can adjust the value in the Line **S**pacing box by clicking on the **up** or **down arrows** beside it.

> Pressing **F4** will indent a paragraph without having to bother with all those menus.

> To indent from both margins fast, press **Shift+F4**.

you format a paragraph's margins. A *paragraph's margins?* Yup. This just refers to the white space above and below a paragraph (i.e., the spacing between paragraphs) and to the left and right of a paragraph (i.e., between the paragraph and the left and right page margins). As an added bonus, you can also indent the first line of a paragraph.

Here's how it's done:

1. Select a block in the paragraph you want to work with.

2. Pull down the Layout menu and select the Margins command. You'll see the Margin Format dialog box on the screen.

3. Use the options in the **Paragraph Margins** group to make your adjustments. You should note three things here:

    - The Left Margin Adjustment and Right Margin Adjustment are relative to the current page margins. So if you enter **1"** and the page margins are 1 inch, the paragraph will be indented 2 inches.

    - The First Line Indent is relative to the left paragraph margin.

    - The Paragraph Spacing refers only to the number of spaces above and below the paragraph. Don't confuse this with the line spacing we looked at earlier in this chapter.

4. When you're done, select **OK** to return to the document.

The Least You Need to Know

This chapter walked you through some of WordPerfect's line and paragraph formatting options. It is, as I said, somewhat confusing at times, so I think a brief recap is in order:

- If you want to format just a paragraph, block off some text in the paragraph (a letter or two will do). Otherwise, WordPerfect formats everything from the cursor position on down.

- To set tab stops, select the **T**ab Set command from the **L**ayout menu and use the Tab Set dialog box to enter your tabs.

- To justify text, pull down the **L**ayout menu, select the **J**ustification command, and then choose the justification option you need from the cascade menu that appears.

- To change the spacing between the lines in a paragraph, select the **L**ayout menu's **L**ine command. In the **Line Format** dialog box, enter the number of spaces you want in the Line **S**pacing text box.

- You can indent text either from the left margin or from both margins. Just select the **A**lignment command from the **L**ayout menu, and select the appropriate option from the cascade menu.

- To set paragraph margins, pull down the **L**ayout menu and select the **M**argins command. Enter your new margin values in the **Margin Format** dialog box.

Chapter 14
Making Your Pages Look Good

In This Chapter

- Making adjustments to the page margins
- Creating your own page breaks
- Using WordPerfect's new page mode
- Adding and formatting page numbers
- Defining headers and footers
- Sad stories of widows and orphans

Well, lets see: we've looked at formatting characters, lines, and paragraphs. So, since logic is an occasionally useful tool that I succumb to from time to time, we'll now graduate to full-fledged *page formatting*. This is the stuff—we're talking things like margin adjustments, page numbers, headers, and footers—that can add that certain *je ne sais quois* to your documents. (Of course, adding fancy foreign terms in italics also helps, but I'll leave that up to you.) This chapter takes on these topics and more.

> **OOPS!**
> As usual, if any of this formatting stuff gets out of hand, immediately select the **Edit** menu's **Undo** command (or press **Ctrl+Z**) to bring everything back in line.

Adjusting Page Margins

The *page margins* refer to the white space that surrounds your text on a page. There are, then, four margins altogether: at the top and bottom of the page, and on the left and right sides of a page. By default, WordPerfect decrees each of these margins to be one inch, but you can override that, if you like. Why would you want to do such a thing? Here are a few good reasons:

> **TECHNO NERD TEACHES**
>
> When the last line of a paragraph appears by itself at the top of a page, it's called, sadly, a *widow*. If you get the first line of a paragraph by itself at the bottom of a page, it's called an *orphan*. (No, I don't *know* who comes up with this stuff.) WordPerfect, mercifully, lets you prevent these pathetic creatures from inhabiting your documents. Just pull down the **L**ayout menu, select **O**ther, and then activate the **W**idow/Orphan Protect check box.

- If someone else is going to be making notes on the page, it helps to include bigger left and right margins (to give them more room for scribbling).

- Smaller margins all around mean that you get more text on a page. On a really long document, this could save you a few pages when you print it out.

- If you have a document that's just slightly longer than a page (say by only a line or two), you could decrease the top and bottom margins just enough to fit the wayward lines onto a single page.

Before changing the margins, you need to decide how much of the document you want affected. WordPerfect adjusts the margins—either from the current paragraph to the end of the page, or only for any paragraphs that are part of a highlighted block. So, for example, if you want to adjust the margins for the entire document, place the cursor at top of the first page (by pressing **Home,Home,up arrow**).

> **By the Way . . .**
>
> If you just want to change the margins for a single paragraph, refer back to Chapter 13, "Formatting Lines and Paragraphs," for the appropriate steps.

When you're ready, pull down the **Layout** menu and select the **Margins** command. The Margin Format dialog box appears, as shown here.

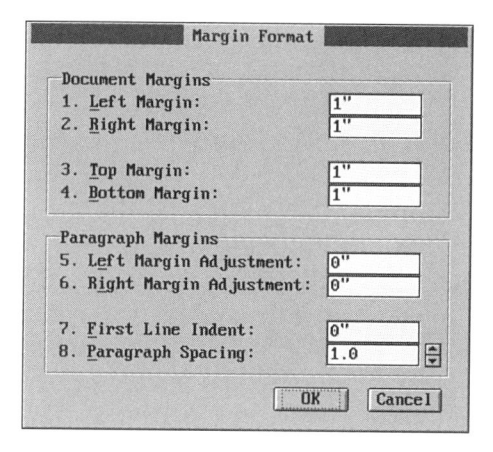

Use the Margin Format dialog box to set your page margins.

You use the text boxes in the Document Margins group to set your margins. For example, to adjust the top margin, enter a number in the **Top** Margin box. (Note that these numbers are measured in inches from the edge of the page. You don't have to bother with the inch sign (") though; WordPerfect adds it for you.) When you're done, select **OK**.

OOPS!

If you plan to print a document on a laser printer, keep in mind that most lasers can't print anything that's closer to the edge of the page than half an inch or so.

By the Way . . .

When you adjust your margins, you'll notice that the status line's Ln and Pos indicators are affected as well. For example, if you set the top margin to half an inch, the **Ln** indicator will display **0.5"** when you're at the top of a page.

Dealing with WordPerfect's Page Breaks

As you may know by now, WordPerfect signals the start of a new page by running a line across the screen (it's called a *page break*). Text that appears above the line prints on one page, and text below the line prints on the

> **SPEAK LIKE A GEEK**
>
> Page breaks that adjust themselves automatically are *soft page breaks*.
>
> A page break that doesn't move is called a *hard page break*.

> **E-Z**
>
> Forget all those pull-down menu commands. Just press **Ctrl+Enter** to set a hard page break.

> **5.1**
>
> You can take a look at page numbers, headers, and such in WordPerfect 5.1 by pulling down the **F**ile menu, selecting the **P**rint command, and then selecting **V**iew Document from the Print menu. Note, however, that you can't make changes to the document while viewing it in this manner.

next page. This text arrangement is not set in stone, of course. If you insert a new paragraph or change the margins, the text on both sides of the page line moves accordingly.

But what if you have a line or paragraph that *has to* appear at the top of a page? You could fiddle around by pressing Enter enough times, but WordPerfect gives you an easier way. Just position the cursor where you want the new page to begin, pull down the Layout menu, select the **A**lignment command, and then select the Hard **P**age command. WordPerfect creates a new page and marks the break with a *double* line. Now, no matter how much stuff you insert on the previous pages or how you adjust the margins, the text just below the double line always remains at the top of that page.

To delete a hard page break, you have two options:

- Position the cursor at the beginning of the line below the break and press **Backspace**.
- Position the cursor at the end of the line above the break and press **Delete**.

A Note About Page Mode

Many of the formatting options you'll be learning about in the rest of this chapter won't actually appear on your screen. Things like page numbers, headers, and footers only appear once you've printed the document. If you'd like to take a look at these before you print (and you use version 6), switch to *page mode*. This mode shows you just what your page will look like when it's printed, including the otherwise-hidden formatting options. All you do is pull down the View menu and select the P**a**ge Mode option.

> **By the Way . . .**
> Another way to see what your page looks like is WordPerfect's Print Preview feature. Peek ahead to Chapter 16, "Getting It Down On Paper: Printing Documents," for the Print Preview particulars.

Adding Page Numbers

WordPerfect's status line tells you which page you're on when you ramble through a document on screen, but what happens when you print it out? To avoid getting lost in large documents, you should add page numbers that'll appear on the hard copies. Once you tell WordPerfect that you want page numbers, the program tracks everything for you.

Everything happens inside the Page Numbering dialog box, so you need to display that first. Just select the **Page** command from the **Layout** menu, and then select the Page Numbering option.

Positioning the Page Numbers

The first decision you have to make is where you want your numbers to appear on the page. WordPerfect, ever eager to please, gives you no less than eight (that's right, *eight*) possibilities. To check them out, select the Page Number **P**osition option at the top of the Page Numbering dialog box. This displays the Page Number Position dialog box, shown here.

As you can see, most of the options are straightforward. You can position the numbers on the top or bottom of the page, and in each case you can choose between the left, center, or right side of the page. Two other choices—Alternating, **T**op and Alternating, **B**ottom—may require a bit more explanation. These options mean that WordPerfect will switch the position of the numbers depending on whether the page is odd or even.

For example, the Alternating, Top option places the numbers on the top right for odd pages and the top left for even pages (which is, you'll notice, the way this book is formatted).

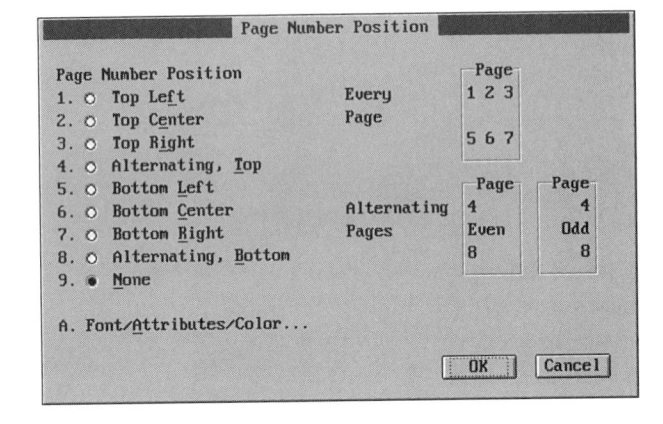

WordPerfect's Page Number Position dialog box gives you all kinds of ways to position your page numbers.

```
                    Page Number Position
Page Number Position                        ┌Page─┐
  1. ○  Top Left              Every         │1 2 3│
  2. ○  Top Center            Page          │     │
  3. ○  Top Right                           │5 6 7│
  4. ○  Alternating, Top                    └─────┘
  5. ○  Bottom Left                      ┌Page┐ ┌Page┐
  6. ○  Bottom Center         Alternating│ 4  │ │  4 │
  7. ○  Bottom Right          Pages      │Even│ │ Odd│
  8. ○  Alternating, Bottom              │ 8  │ │  8 │
  9. ●  None                             └────┘ └────┘

  A. Font/Attributes/Color...
                                        [  OK  ] [Cancel]
```

After you've marveled at the sheer wealth of choices available to you, pick the one you want, and then select **OK** to return to the Page Numbering dialog box.

> ### By the Way . . .
> Rather than just using a number all by itself, you can add some text to go along with your page numbers. So, for example, you could add the word **Page** or even something like **My Great American Novel**. All you do is type what you want in the Page Number Format text box. It's usually best to insert the text before the **[page #]** code that's already in there.

Setting the Page Number

5.1 In version 5.1, once you have the Page **N**umbering menu displayed, press the number that corresponds to the position you want, and then press **F7** to exit.

Most of the time you'll just start at page 1 and go from there. However, you're free to start the page numbers at whatever number you like. This is great if your document is a continuation of an existing project (such as a new chapter in a book). If the rest of the project has 100 pages, then you'd start this document at page 101.

Select the Page Number option to display the Set Page Number dialog box, and then enter the starting number in the New Number text box. Select **OK** to return to the Page Numbering dialog box.

> **By the Way . . .**
> You're not restricted to using plain old numbers. When you're in the **Set Page Number** dialog box, check out the Numbering **M**ethod option. You'll see that you can use letters (upper- or lowercase) or even Roman numerals.

> **Put It to Work**
>
> In general, you shouldn't work with documents any larger than a couple of dozen pages or so. Not only might you run out of memory, but humongous documents are just a pain to work with. Ideally, you should break monster projects into manageable chunks—a chapter per document is usually okay.
>
> Happily, WordPerfect includes lots of page numbering options that are great for keeping track of these large projects. For example, you can include chapter numbers in your documents. In the **Page Numbering** dialog box, place the cursor in the Page Number **F**ormat text box, and then either press **F5** or click on the **Number Codes** button. Select **C**hapter Number from the dialog box, and press **Enter**. A new code—**[chpt #]**—appears. Add some text so you know which number is which, like so:
>
> **Chapter [chpt #] Page [page #]**
>
> WordPerfect won't increment these numbers automatically, so you'll need to use the **C**hapter option to adjust them yourself.
>
> *continues*

> *continued*
>
> If your project is a multi-volume deal (my, you *are* prolific, aren't you?), you can do the same thing with volume numbers.

5.1 To set the page number in 5.1, select Page **N**umbering from the Page Numbering menu, and then select **N**ew Page Number. Enter the number you want, and then press **F7** to exit.

Centering Text Between the Top and Bottom

If you've read Chapter 13, "Formatting Lines and Paragraphs," then you know how to center text between the left and right margins. WordPerfect also lets you center between the top and bottom margins, which is great for things like title pages, résumés, and short business letters.

First move to the page you want to center, then select **P**age from the Layout menu. To center only the current page, select the Center Current Page check box. If you want every page in the document centered, activate the Center **P**ages check box.

5.1 Inconveniently, version 5.1 will center only one page at a time. Select **P**age from the **L**ayout menu, choose the **C**enter Page option, and then press **F7** to exit.

Setting Up Headers and Footers

Take a look at the top of the page you're reading now. Above the line that runs across the top you'll see a page number and some text (on the even pages, you see the part number and part name; on the odd pages, it's the chapter number and chapter name). These are examples of *headers*—sections of text that appear at the top margin of every page.

WordPerfect lets you include headers in your own documents, just like the pros. You can put in the usual stuff—page numbers (as described in the last section), chapter titles, and so on—but you're free to add anything you like: your name, your

5.1 Adding a header or footer in version 5.1 isn't all that different from doing it in version 6. You do start differently, however: select the **L**ayout menu's **P**age command, and then select the **H**eaders or **F**ooters option.

company's name, your dog's name, whatever. And you can even do *footers*, as well. A footer is the same as a header, only it appears at the bottom of each page (makes sense).

To add a header or footer, follow these steps:

1. When you add a header or footer, WordPerfect uses it for all the pages from the current page to the end of the document. So the first thing you need to do is position the cursor somewhere in the first page you want to use.

2. Pull down the Layout menu and select the Header/Footer/Watermark command. The Header/Footer/Watermark dialog box, shown here, appears.

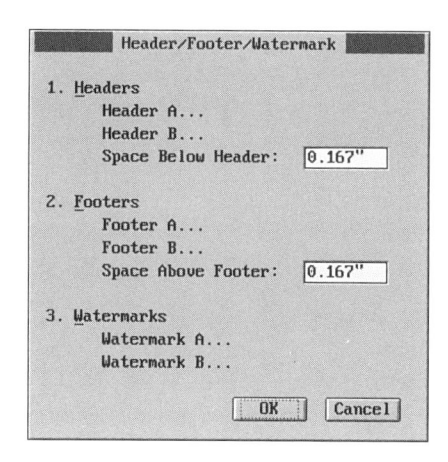

> **TECHNO NERD TEACHES**
>
> A *watermark*, in case you're wondering, is a translucent image or section of text that prints over the top of existing text on a page. You can use them to add logos, descriptive comments (e.g., "SAMPLE" or "TOP SECRET"), or to control people's minds with subliminal messages (yeah, right). If you'd like to check them out, follow the same basic steps that you use for a header or footer. (Note, however, that you need a PostScript printer to successfully print out watermarks.)

The Header/Footer/Watermark dialog box.

3. Select **H**eaders to add a header, or **F**ooters to add a footer.

4. You can define up to two headers or footers (A and B) per page, so you now need to select which header or footer to add. For example, to define header A, select Header **A**.

5. You can choose to place your headers or footers on all pages, or only on odd or even pages. Select the appropriate option from the dialog box, and then select the **Create** button.

6. WordPerfect then presents you with a blank editing screen. Just type in the header text you want to use. Feel free to use any character or line formatting options (fonts, bold, justification, etc.). You can, if you like, add several lines of text. Just remember that the bigger the header or footer, the less room you'll have for your regular text.

7. When you're done, press **F7** to return to the document.

> ### The Least You Need to Know
> This chapter walked you through some of WordPerfect's page formatting options. Here's a recap of what you really need to know to make your life complete:
>
> - To adjust the page margins, pull down the **Layout** menu, select the **Margins** command, and then enter the new margin values in the **Margin Format** dialog box.
>
> - A *soft page break* is a page separator that WordPerfect adds automatically to your documents. It's based on the current margin settings. A *hard page break* is a break you enter yourself. It remains in position even if you enter text above it or change the margins. To add a hard page break, position the cursor and press **Ctrl+Enter**.
>
> - To add page numbers to a document, first select the **Layout** menu's **Page** command, and then select the Page **N**umbering option. In the Page Numbering dialog box, select Page Number **P**osition to position the page numbers, and Page **N**umber to set a starting page number and format.
>
> - Centering text between the top and bottom margins is a breeze. Just select **P**age from the **L**ayout menu, and then activate either the **C**enter Current Page or Center **P**ages check box.

- If you need to add headers or footers to a document, select the **H**eader/Footer/Watermark command from the **L**ayout menu, and run through the options in the dialog box that appears.

- To see formatting options such as page numbers, headers, and footers, switch to *page mode* by selecting the **Pa**ge Mode command from the **V**iew menu.

Chapter 15
Other Ways to Look Good

In This Chapter

- Adding and formatting dates and times in a document
- Creating footnotes, endnotes, and comments
- Using hyphenation for fun and profit
- Working with different paper sizes
- Miscellaneous ways to fool people into thinking you know what you're doing

This chapter will be your formatting graduate school. The last three chapters covered the grade school of formatting characters, the high school of formatting lines and paragraphs, and the college of formatting pages. Now you get to do post-graduate work with things like dates, footnotes, and hyphenation. Believe me, people will be *very* impressed. Will this be as hard as graduate school? No way. You'll still just be learning the basics in the same non-technical fashion that you've come to know and love.

> If you press **Shift+F5**, WordPerfect displays the Date dialog box with the same options as the cascade menu.

Inserting the Date and Time into a Document

If you need to add a date to a document (if you're just starting a letter, for example), don't bother typing it yourself; let WordPerfect do it for you. All you do is position the cursor where you want the date to appear, pull down the Tools menu, and select the Date command. A cascade menu appears with three date commands:

Text   This command inserts the date just as though you typed it yourself.

Code   This command inserts a special code that tells WordPerfect to always display the *current* date. This means that the date will change if you open the document tomorrow, next week, or next month.

Format   WordPerfect has no less than eight date formats, including one that inserts the time only and another that inserts both the date *and* time.

Select Text or Code to insert the date. To get a different date style (or the time), select Format, pick out the style you want, and then select **OK**.

Put It to Work

One of the most common uses for the date and time in a document is to keep track of revisions. Some documents may go through a dozen amendments or more, so it becomes crucial to know which version you're dealing with. By including the codes (not just text) for the date and time, WordPerfect updates everything each time you work on the file, so you always know when it was last modified.

The ideal place for these date and time codes is a header or footer (which I covered in Chapter 14, "Making Your Pages Look Good"). When you're in the header or footer editing screen, just add the date and time as described in this section (make sure you use the **C**ode command).

Adding Footnotes and Endnotes

One of the best ways to make people think you worked *really* hard on a document is to include *footnotes* at the bottom of the page. Footnotes say "Hey, this person took the time and effort to write this little parenthetical note for my edification or amusement. I think I'll take him out to lunch."

If you've ever tried adding footnotes to a page with a typewriter, then you know what a nightmare it can be, trying to coordinate the size of the note with the regular page text. And if you need to change your footnote numbers? Forget about it.

WordPerfect changes all that by making footnotes as easy as typing text. The program arranges things so that your pages accommodate any size footnote perfectly, and it'll even manage the footnote numbers for you—automatically! But wait, there's more! WordPerfect can also do *endnotes*, if you prefer them over footnotes. Endnotes are less convenient for the reader, but they're good for longer entries that would otherwise take up too much space in a footnote.

Creating Footnotes and Endnotes

Since a footnote or endnote always refers to something in the regular text, your first task is to position the cursor where you want the little footnote/endnote number to appear. Once you've done that, pull down the Layout menu and select either the Footnote or Endnote command. In the cascade menu that

OOPS!

If the date or time that appears is wrong, don't blame WordPerfect; your computer is the one who's supposed to keep track of these things. If it has fallen down on the job, there's a way to fix it—if you don't mind attempting a DOS command or two. (Yes, a shudder *is* the appropriate reaction at this point.) The next time you're at the DOS prompt, type **date** and press **Enter**. DOS shows you the current date and prompts you for a new one. Type in the date, with the **mm-dd-yy** format that DOS uses (you need to include the dashes), and press **Enter**. To fix the time, type **time**, press **Enter**, and enter the correct time in DOS's **hh:mm** format.

SPEAK LIKE A GEEK

A *footnote* is a section of text placed at the bottom of a page. An *endnote* is a section of text placed at the end of a document. Both footnotes and endnotes usually contain asides or comments that embellish something in the regular document text.

appears, select **Create**. WordPerfect displays the footnote or endnote editing screen with the note's number. Enter your text (feel free to use any character or line formatting options), and press **F7** when you're done. WordPerfect returns you to the document and displays the same number at the cursor position.

> **By the Way . . .**
> If you want to see your footnotes or endnotes, put WordPerfect in page mode by selecting **P**age Mode from the **V**iew menu (you need version 6 for this). Alternatively, you can use the Print Preview feature (see Chapter 16, "Getting It Down on Paper: Printing Documents").

Editing Footnotes and Endnotes

If you need to make changes to a footnote or endnote, select Footnote or Endnote from the Layout menu, and then choose Edit from the cascade menu. In the dialog box that appears, enter the number of the footnote or endnote that you want to edit, and then select **OK**. WordPerfect displays the appropriate edit screen for you to make your changes. Press **F7** when you're done.

Adding Comments to a Document

When you're writing, you may need to make a quick note to yourself about something related to the text. Or, other people may be reading your work on screen and they might want to make some snarky remarks for you to see. In either case, you can use WordPerfect's document comments feature to handle the job. Comments are text that appear in boxes on the screen, but they don't print out.

To add a comment, first position the cursor where you want the comment to appear. Then select Comme**n**t from the **L**ayout menu, and Create from the cascade menu. WordPerfect displays the comment editing screen where you can type your text (and add some formatting options, if you like). Press **F7** when you're done and you'll see the comment displayed inside a box, as you can see here.

WordPerfect places document comments inside a box. These comments don't appear when you print the file.

If you need to edit a comment, position the cursor on the first line below the command, select Comme**n**t from the Layout menu, and then select Edit from the cascade menu. When the editing screen appears, make your changes, and then press **F7** to exit.

> ### Put It to Work
>
> One of the keys to productive writing is to build up some momentum. If you're on a roll, but you get stuck on a particular idea or phrase (or if you come across a fact you need to check), don't get bogged down trying to solve it. Ignore it for now and keep going; you can always come back later on and fix things up.
>
> Before moving on, though, you should probably make a quick note or two, just to get your ideas down so you don't forget them. Comments, of course, are perfectly suited to this.

Using Hyphenation to Clean Up Your Documents

As you've seen by now, WordPerfect's word wrap feature really makes typing easier, because you don't have to worry about a looming right margin the way you do on a typewriter. If you're in the middle of a word when the margin hits, WordPerfect just moves the whole thing to a new line. While this is convenient, it can make your document look ragged if the word is a large one.

For example, take a look at the first paragraph here.

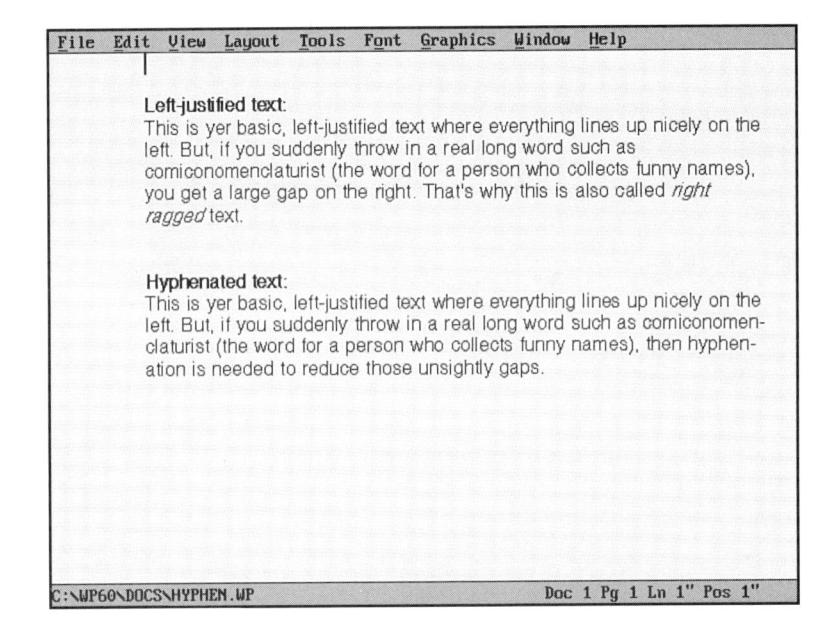

Hyphenation can reduce the gaps produced by some longer words.

As you can see, the second line has a large gap on the right because the next word—*comiconomemclaturist*—was too long to fit. One solution would be to use full justification (where text is aligned with both the left and right margins; see Chapter 13, "Formatting Lines and Paragraphs"). This often works, but you sometimes end up with lines that look unnatural.

Often a better solution is *hyphenation*, where WordPerfect takes any long words that won't fit at the end of a line, splits them in two, and adds a hyphen. The second paragraph above is hyphenated.

Follow these steps to add hyphenation to your document:

1. WordPerfect adds hyphenation from the current paragraph down to the end of the document. Position the cursor appropriately or, if you only want to hyphenate the current paragraph, select a block inside the paragraph (a letter or two will do).

2. Select the **L**ayout menu's Line command to display the Line Format dialog box.

3. Activate the H**y**phenation check box and then select **OK**. WordPerfect examines the text, and if it finds any suitable candidates for hyphenation, it displays the Position Hyphen dialog box (see below) that shows you where the hyphen will go.

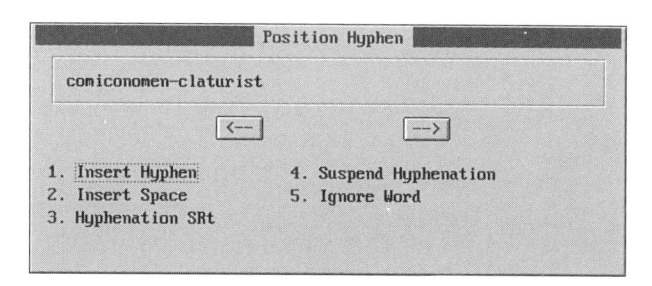

When WordPerfect finds a word that needs hyphenating, it displays the word in the Position Hyphen dialog box.

By the Way . . .

Positioning hyphens in a large document can be a pain. See Chapter 19, "Cool Tools to Make Your Life Easier," to learn how to tell WordPerfect to hyphenate everything without prompting you.

4. If you don't like where WordPerfect will break up the word, use the **left** or **right arrow** keys to move the hyphen location.

5. Select **Insert Hyphen** to, well, insert the hyphen.

6. If WordPerfect finds any more words to hyphenate, you'll have to keep repeating steps 4 and 5.

OOPS!

If you plan to print out any document where you've changed the paper size, don't forget to add the appropriate paper to your printer.

You may have noticed that the Hyphenation group in the Line Format dialog box also included a Hyphenation Zone option. You don't need to know about this to use hyphenation, but I'll give a quickie explanation for the curious.

Basically, these zones just control the amount of hyphenation in a document. The left zone is the space immediately to the left of the right margin. The right zone, then, is the space to the right of the right margin (are you sure you want to know this?). The size of each zone is a percentage of the line length. For example, the left zone is usually 10%, so if the line is 6.5 inches long, the left zone is .65 inches.

If a word begins before the left zone and continues past the right zone, WordPerfect will try to hyphenate it. If it begins after the left zone, it gets wrapped to the next line, no matter what. So, if you want more hyphenation in a document, decrease the size of each zone.

Working with Different Paper Sizes

You'll probably do most of your work on good old 8 1/2-by-11-inch paper. However, should the mood strike you, WordPerfect lets you set different paper sizes. For example, you could switch to 8 1/2-by-14-inch legal size, or envelopes, or just about anything you want. You can also select a different *orientation*. Normal orientation has the lines running across the short side of the page, but if you prefer to have the lines run across the long side of the page, you can.

E-Z

If you just have a word or two that you want to hyphenate, forget all this rigmarole. Instead, position the cursor where you want the word broken up, and press **Ctrl+-**. This adds a so-called *soft hyphen*: if you alter the position of the word, the hyphen disappears.

SPEAK LIKE A GEEK

Having the lines run across the short side of a page is called *portrait orientation*. When you turn things around and have the lines run across the long side of the page, it's called *landscape orientation*.

To change the paper size or orientation, select **P**age from the **L**ayout menu to display the Page Format dialog box. Select the Paper **S**ize/Type option, and you'll see the Paper Size/Type dialog box. Use the **up** and **down arrow** keys to highlight a selection in the **P**aper Name box. The Paper Details area tells you everything you need to know about the highlighted paper. When you've got the one you want, press **Enter**.

> ## The Least You Need to Know
> This chapter took you on a quick graduate course of some other WordPerfect formatting options. Here's a review before the final exam:
>
> - ☞ To add either the date or the time to a document, pull down the **T**ools menu and select the **D**ate command. In the cascade menu, select **T**ext to insert a date that won't change, or **C**ode to tell WordPerfect to always show the current date.
>
> - ☞ Footnotes and endnotes are handy ways to add information to a document without cluttering the text. Select either **F**ootnote or **E**ndnote from the **L**ayout menu, select **C**reate, and then fill in the note. Press **F7** when you're done.
>
> - ☞ Comments are an easy way to include notes to yourself or others in a document. Select Commen**t** from the **L**ayout menu, and then select **C**reate from the cascade menu. When the editing screen appears, add your text and then press **F7** to exit.
>
> - ☞ Use hyphenation to clean up some of the gaps caused by long words. Select the **L**ayout menu's **L**ine command and then activate the Hyphenation check box.
>
> - ☞ To work with a different paper size, select the **P**age command from the **L**ayout menu, and then select the Paper **S**ize/Type option. Pick out the paper you want to use from the dialog box that appears.

Part IV
Working with Documents

In WordPerfect, you don't work with anything so humdrum as a file. Uh-uh. Instead, you work with documents, which, you've got to admit, sure sounds impressive, doesn't it? Why, it's enough to turn even the humblest memo into a virtual magnum opus.

The topics in this part look at the "forest" of your documents as a whole, rather than the "trees" of the individual characters, words, and pages. You'll learn about printing (Chapter 16), working with multiple documents and document windows (Chapter 17), and WordPerfect's File Manager (Chapter 18).

Chapter 16

Getting It Down on Paper: Printing Documents

In This Chapter

- The basic printing steps
- Printing a selection of pages
- Printing an unopened document right from your hard disk
- Using WordPerfect's cool Print Preview feature
- Selecting a different printer
- Magic, mirrors, movie trailers, and other miscellaneous mumbo-jumbo

Okay, you've managed to peck out a few words on the keyboard, and maybe even gotten used to the idea of not pressing Enter at the end of each line. You've struggled through all those pull-down menus and dialog boxes, you've got a few editing skills down pat, and you've even managed to add a bit of formatting to perk things up a bit. Now what? Ah, now it's hard copy time. Now you print out your creation for all to see. This is one of my favorite parts because, now matter how much I work with computers, I still feel like it's all hocus-pocus—just a bunch of smoke and mirrors. I don't feel right until I see those pages come slithering out of my printer. To that end, this chapter takes you painlessly through the basics of printing with WordPerfect.

Basic Printing

Without further ado, lets get right to the basic steps that let you print a document in WordPerfect:

1. Make sure your printer is ready to go:
   - Is it plugged in to both the wall and your computer?
   - Is it turned on?
   - Is it *on line*? (Most printers have an "On Line" light that'll tell you. If the light isn't on, press the **On Line** button.)
   - Is there enough paper for your document?

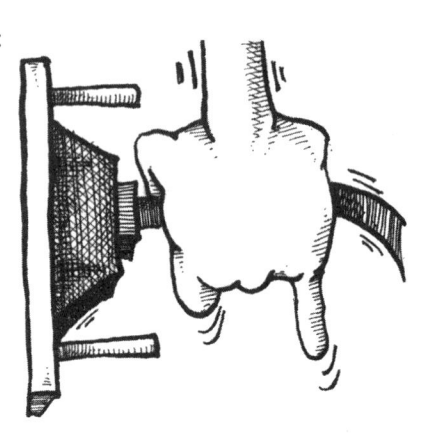

2. Once your printer is warm and happy, you need to decide how much of the document you want to print:
   - If you want to print the whole thing, go ahead and skip to Step 3.

> **OOPS!**
>
> In this section, I'm assuming you've already set up a printer within WordPerfect (normally you do this during installation). If, when you display the Print/Fax dialog box as described on the next page, the Current Printer area says **NO PRINTER SELECTED**, then you don't have a printer set up. You'll need to rerun the installation program, and install one from there. To remedy this, choose **Select** from the **Print/Fax** dialog box, choose **Add Printer** from the **Select Printer** dialog box, and then highlight your printer from the list that appears and press **Enter**.

> **By the Way . . .**
>
> WordPerfect kindly lets you print documents that aren't even open. The section titled "Printing an Unopened Document," gives you the scoop.

   - If you want to print only a single page, place the cursor anywhere on the page.
   - If you want to print a block, select the block. (You select a block by pressing **Alt+F4** or **F12**, and then using the **arrow** keys to highlight what you

Chapter 16 • Getting It Down on Paper: Printing Documents **157**

need. If you have a mouse, just drag it over the appropriate text. See Chapter 10, "Block Partying: Working with Text Blocks," for details.)

3. Pull down the File menu and select the Print/Fax command. You'll see the Print/Fax dialog box, shown here.

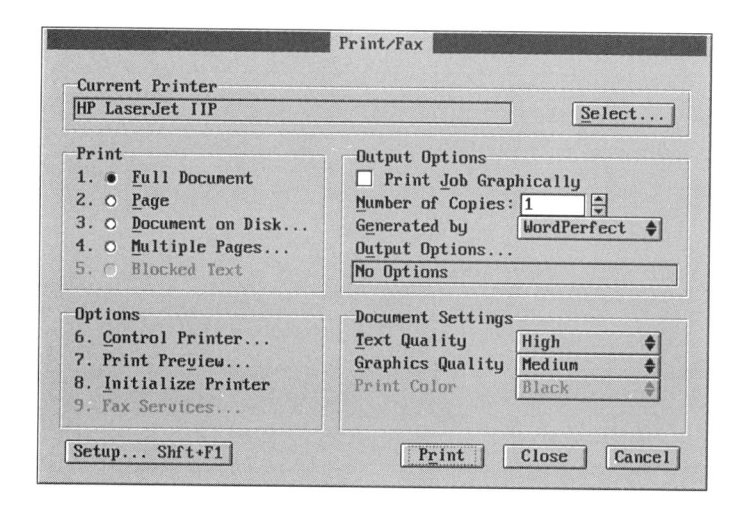

> **Shift+F7** is the shortcut key combo for the **Print** command.

WordPerfect's Print/Fax dialog box contains all the options you need to print your documents.

4. Use the Print group's radio buttons to tell WordPerfect what to print. Full Document prints everything, **P**age prints only the current page, and Blocked Text prints only the currently selected block. For the Document on Disk option, see "Printing an Unopened Document," later in the chapter. For the Multiple Pages option, see "Printing Multiple Pages."

5. If you need more than one copy, enter the number you want in the Number of copies text box.

6. Use the Text Quality option to set how nice you want your text to look. If you're printing a final draft, select High for the best looking output. If you're just printing out a copy to see how things look, you can save some ink (or toner, if you have a laser printer) by selecting Medium or even Draft quality.

TECHNO NERD TEACHES

If you're printing more than one copy of a document that's several pages long, you might want to take a look at the Generated by option. This control specifies whether you want WordPerfect or the printer to generate the multiple copies. For example, suppose you want three copies of a two-page document. If WordPerfect generates the copies, things take a little longer, but the copies get *collated*, which means that the entire document gets printed one copy at a time. If the printer does it, the job will print faster, but you'll get three copies of page 1, and then three copies of page 2.

OOPS!

Make sure you type the page numbers in numerical order (that is, ascending—no countdowns, please). WordPerfect will choke if you enter something like 8-3 or 6,1.

7. When you've finished picking your options, select the Print button to set everything in motion.

Printing Multiple Pages

If you only need to print a few pages from a document, select **Print/Fax** from the File menu and then select the Multiple Pages option in the **Print**/Fax dialog box. In the Print Multiple Pages dialog box that appears, use the Page/Label Range option to specify the pages you want printed. The following table shows you how to enter the page numbers (the letters *a*, *b*, and *c* represent page numbers you can enter):

Use	To print
a	Page *a*
a, b, c	Pages *a*, *b*, and *c*
a-b	Pages *a* to *b*
a-	From page *a* to the end of the document
-a	From the beginning of the document to page *a*
a, b, c-d	Pages *a* and *b*, and pages *c* to *d*

The Print Multiple Pages dialog box gives you several other options, as well:

☞ If you've been using chapter or volume numbers, use the Chapter(s) or Volume(s) text boxes to specify which ones you want to print.

☞ If you need to print only odd or even pages, select the appropriate setting from the Odd/Even Pages option.

☞ If you want the last page in the range printed first (which is handy if your printer spits out the pages face up), activate the Descending Order check box.

> **By the Way . . .**
> You can use the **Descending Order** option even if you're printing the entire document. Just make sure the **Page/Label Range** says **(all)**.

What's Wrong with This Picture?

To get you more comfortable with this multiple page printing thing, here are some sample page ranges. Just write in what pages you think will print (assume it's a five-page document).

Page Ranges:

1. 1-2,4-   Pages printed:
2. 2-4   Pages printed:
3. 1-   Pages printed:
4. 3-2   Pages printed:
5. -4   Pages printed:
6. 1,2,3-5   Pages printed:

Answers:

1. Pages 1, 2, 4, and 5 print.
2. Pages 2, 3, and 4 print.
3. Everything prints (pages 1, 2, 3, 4, and 5).
4. Nothing prints (the range has to be specified in numerical order).
5. Pages 1, 2, 3, and 4 print.
6. Everything prints.

Printing an Unopened Document

One of WordPerfect's nice time-saving features is the ability to print an unopened document. This saves you from having to go through the whole hassle of opening the file, printing it, and then closing it again.

Just select **Print/Fax** from the File menu and then select the **Document on Disk** option. You'll see the Document on Disk dialog box appear. Just enter the name of the file you want to print in the Document Name text box. (If you're not sure of the name, select the **File List** button—or press F5—press **Enter**, and then use the File Manager to find the document. See Chapter 18, "Using the File Manager," to get the grisly details.)

When you're ready, select **OK**. WordPerfect displays the Print Multiple Pages dialog box, so you can specify a print range, if you like. Enter your options and then select **OK**. Once you're back in the **Print**/Fax dialog box, select the Print button.

Canceling a Print Job

If you send a job to the printer and then decide you don't want to print it after all, WordPerfect lets you cancel any job in midstream. Here are the steps you need to follow:

1. Select **Print/Fax** from the File menu to display the Print/Fax dialog box, and then select the Control Printer option. This displays the Control Printer dialog box, as shown here.

2. Use the **up** or **down arrow** keys to highlight the job you want to cancel, and then press asterisk (*) to mark it. Repeat this for each job you want to blow away.

3. When you have all the jobs you want to cancel marked, select Cancel Job. WordPerfect asks if you're sure.

4. Select **Yes** to cancel the jobs.

5. Select **Close** to return to the Print/Fax dialog box.

Chapter 16 • Getting It Down on Paper: Printing Documents **161**

WordPerfect's Control Printer dialog box keeps you apprised of your print jobs, and lets you cancel them at any time.

Current print jobs

By the Way . . .

The Control Printer dialog box has all kinds of other neat info. For example, you can watch the Current Job group options to see how a print job is making out. And if something goes wrong with the job, you'll see a message and WordPerfect will tell you what you need to do.

Using Print Preview

One of my favorite things about going to the movies is watching the trailers for upcoming films. Maybe that's why I like WordPerfect's Print Preview feature. It's like a trailer for the document you're about to print (without all the hype). You see exactly what your printout will look like, headers, footers, page numbers and all. True, version 6's graphics and page modes let you see all

162 *Part III • Working with Documents*

that stuff, too. But Print Preview shows you the big picture: you see a full page on your screen, so you can see how the whole thing fits together.

You can crank up Print Preview in one of two ways:

- ☞ Select Print Preview from the File menu.
- ☞ If you're already in the **Print**/Fax dialog box, select the Print Preview option.

Here's a picture of the screen you'll see.

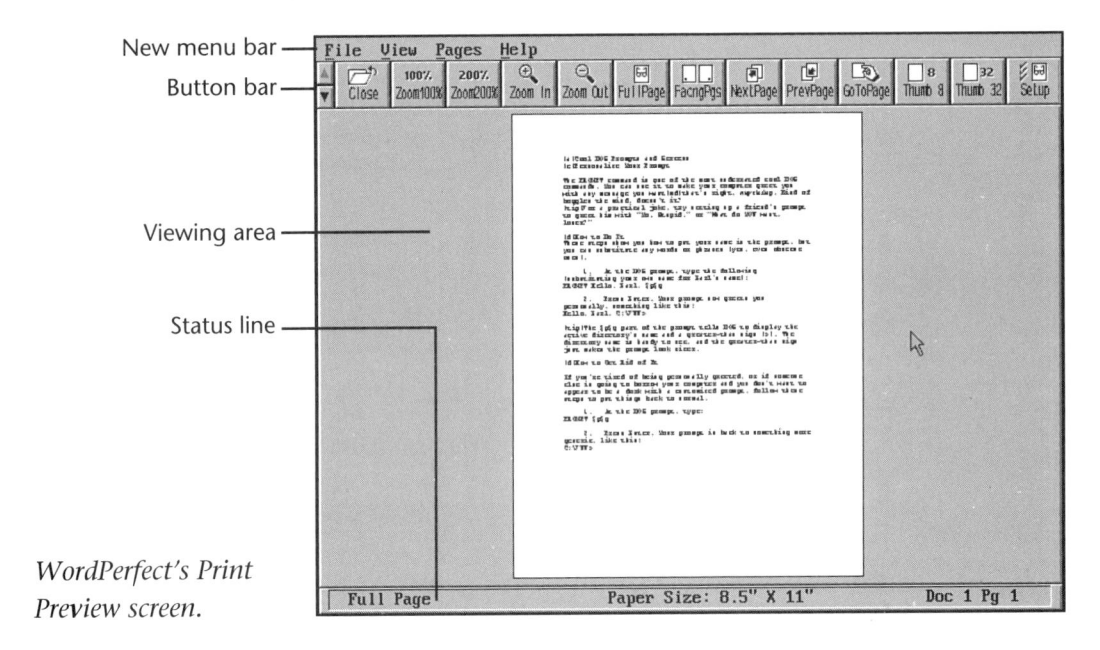

WordPerfect's Print Preview screen.

- New menu bar
- Button bar
- Viewing area
- Status line

This screen is a little different from the one you're used to, so lets go through the parts:

Menu bar Print Preview has a scaled-down menu bar, but you use it just like the regular one.

Button Bar This strange beast lets mouse users access the Print Preview functions easily. I won't discuss this here, but if you want to know more, take a peek at Chapter 19, "Cool Tools to Make Your Life Easier."

Viewing area This is where WordPerfect displays your document. You can "zoom" in and out to see more detail or less detail.

Chapter 16 • Getting It Down on Paper: Printing Documents 163

Status line Print Preview's status line shows slightly different info from what you see on the normal one. You see the current View (Full Page, 100%, etc.), the paper size, and the usual Doc and Pg values.

The next couple of sections show you how to use different Print Preview views, and how to navigate your document. When you're finished with Print Preview, pull down the File menu and select Close.

Selecting Different Views

Print Preview normally displays your documents one page at a time in *Full Page View*, which scales down each page so that you can see the whole thing on your screen. This is great for checking out the overall layout of each page, but if you need to see more detail or more pages at once, you need to select the appropriate command from the View menu. Here's a summary:

> You can also exit Print Preview simply by pressing **Esc** or **F7**.

Select	To
100% View	See each page at the actual printed size.
200% View	See each page at twice the actual printed size.
Zoom **In**	Increase the size of the page by 25%.
Zoom **Out**	Decrease the size of the page by 25%.
Facing Pages	View two consecutive pages at once.
Thumbnails	Display several pages at once. A cascade menu appears from which you can select the number of pages you want to view.

Navigating Your Document

To see other pages in your document, use the commands in the **Pages** menu. To go back one page, select **Previous Page**; to go forward one page, select **Next Page**; to go to any page, select **Go To Page**, enter a number in the **Go To Page** dialog box, and then select **OK**.

Selecting a Different Printer

If you're lucky enough to have more than one printer, you can switch between them in WordPerfect fairly easily.

You may have noticed when printing that the Print/Fax dialog box shows you the name of the currently selected printer in the Current Printer area. To change this, choose the **S**elect button beside it. This displays the Select Printer dialog box. Use the **up** and **down arrow** keys to highlight the printer you want (or just click on it with your mouse) and then choose the **S**elect command.

> ### The Least You Need to Know
>
> This chapter showed you how to get hard copies of your WordPerfect documents. Since you'll likely be doing a lot of printing with WordPerfect, a quick review of the basics wouldn't hurt:
>
> - Before printing, make sure your printer is ready for action. Check to see if it's plugged in, the cables are secure, it's turned on (and on line), and that it has enough paper to handle the job.
>
> - To print, pull down the **F**ile menu and select the Print/Fax command (or just press **Shift+F7**). Enter your options in the **Print**/Fax dialog box, and then select the Print button.
>
> - You don't need to print the entire document each time. If you like, you can print just a block, the current page, or a range of pages. For the latter, select the **M**ultiple Pages option and enter pages you want to print in the dialog box.
>
> - To print an unopened document, select the **D**ocument on Disk option from the **Print**/Fax dialog box. Enter the name of the file you want printed and then select **OK**. Enter the pages to print, select **OK**, then select Print.

- Print Preview lets you see exactly how your document will look when it's printed. Just select the Print Preview command from the File menu or, if you're in the Print/Fax dialog box, select the Print Preview option.

- To select a different printer, choose the Select button in the Print/Fax dialog box, highlight the printer you want, then choose the Select option.

Chapter 17
Working with Multiple Documents

In This Chapter

- The fastest ways to switch between open documents
- Using version 6's window frames
- Using frames to move, size, close, and arrange windows
- Fascinating juggling lore

Remember the minor juggling craze that bounced around the country a few years ago? Well, your faithful scribe was one of many who jumped on that strange bandwagon. No, I didn't become any kind of expert (or run off and join the circus), but I did learn the basic three-ball pattern. I've kept it up to this day—and will, on a dare, attempt to juggle three of just about anything (which, believe me, has scared the heck out of many a party hostess).

If you missed that particular craze, WordPerfect lets you do some juggling of your own. In version 6, you can open as many as *nine* documents at once (the maximum is two in version 5.1). This not only lets you work with several documents at once, but it's great for quickly comparing two or more documents, or pasting info between files. Best of all, everything's blindingly simple, as you'll soon see.

> **By the Way . . .**
> Nine is a lot of documents, but it's still short of the official world's record for juggling, which is a mind-boggling *eleven* rings at once. How do I know? Don't ask.

Switching Among Multiple Documents

Opening several documents is easy: for each one, just use the File menu's Open command and enter the name of the file. WordPerfect sets up a new work area for the file and updates the Doc number on the status line. But once you have them open, you need some way of switching among them. As you might expect by now, WordPerfect has about a million ways to do this. Here's a sampling:

> **E-Z** Press **Shift+F3** to alternate quickly between the current document and the last one you used.

> **E-Z** The shortcut key combo for the Switch To command is **Home,0**.

- ☞ To cycle through the documents, select either Next or Previous from the Window menu.
- ☞ To switch between the current document and the last one you worked with, select the Window menu's Switch command.
- ☞ To switch to a specific document number, press **Home** and then the number. For example, to display document 2 on the screen, press **Home,2**.
- ☞ To see a list of all the open documents, select the Switch To command from the Window menu. WordPerfect displays the Switch To Document dialog box. As you can see here, each document is listed along with its number. Just press the appropriate number to switch to the file you need.

Chapter 17 • Working with Multiple Documents — 169

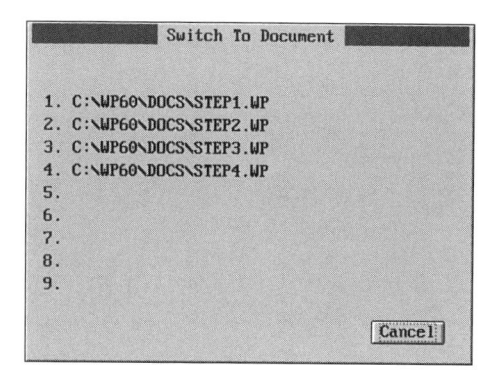

```
          Switch To Document
  1. C:\WP60\DOCS\STEP1.WP
  2. C:\WP60\DOCS\STEP2.WP
  3. C:\WP60\DOCS\STEP3.WP
  4. C:\WP60\DOCS\STEP4.WP
  5.
  6.
  7.
  8.
  9.
                              [Cancel]
```

The Switch To Document dialog box displays a list of all the open documents. Select a number to see the document on screen.

Put It to Work

One of the benefits of multiple open documents is that you can share text among them. There are endless uses for this capability, but here's a sampler:

- ☛ You could take sections of a report and use them in a memo or letter.

- ☛ If you have one or more files organized as a project, you could take chunks out and use them to create a summary document.

- ☛ You could create a document to hold boilerplate (bits of often-used text), and keep it open all the time. You could then copy stuff from the file (or add more things to it) at will.

The good news is that this is all extremely simple to do. Here are the basic steps:

1. Open the appropriate files, and display the document that has whatever text you need.

2. Block the text (if you need some blocking basics, refer back to Chapter 10, "Block Partying: Working with Text Blocks").

continues

> *continued*
>
> 3. Use the appropriate Edit menu command to cut or copy the text (this was also covered in Chapter 10).
> 4. Switch to the document that you want to receive the text.
> 5. Position the cursor where you want the text to appear, and then paste it.

WordPerfect's Adjustable Windows

As I've said, every time you open a document, WordPerfect sets up and displays the file in a new work area. In WordPerfect parlance, these work areas are called *windows*. This makes some sense, I suppose. After all, at any one time, the screen can only show you a part of a document, so it's like looking through a window at your text.

If you have version 6, then you can think of your computer as a room with nine different windows. As you've just seen, you can display a document in any of these windows, and just switch among them.

> **5.1**
>
> If you have two open documents in version 5.1, you can switch between them by selecting **Switch Document** from the **Edit** menu, or by pressing **Shift+F3**. You can also split the screen and display both documents at once. Just select **Window** from the **Edit** menu or press **Ctrl+F3**.

> **SPEAK LIKE A GEEK**
>
> The window you're currently working in is called the *active window*.

Framing a Window

The problem with windows is that normally you can look through only one at time on your screen. It would be nice, on occasion, to be able to see maybe a couple of documents at the same time.

Sound impossible? Hah! With version 6's new *window frames*, it's easier than you think. What does framing do? Well, it puts a border around a window that lets you do all kinds of crazy things:

- ☞ Change the size of the window.
- ☞ Move the window to a different location.
- ☞ Make the window really small so it's out of the way.
- ☞ Make the widow really big so you can't see anything else.

To access this voodoo, just pull down the **W**indow menu and select the Frame command. As you can see here, your window will suddenly sprout a border with various funny symbols on it.

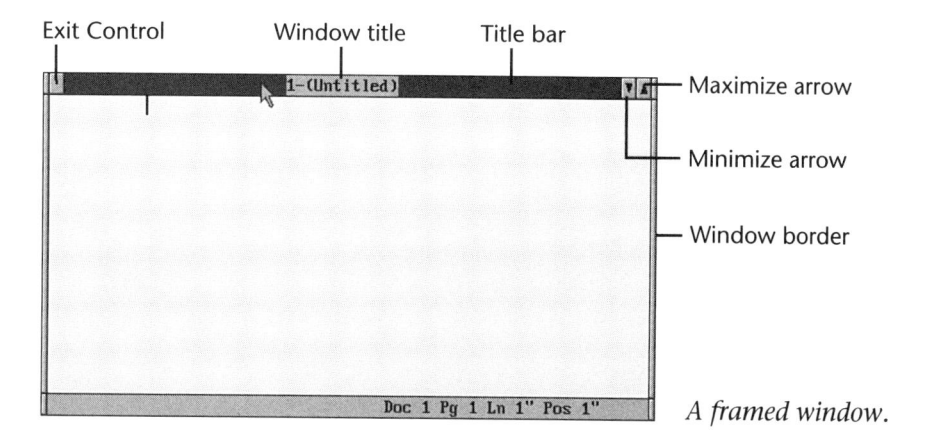

A framed window.

Anatomy of a Window

Here's a summary of the new features you get when you frame a window (I'll talk about things like moving and sizing windows later in the chapter):

Window title This shows you the name of the document and the document number.

Title bar You can use this area to move the window with a mouse.

Border You can use the sides and bottom to change the size of the window with a mouse.

Maximize arrow This arrow is used to increase the window to its largest extent (i.e., the normal window view you get when you open a document).

Minimize arrow This arrow decreases the window to its smallest size.

Exit Control This button closes the document.

Adjusting Your Windows

Okay, so now you know how to frame a window. I know what you're thinking: "How does this affect *me*?" Well, it's quite simple, really: a framed window is an *adjustable* window, which means you can move it around, make it different sizes, and more. In other words, you have *control* over what you see on your screen. The next few sections show you how to use that control.

> ### By the Way . . .
> Once you start playing around with windows, you may end up with several, scattered willy-nilly about the screen; you may forget which one is the active window. Here are two things to look for:
>
> - The blinking cursor.
> - The title bar with the darker color.

Sizing Up Your Windows

If you'd like to see a couple of windows on screen at the same time, one way to do it is to change the size of each window so they both fit. This is (by far) easiest with a mouse, but the keyboard will do in a pinch.

The secret to sizing a window with the mouse is to use the *borders* that appear when you frame the window. All you do is drag the appropriate border so it's the size you want. You can use the left and right borders to adjust the sides, or the status line to adjust the bottom. As you're dragging, WordPerfect displays a dotted line to show you the new size. When things look about right, release the mouse button, and WordPerfect redraws the window in the new size.

Chapter 17 • Working with Multiple Documents **173**

> **By the Way . . .**
> Here's a refresher course on dragging the mouse, in case you forgot. First, position the pointer over the object you want to drag (a window border, in this case), then press and hold down the left mouse button. Now move the mouse to wherever you want to go, and then release the button.

If you prefer to use the keyboard, you need to follow these steps:

1. Switch to the window you want to size.

2. Press **Ctrl+F3** to display the Screen dialog box, and then select the **W**indow option. WordPerfect displays the Window dialog box.

3. Select the **S**ize option. A dotted outline appears around the window.

4. Use the **arrow** keys to size the window outline.

5. Once the outline is the size you want, press **Enter**. WordPerfect redisplays the window in the new size.

> **E-Z**
> It's possible to size two borders at the same time. All you have to do is position the mouse pointer on a window corner. When you drag the mouse, the two sides that create the corner will move.

> **OOPS!**
> If you decide you don't want the window resized after all, just press **Esc**.

Windows on the Move

One of the problems with having several windows open at once is that they have a nasty habit of overlapping each other. And it never fails that what gets overlapped in a window is precisely the information you want to see. (Chalk up another one for Murphy's Law, I guess.) Instead of cursing WordPerfect's ancestry, you can try moving your windows around so they don't overlap (or so they overlap less).

Things are, once again, *way* easier with a mouse: all you do is drag the window's title bar. As you do, WordPerfect displays a dotted outline of the window. When you've got the outline where you want it, just release the mouse button, and WordPerfect redisplays the window in the new location.

If you use a keyboard, here are the steps to follow:

1. Switch to the window you want to move.
2. Display the Screen dialog box by pressing **Ctrl+F3**, and then select the **W**indow option. The Window dialog box appears.
3. Select the **M**ove option. A dotted outline appears around the window.
4. Use the **arrow** keys to move the window outline.
5. Once the outline is in the location you want, press **Enter**. WordPerfect redisplays the window in the new location.

> **OOPS!**
> If you change your mind about moving the window, you can press the **Esc** key at any time.

Letting WordPerfect Do the Work: Cascading and Tiling

All this moving and sizing stuff is fine for people with time to kill. The rest of us just want to get the job done and move on. To that end, WordPerfect includes Cascade and Tile commands that'll arrange your windows for you automatically.

> **By the Way . . .**
> Speaking of having time to kill, did you know that the world's record for the longest time juggling three objects without a drop is mind-numbing 8 hours, 57 minutes?

The Cascade command arranges your open windows in a cool, waterfall pattern. This is good for those times when you want things nice and neat, but you don't need to see what's in the other windows. To cascade your windows, select the Cascade command from the **W**indow menu.

> **By the Way . . .**
> The basic three-ball pattern that you see most jugglers using is also called a *cascade*. Just a coincidence? I wonder.

The Tile command divides up your screen and gives equal real estate to each window, as shown here.

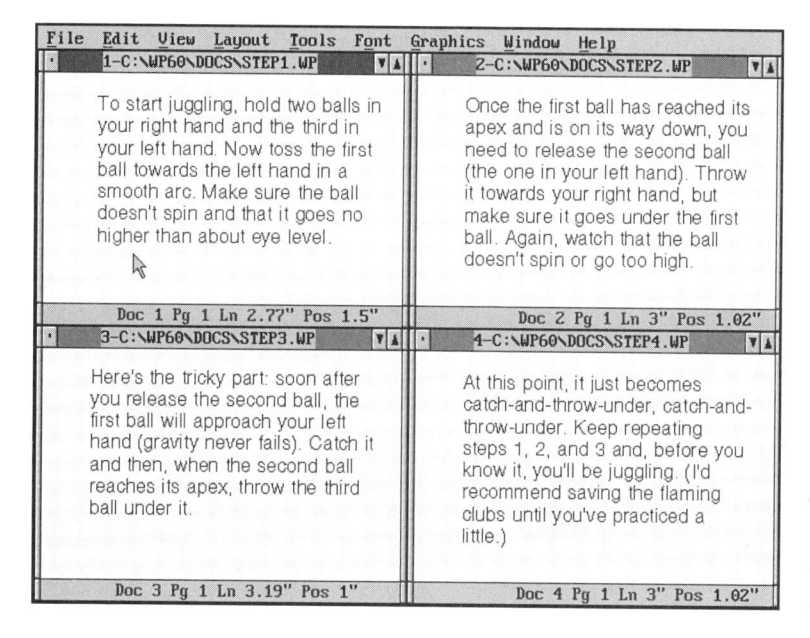

*The **Tile** command gives each of your open windows an equal amount of screen space.*

This pattern lets you work in one window and still keep an eye on what's happening in the other windows (you never know what those pesky little devils might be up to). To tile your windows, select the Tile command from the **Window** menu.

The Minimalist Approach: How to Minimize a Window

You'll often find you have some windows you know you won't need for a while. You could move them out of the way or make them smaller, but that takes time, and our goal is always to make things as easy as possible. Fortunately, there's an alternative: you can *minimize* the window down to a miniscule rectangle.

If you use a mouse, you can minimize a window in no time at all, simply by clicking on the frame's **minimize arrow** (the one pointing down).

It takes a teeny bit more effort if you're using the keyboard. In this case, you need to pull down the Window menu and select the Minimize command.

Taking It to the Max: Maximizing a Window

If you get tired of all this "frame" monkey business, you can *maximize* a window to its normal size.

If you use a mouse, all you have to do is click on the window's **maximize arrow** (the one pointing up). From the keyboard, pull down the Window menu and select the Maximize command.

Closing a Window

When a window is framed, you'll see a dot in the upper left corner. This is called the *Exit Control* and, if you have a mouse, you can close the window simply by clicking on the **Exit Control**. If you've made changes to the document, WordPerfect will, of course, ask you to save them as it normally does.

> ### The Least You Need to Know
> This chapter gave you the lowdown on using multiple documents in WordPerfect. You learned some basic techniques for switching among open documents, and for using WordPerfect's window frames. Here's the highlight film:
>
> ☞ To switch between windows, you can use the various **W**indow menu commands (**N**ext, **P**revious, **S**witch, or **S**witch To) or you can press **Home** and then the document number.

- Select **F**rame from the **W**indow menu to display a frame around a document window.

- To size a framed window, drag the left, right, or bottom border. You can also press **Ctrl+F3**, **1**, **S**, and use the **arrow** keys.

- To move a framed window, drag the title bar to the location you want. From the keyboard, press **Ctrl+F3**, **1**, **M**, and use the **arrow** keys.

- If you'd prefer WordPerfect to arrange your windows for you, select either the **C**ascade or **T**ile commands from the **W**indow menu.

- To reduce a window to its smallest size, click on the **minimize arrow** or select **M**inimize from the **W**indow menu. To increase a window to its largest size, click on the **maximize arrow** or select the **W**indow menu's **M**aximize command.

Chapter 18
Using WordPerfect's File Manager

In This Chapter

- Starting and navigating File Manager
- A quick briefing on files and directories
- Using File Manager to open, retrieve, and view documents
- Other file fun: copying, moving, renaming, and deleting
- A snappy analogy designed to knock some sense into all this DOS mumbo-jumbo

What I'm about to tell you is explicit and unexpurgated, and may therefore be offensive to some. You may want to remove small children from the room before continuing . . . Okay, here it is: WordPerfect is a DOS program; WordPerfect documents are, in fact, DOS files; these files exist in DOS directories. You cannot escape DOS; it knows where you live and where you work. DOS, death, and taxes: the three constants in life.

Why the scaremongering? Because, sooner or later (hopefully later), you're going to have to deal with DOS in some way. You're going to need to copy or rename a file, or create a directory, or delete the detritus that has accumulated over the years.

But friends, I'm here today to tell you there's good news. I'm here to tell you that, yes, you have to deal with DOS—but, no, you don't have to deal with DOS *directly*. WordPerfect's File Manager tames the DOS beast, and while it may not make this stuff any more pleasant, it *does* make it easier. This chapter tells you everything you need to know.

> E-Z
>
> The shortcut key for the File Manager command is **F5**.

Starting File Manager

There's no time like the present, as they say, so let's get right to it. To start File Manager, pull down the **F**ile menu and select the **F**ile Manager command. You'll see the Specify File Manager List dialog box, which prompts you about something called a *directory*. I'll be explaining directories a little later on, so if you're not sure what to do, just select **OK**. Eventually, you'll see the File Manager screen, which will look something like (but not exactly like) the one shown here.

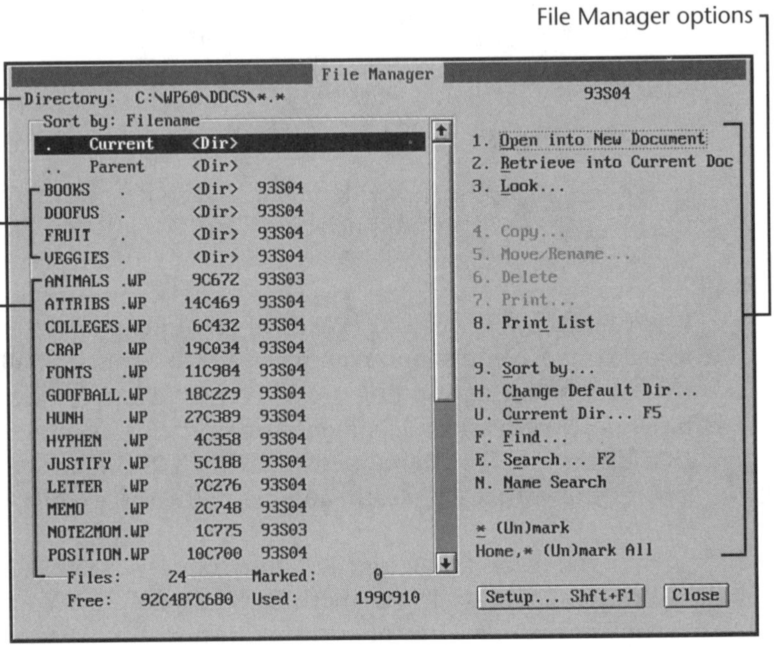
File Manager options
Current directory
Subdirectories
Files in the current directory
File Manager
Directory: C:\WP60\DOCS*.*
93S04
Sort by: Filename
. Current <Dir>
.. Parent <Dir>
BOOKS . <Dir> 93S04
DOOFUS . <Dir> 93S04
FRUIT . <Dir> 93S04
VEGGIES . <Dir> 93S04
ANIMALS .WP 9C672 93S03
ATTRIBS .WP 14C469 93S04
COLLEGES.WP 6C432 93S04
CRAP .WP 19C034 93S04
FONTS .WP 11C984 93S04
GOOFBALL.WP 18C229 93S04
HUNH .WP 27C389 93S04
HYPHEN .WP 4C358 93S04
JUSTIFY .WP 5C188 93S04
LETTER .WP 7C276 93S04
MEMO .WP 2C748 93S04
NOTE2MOM.WP 1C775 93S03
POSITION.WP 10C700 93S04
Files: 24 Marked: 0
Free: 92C487C680 Used: 199C910
1. Open into New Document
2. Retrieve into Current Doc
3. Look...
4. Copy...
5. Move/Rename...
6. Delete
7. Print...
8. Print List
9. Sort by...
H. Change Default Dir...
U. Current Dir... F5
F. Find...
E. Search... F2
N. Name Search
* (Un)mark
Home,* (Un)mark All
Setup... Shft+F1
Close

WordPerfect's File Manager.

The File Manager screen looks pretty complicated, but it all boils down to two areas: the available options on the right and a list of files in the current directory on the left. Before moving on, let's take a closer look at *files* and *directories*.

Files and Directories: A Brief Primer

When people ask me to explain files and directories to them (well, no, it doesn't happen all *that* often), I always tell them to think of their computer as a house. Not just any old house, mind you, but one with all kinds of servants waiting to do their bidding. (People usually start warming up to the analogy at this point.) The inside of the house—you can think of this as the computer's hard disk—has maids, valets, cooks, and so on; these are the programs (such as WordPerfect) installed on the hard disk. Outside the house there are gardeners, landscapers, and chauffeurs; these are the devices attached to the computer (such as the keyboard, printer, or modem).

In the simplest possible terms, your computer's *files* are equivalent to the various elements in the house. As I've said, the people (the servants) are the files that run your programs. The inanimate objects in the house—the furniture, appliances, utensils, and so on—are the data files (such as a WordPerfect document) used by you or your software.

Imagine, for a moment, that this house had no rooms, and that all the stuff inside was just scattered randomly throughout. Clearly, trying to *find* anything in such a place would be, if not impossible, at least frustrating. The problem, of course, is that there's no organization. A normal house has many different rooms, and usually everything in one room is related in one way or another. So, if you were looking for either cooking utensils or food, you'd probably look in the kitchen instead of the bedroom. (I said *probably*. You might also look under the sofa, depending on your housekeeping habits.)

Your computer's hard disk also contains a number of "rooms," and these are called *directories*. In a properly organized hard disk, each directory normally contains a number of related files. For example, your

182 Part IV • *Working with Documents*

SPEAK LIKE A GEEK

A *byte* is computerese for a single character of information. So for example the phrase "This phrase is 28 bytes long" is, yes, 28 bytes long (you count the spaces too, but not the quotation marks, silly).

E-Z

If you have a mouse, you can open a document quickly just by double-clicking on it.

WordPerfect directory contains all the files that WordPerfect uses (and, possibly, some of your documents). You may also have separate directories for other programs installed on your computer.

Let's extend the analogy a little further. Some rooms in a house have a smaller room attached to them (such as a walk-in closet in a bedroom, or a dining room in a living room). Even storage spaces such as pantries and cupboards are "room-like" because they store objects. All of these are examples of what we could call "subrooms." Directories can also have "subrooms," and these are called—you guessed it—*subdirectories*.

Anatomy of the File List

So, to apply all this to File Manager, the file listing on the left is really just an inventory of objects in one of your hard disk's rooms (probably your WordPerfect directory). You'll see all kinds of objects listed, but they all fall into two categories: subdirectories and files.

A subdirectory entry from the File Manager list.

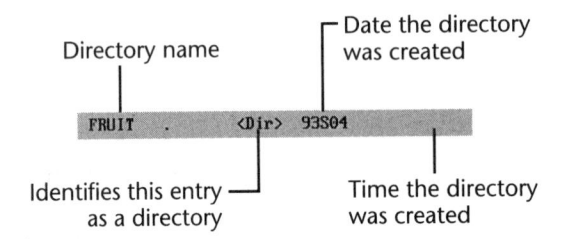

```
FRUIT    .      <Dir>  93S04
```

Directory name | Date the directory was created
Identifies this entry as a directory | Time the directory was created

Subdirectories

If the current directory has any subdirectories, they'll be displayed at the top of the list. As you can see here, a typical subdirectory entry has a <DIR> identifier, as well as the date and time the subdirectory was created.

Files

The rest of the list displays the files in the current directory. Here's a typical entry that shows the file's name and extension, its size in bytes, and the date and time it was last modified.

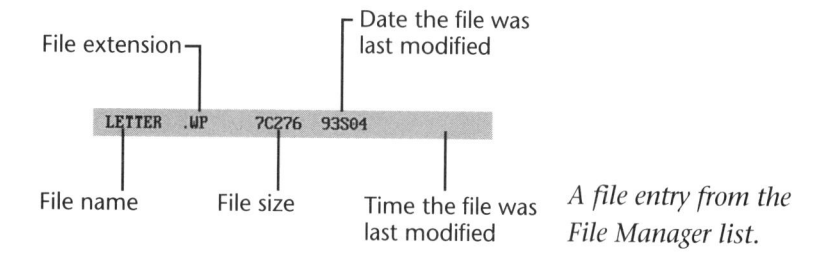

Chapter 18 • Using WordPerfect's File Manager **183**

```
          File extension ┐   ┌ Date the file was
                         │   │ last modified
          LETTER    .WP    7C276   93S04
            │        │       │       │
         File name  File size  Time the file was
                              last modified
```
A file entry from the File Manager list.

> **By the Way . . .**
> For more info on file names, refer back to Chapter 7, "Day-to-Day Drudgery I: Saving, Opening and Closing."

Navigating the File List

The basic idea behind File Manager is that you highlight a file in the file list, and then do something to it (copy it, delete it, whatever). The following table lists some of the keys you can use to navigate the file list.

Press	To Move
Up or down arrow	Up or down one file
Page Up or Page Down	Up or down one screenful
Home,Home,up arrow	To the top of the list
Home,Home,down arrow	To the bottom of the list
N+letter	To the first file that starts with *letter*
Enter on a directory	To the directory

If you have a mouse, you can use three methods to navigate the list:

- ☛ To highlight a file on the screen, point the mouse at the file.
- ☛ To move to another part of the list, use the scroll bars.
- ☛ Double-click on a directory name to move to the directory.

> **TECHNO NERD TEACHES**
>
> What's with the dot (.) and double-dot (..) deals at the top of the list? Well, these are just DOS shorthand symbols. The dot represents the current directory, and the double dot represents the so-called *parent* directory—the directory out of which the current directory has sprung. For example, suppose you had a directory named BEDROOM that had a subdirectory named CLOSET. BEDROOM would then be the parent directory of CLOSET (and CLOSET would be the *child* directory of BEDROOM; no, I don't know who the heck makes up this stuff).

> **5.1**
>
> In 5.1, highlight the file you need, and then select **Retrieve**. If you already have a file open, you'll see the following prompt in the status line:
>
> **Retrieve into current document? No (Yes)**
>
> Press **N** to open the document in a new work area, or **Y** if you want to combine the files.

> **By the Way . . .**
>
> If you need some scroll bar basics, trek back to Chapter 8, "Day-to-Day Drudgery II: Navigating Documents," to get the scoop.

What You Can Do with File Manager

Yeah, I know what you'd *like* to do with File Manager, but I'll let you handle that on your own. Otherwise, File Manager can be quite useful. The following sections take you through some of the more common tasks that'll crop up from time to time.

Opening and Retrieving Documents

You normally open a document by selecting the File menu's Open command and then entering the name of the file. But what if you don't remember the name of the file? Or it's in a different directory? Or you're not sure how to spell it? The solution to these problems is simple: use File Manager to highlight the document you need, and then select the Open into New Document option. If you want to retrieve the document, instead, you need to select the Retrieve into Current Doc option.

Looking at a Document

I *hate* opening the wrong document. It means that not only have I wasted the time it took to open the file, but now I have to close it and go hunting around for the correct one. What a bother. Happily, you can avoid this fate by using WordPerfect's Look feature. Look lets you examine a document first and *then* decide if you want to open it or not.

All you do is highlight the file and then select the Look option. WordPerfect puts the document on screen and displays a menu of options at the bottom. If the file is the one you want, select the Open option. To view other files in the list, use the Next and Previous options. If you just want to return to File Manager, select OK.

> The Look feature is designed mostly for displaying WordPerfect documents. If you happen to select a different type of file accidentally, you may end up with a royal mess on the screen. Not to worry; just select OK to get the heck out of there.

> **By the Way . . .**
> If you want to see more of a file displayed by Look, just use the usual WordPerfect navigation keys or, if you have a mouse, the scroll bar. (This is all covered in Chapter 8, "Day-to-Day Drudgery II: Navigating Documents.") Look also has a neat Scroll feature: just select the Scroll option, and WordPerfect scrolls through the file. Press Esc to stop the scrolling.

Copying Files

If you need to make a copy of a file on a floppy disk or in another directory, File Manager's Copy option will do the job. Just highlight the file and then select Copy. You'll see Copy dialog box, shown here.

Use the Copy dialog box to make a copy of a file.

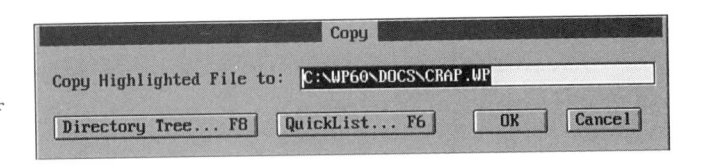

Enter the destination for the file in the Copy Highlighted File To text box. To be safe, always include the drive and directory. When you're ready, select **OK** to start the copy.

> ### Put It to Work
>
> You can use File Manager's **C**opy option as a (very) basic backup command. Place a formatted floppy disk in the appropriate disk drive, mark your documents (see the section titled "Selecting Multiple Files," later in this chapter) and then run **C**opy. In the **C**opy Highlighted File To text box, enter **a:** if the disk is in drive A, or **b:** if it's in drive B.
>
> You can make backing up a little easier by changing a couple of File Manager setup options. In File Manager, press **Shift+F1** to display the File Manager Setup dialog box. Select both the **D**escending Sort and **WP** Documents Only check boxes, and select **D**ate/Time in the group labeled "**S**ort List by." Select **OK** to exit; you'll see only WordPerfect documents in the list, *and* they'll be sorted by date. How does this help? Well, the documents you worked on most recently will appear at the top of the list. Since these are the ones you're most likely to back up, it's easy just to mark everything you need and crank up the **C**opy command.

Once you've highlighted a file, you can select the **D**elete option quickly just by pressing **Delete** or **Backspace**.

Moving and Renaming Files

If you want to move a file to a new location, or if you want to just give it a different name, highlight the file and select File Manager's **M**ove/Rename option. This displays the Move/Rename dialog box and all you do is enter the new name or the new location in the New Name text box. When you're done, select OK.

Deleting Files

As you're learning WordPerfect, you'll probably create all kinds of garbage files while you practice the program's features. This is fine, but after awhile these files can really clutter up your hard disk, which makes finding stuff in File Manager a real needle-in-a-haystack exercise. You can use File Manager's **Delete** option to do periodic housecleanings. Just highlight a file you want to scrap, and then select the **Delete** option. WordPerfect will ask you to confirm that you want to delete the file. Select **Yes** to delete or **No** to cancel.

Unless you have special "undelete" software (or at least version 5 of DOS), deleted files are gone for good, so you should be absolutely sure you can live without a file before expunging it. If you have *any* doubts, whatsoever, use the Look feature to take a peek at the file's contents. (If you have DOS 5 or later and you do happen to delete a file accidentally, you may be able to recover it. To learn how, I'd suggest picking up a copy of *The Complete Idiot's Guide to DOS* by the most excellent Jennifer Flynn.)

Selecting Multiple Files

You can perform many File Manager operations (such as opening, copying, and deleting) on a single file or on multiple files. While you can only highlight one file at a time, you can *mark* other files and File Manager will include them in the operation.

To mark a file, just highlight it and press asterisk (*). You'll see an asterisk appear beside the file name. To unmark a file, just highlight it and press * again. If you need to mark *every* file, press Home,*. To unmark all files, press Home,* again.

> **5.1**
> Selecting the **C**opy option in version 5.1's File Manager produces the following prompt at the bottom of the screen:
>
> **Copy this file to:**
>
> Type in the name of the destination and press **Enter**.

> **OOPS!**
> Don't move or rename any of the files in your main WordPerfect directory (unless it's a document that you created yourself). WordPerfect expects things to be named a certain way and if something is off by even a letter, the program will complain and moan something fierce (or it may refuse to run altogether). The safest course is to move or rename only those files that you know you've created yourself.

> **E-Z**
> To mark and unmark a file, you can also just press the Spacebar.

> ### By the Way . . .
> If you have multiple files marked and you select a File Manager option, WordPerfect will usually ask you to confirm that you want to perform the operation on the marked files. Just select **Yes** to use the marked files, or **No** to perform the operation on only the currently highlighted file.

> ### The Least You Need to Know
> This chapter gave you a quick tour of File Manager WordPerfect's answer to DOS. Here's a brief rundown of what was important:
>
> - To start File Manager, select **F**ile Manager from the **F**ile menu (or press **F5**), enter the directory you want to see, and then select **OK**.
>
> - File Manager shows you a list of the files in the current directory. This is analogous to looking at a list of the inventory in the room of a house.
>
> - To work with a file, highlight it and then select one of File Manager's options (**C**opy, **M**ove/Rename, **D**elete, etc.).
>
> - To select multiple files, you need to mark each one individually. Just highlight each file in turn and press asterisk (*). Press asterisk again to unmark a file.

Part V
WordPerfect Tools

WordPerfect is one of those programs that you can accessorize. Oh, sure, it looks fine in its basic outfit—but add a bauble here, a trinket there, and you get a whole new look. And the real good news is that this new look also makes WordPerfect easier to use, and more powerful. Too good to be true? Nah! Just try on the three chapters in this section for size, and you'll see!

Chapter 19
Cool Tools to Make Your Life Easier

In This Chapter

- Using the Ribbon to access formatting options
- Using the Button Bar to access common commands
- Customizing WordPerfect's windows
- Customizing the mouse
- Customizing the screen colors
- Lots of cool version 6 stuff that's sure to make version 5.1 users insanely jealous

I remember a line from a commercial that was on a few years back for some cold remedy: "Why suffer through a long cold when you can lessen your misery with *x*?". And so I ask *you*: Why suffer through WordPerfect when you can lessen your misery with a few tools and setup options? This, after all, has been one of the goals of this book: to help you get your work done with a minimum of fuss and bother. This chapter mines WordPerfect's menus to uncover a few gems that will allow you to do just that.

The Ribbon: Easy Formatting Access

WordPerfect's philosophy, as I've said before, is to get the heck out of your way so you can get down to the business of writing. While this is a good strategy for professional word jockeys, it leaves a lot to be desired for working stiffs like you and me who just want to get our tasks done quickly. The problem is that everything is hidden either by several layers of pull-down menus and dialog boxes, or by absurd key combinations that nobody can (or *should*) ever remember.

Ironically, one of the things buried in the pull-down menus (provided you have version 6, that is) is a tool that lets you use the menus less often. It's called the *Ribbon*, and you can see it by selecting the **View** menu's **Ribbon** command. It appears just below the menu bar and looks like this:

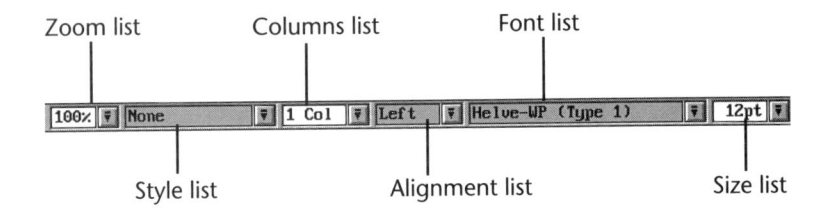

WordPerfect 6's Ribbon.

Working with the Ribbon

The Ribbon is a collection of drop-down lists that give you easy mouse access to some of WordPerfect's formatting features. All you do is select a block (if necessary), and then use your mouse to select what you need from the Ribbon. Here's a rundown of the available options:

> **By the Way . . .**
> If you need a refresher course on using drop-down lists, truck back to Chapter 6, "Talking to WordPerfect's Dialog Boxes."

The Zoom List

Normally, WordPerfect displays your document pages at more or less life size. If you're in graphics mode or page mode, however, you can enlarge or reduce the size of each page with WordPerfect's Zoom feature.

> **By the Way . . .**
> To switch to graphics mode, select **Graphics** Mode from the **View** menu. For page mode, select the **View** menu's **Page** Mode command.

The following table outlines the various Zoom options (note that these options have no effect on what your documents look like when you print them out):

Select	To
50% or 75%	Reduce the size of the page.
100%	See the page at normal size.
125%, 150%, or 200%	Increase the size of the page.
Marg	Increase the size of the page so that the area between the margins takes up the full width of the screen.
Wide	Increase the size of the page so that the area between the left and right edges (including the margins) takes up the full width of the screen.
Full	Reduce the size of the page so you can see the entire page on the screen.

> **By the Way . . .**
> Just so you know, you can also use the Zoom feature by selecting **Zoom** from the **View** menu and picking an option from the cascade menu that appears. "Marg" in the Zoom list corresponds to the **Margin Width** command; "Wide" corresponds to **Page Width**; and "Full" corresponds to **Full Page**.

The Style List

In WordPerfect, a *style* is a collection of formatting options. This is a large and slightly advanced topic, so I won't cover it in this book. However, that doesn't mean you can't take advantage of the convenience of the Style drop-down list. WordPerfect comes with several predefined styles that you can use any time you like. The three basic styles (called "Level 1," "Level 2," and "Level 3") add paragraph numbers and various levels of indentation.

Each of these options formats a paragraph only; you just position the cursor anywhere in the paragraph, and then select the style you want from the Ribbon.

> **By the Way . . .**
> If you'd like to take a stab at styles yourself, select the **Layout** menu's **Styles** command (or just press **Alt+F8**).

The Columns List

WordPerfect lets you organize your text into columns, just like the ones you see in magazines and newspapers. I won't cover this topic in any kind of depth, but the basics are easy enough to pick up. If you elect to use, say, two columns, WordPerfect divides each page in two (although you can't tell this by looking), which affects your document in two ways:

- Any existing text from the current paragraph to the end of the document is organized into two columns. The first column runs down the left of each page, and then the text snakes back up to the top of the page for the next column.

- As you type new stuff, the text wraps about halfway across the page. When you hit the bottom of the left column, you leap back up to the top of the right column, and continue from there.

To use the Columns list, position the cursor where you want the columns to start and then select one of the list's options.

> **By the Way . . .**
> To see a few more column options, select **Columns** from the Layout menu (or press **Alt+F7**).

The Alignment List

The Alignment list works just like the Layout menu's Alignment command (this was covered back in Chapter 13, "Making Your Lines and Paragraphs Look Good").

The Font List

You normally choose a different font by selecting the Font command from the Font menu, and then picking out the one you want from the Font drop-down list. (Chapter 12, "Making Your Characters Look Good," spells out the details.) Well, the Ribbon lets you cut out the middleman and access the Font drop-down list directly.

The Size List

Changing the characters to a specific point size is just as involved as changing the font (again, see Chapter 12 for the complete steps). Why go through all that, when you can set the size right from the Ribbon? Beats me.

The Button Bar: Easy Command Access

If you thought the Ribbon was cool, wait until you get a load of version 6's new *Button Bar*. Just select the Button Bar command from the View menu to check it out. As you can see here, the Button Bar is a collection of buttons with cute little pictures and hard-to-read text.

> **By the Way . . .**
>
> Although you get a Button Bar in text mode, it's pretty pathetic. To get the neat pictures, make sure you're in either graphics mode or page mode.
>
> WordPerfect's Print Preview also has a Button Bar. It has some different buttons, but it works the same way.

WordPerfect 6's Button Bar. — Scroll arrows

OOPS!
Sorry keyboard users, the Button Bar is only accessible with a mouse.

TECHNO NERD TEACHES
You can customize the position and style of the Button Bar. Select Button Bar **S**etup from the **V**iew menu, and then choose the **O**ptions command from the cascade menu that appears. In the **Button Bar Options** dialog box, select a position (**T**op, **B**ottom, **L**eft Side, or **R**ight Side) and a style (**P**icture and Text, Picture **O**nly, or Text On**l**y), and then select **OK**.

Each of the buttons you see represents a common WordPerfect task. All you have to do is click on a button, and WordPerfect executes the task. For example, clicking on the Print button displays the Print dialog box. To see more buttons, click on the downward-pointing arrow on the left side of the Button Bar. To get back, click on the upward-pointing arrow.

Have It Your Way: Customizing WordPerfect

WordPerfect works fine right out of the box, but it includes all kinds of customization options that let you set up the program the way *you* want it. The next few sections take a look at some of these options.

Customizing WordPerfect's Windows

As you learned in Chapter 17, "Working with Multiple Documents," WordPerfect version 6 displays each open document in its own window.

You can have all kinds of fun with these windows by adding things like scroll bars and frames. In fact, you might have so much fun that you decide you want *every* document you open to use these features. However, selecting everything you need from the pull-down menus each time is a drag. Instead, you can set up a default window setup that WordPerfect will use for each document. To do this, select the Scree**n** Setup command from the View menu. You'll see the Screen Setup dialog box, shown here.

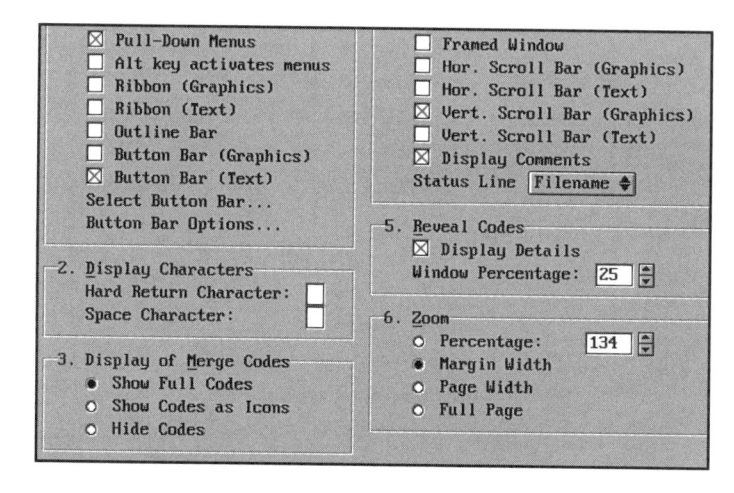

Use the Screen Setup dialog box to customize your document windows.

The Window Options group contains everything you need. Here's a summary of the available options:

Framed Window   As described in Chapter 17, a window frame lets you size, move, and close windows easily. Activate this check box to put a frame around every document window you open.

Horizontal Scroll Bar   Horizontal scroll bars are great for using a mouse to navigate a document that's too wide to fit on the screen (see Chapter 8, "Day-to-Day Drudgery II: Navigating Documents"). This option displays a horizontal scroll bar in every window.

Vertical Scroll Bar   You use vertical scroll bars with a mouse to navigate a document from top to bottom. Activate this check box to display a vertical scroll bar for every document.

Display Comments   Comments are boxed sections of text that appear on the screen, but not in printouts (see Chapter 15, "Other Ways to Look Good"). If you'd prefer *not* to see these comments, deactivate this check box.

Status Line This option controls what WordPerfect displays on the left side of the status line. Your choices are Filename, Font, or Nothing.

Once you've chosen the options you want, select **OK** to put them into effect.

Customizing Your Mouse

As you've seen in this chapter (and in other places in this book), a mouse can be a real time-saver. But its benefits are lost if it's not set up properly, so WordPerfect lets you customize certain aspects of your mouse. Just pull down the File menu, select the Setup command, and then select Mouse from the cascade menu. (If your mouse isn't working, here are the explicit keyboard steps: Alt+F, T, M.) You'll see the Mouse dialog box, shown here.

Use the Mouse dialog box to customize your rodent.

Here's a summary of the available options:

Type This option lets you select a mouse *device driver* (a program that lets WordPerfect talk to your mouse). If your mouse works fine, ignore this option. Otherwise, select it, and then choose your mouse from the list that appears. If you're not sure, choose the Auto Select option.

Port This option is only applicable to certain kinds of mice (called *serial* mice). Again, if your mouse is working, ignore it. Otherwise, just try different values until it does work.

Double-click Interval   This option sets the amount of time you're allowed between two mouse clicks before WordPerfect interprets them as a double click. If you find that your double clicks aren't always recognized, use a higher setting. If two single clicks are sometimes interpreted as a double click, use a lower setting.

> If you press **Shift+F1**, WordPerfect displays a dialog box with the same options as the Setup command's cascade menu.

Acceleration Factor   This option controls how responsive the mouse pointer is to your mouse movements. If you find the pointer is hard to control because it's moving too fast, use a lower setting. If the pointer just seems to creep along, try a higher setting.

Left-handed Mouse   If you're a southpaw, activate this check box to swap the left and right mouse buttons.

Doing WordPerfect's Colors

Lets face it, WordPerfect's basic color scheme is pretty dull (unless, of course, you *like* drab gray)—but that's okay because, after all, this is just a word processor. It's not like you have to wear it in public or anything. However, we can all use a little extra color in our lives occasionally, so WordPerfect gives you a choice of color schemes (or you can even create your own).

To see how it's done, first pull down the File menu, select Setup, and then select Display. The Display dialog box gives you a choice of working with graphics mode colors or text mode colors. Select the appropriate option (I'll assume from here on that you're using graphics mode; in this case, the Graphics Mode Screen Type/Colors dialog box appears).

The Color Schemes box displays a list of the available color schemes (yes, there really is one called "Clown Town"). Highlight the one you want and then choose the Select option. Close the Display dialog to put the new colors into effect.

> Depending on the scheme you chose, you may need to display a dialog box to notice any difference.

If you think you could do a better job of color selection, why not try creating your own scheme? Here are the steps to follow:

1. In the Graphics Mode Screen Type/Colors dialog box, select the Color Schemes box, and then select the Create option. WordPerfect prompts you to enter a name for the scheme.

2. Type in your own silly name for the scheme, and then select **OK**. You'll see the Edit Graphics Screen Colors dialog box.

3. Highlight an item in the **S**creen Elements list, and then select the Color option. The Colors dialog box appears.

4. Use the **arrow** keys to highlight the color you want (or click on the color with the mouse), and then choose the **S**elect button. WordPerfect uses the Sample Colors area to show you what the new color looks like.

5. Repeat Steps 3 and 4 to set the colors for the other screen elements.

6. When you're done, select **OK**, and then close the other dialog boxes to put your new scheme into effect.

> ### The Least You Need to Know
> This chapter took you through a few neat features designed to make your WordPerfect life easier. Here's a recap:
>
> - Use the Ribbon for easy access to some of WordPerfect's formatting options. To display it, select the **V**iew menu's **R**ibbon command.
>
> - The Ribbon contains some cool formatting stuff such as Zoom (which lets you zoom in and out of a document), Styles (which are collections of formatting options), and Columns (which lets you organize your text into two or more columns).

- The Button Bar puts all kinds of WordPerfect commands only a mouse-click away. You display it by selecting the **Button Bar** command from the **View** menu.

- To customize your document windows, select the **View** menu's **Screen Setup** command and make your changes in the **Window Options** section of the **Screen Setup** dialog box.

- If your mouse is being temperamental, run **Setup** from the **File** menu, and select the **Mouse** command. The Mouse dialog box lets you set up the mouse so that it works the way you want it to.

Chapter 20
Using the Spell Checker and Thesaurus

In This Chapter

- Checking your spelling with Speller
- Handling unusual capitalizations and duplicate words
- Looking up words you don't know how to spell
- Using WordPerfect's Thesaurus
- A downright fascinating collection of words

Words. Whether you're a logophile (a lover of words) or a logophobe (one who has an aversion to words), you can't leave home without 'em. Whether you suffer from logomania (the excessive use of words) or logographia (the inability to express ideas in writing), you can't escape 'em. So far, you've seen ways to edit words, ways to organize them, and ways to get them all dressed up for the prom, but when it comes down to using them, well, you're on your own. Now that changes, because in this chapter you'll learn about a couple of tractable tools—Speller and Thesaurus—that'll help you become word-wise (or perhaps even word-perfect). Who knows? With these tools in hand, you may become a full-fledged logolept (a word maniac).

Checking Out WordPerfect's Speller

Nothing can ruin the image of your finely crafted documents more than a few spelling mistakes. In the old days, we could just shrug our shoulders and mumble something about never being good at spelling. With WordPerfect, though, you have no excuses because the darn program comes with a utility called Speller—a built-in spell checker. Speller's electronic brain is stuffed with a 100,000-word strong dictionary that it uses to check your own spelling attempts. If it finds something that isn't right, it'll let you know, and give you a chance to correct it. You can even look up words that you haven't the faintest idea how to spell, and you can add your own words to Speller's dictionary.

> **OOPS!**
> You should save your document before running Speller. Not only might you be making a lot of changes to the document, but it takes time—and if a power failure should hit, you'll lose all your changes.

Cranking Up Speller

Speller can check a single word, a block, a page, everything from the cursor to the end of the document, or the entire document. So the first thing you need to do is position the cursor appropriately:

- If you're checking a word or page, place the cursor anywhere in the word or page.
- If you're checking a block, select the block.

> **By the Way . . .**
> You select a block by pressing **Alt+F4** or **F12** and then using the **arrow** keys to highlight the text. With a mouse, just drag the pointer over the text. Chapter 10, "Block Partying: Working with Blocks of Text," is where you need to look for more block basics.

- If you want Speller to check everything from the cursor, make sure the cursor is where you want it to be.

> **E-Z**
> The shortcut key combo for Speller is **Ctrl+F2**.

To use Speller, pull down the Tools menu, select the **Writing Tools** command, and then, in the

Chapter 20 • Using the Spell Checker and Thesaurus **205**

dialog box that appears, select **S**peller. At this point, one of two things will happen:

- If you selected a block, Speller begins checking the block.

- The Speller dialog box appears. In this case, just tell Speller what you want to check (**W**ord, **P**age, Docu**m**ent, or **F**rom Cursor), and the checking begins.

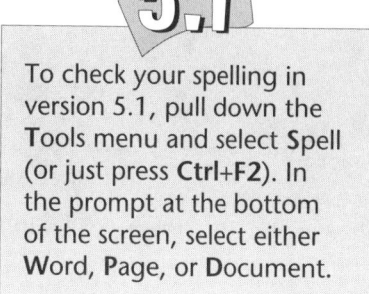

> **5.1**
>
> To check your spelling in version 5.1, pull down the **T**ools menu and select **S**pell (or just press **Ctrl+F2**). In the prompt at the bottom of the screen, select either **W**ord, **P**age, or **D**ocument.

Correcting Spelling Mistakes

If Speller finds something amiss in your document, it'll highlight the word in the text and display the Word Not Found dialog box on your screen, as shown here.

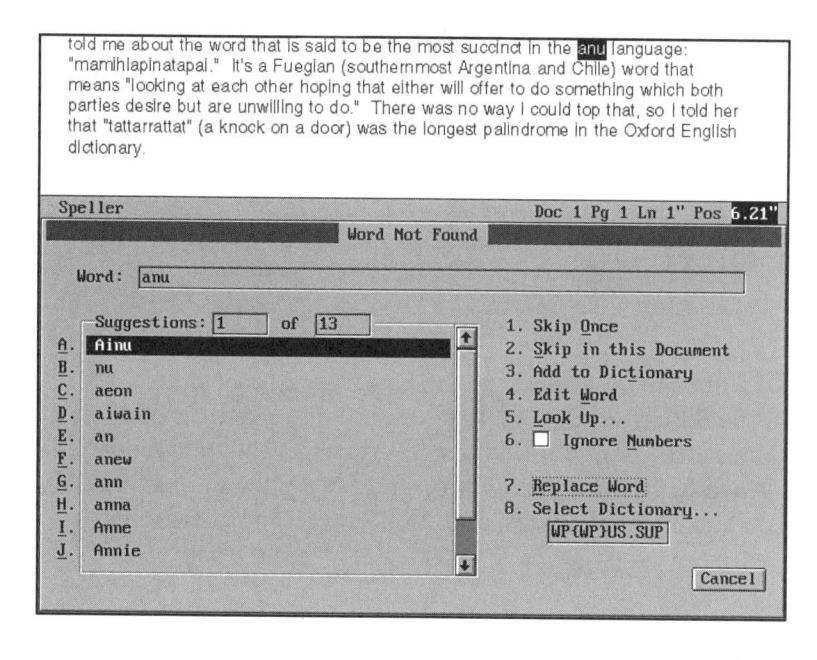

```
told me about the word that is said to be the most succinct in the anu language:
"mamihlapinatapai." It's a Fueglan (southernmost Argentina and Chile) word that
means "looking at each other hoping that either will offer to do something which both
parties desire but are unwilling to do." There was no way I could top that, so I told her
that "tattarrattat" (a knock on a door) was the longest palindrome in the Oxford English
dictionary.
┌─────────────────────────────────────────────────────────────────┐
│ Speller                              Doc 1 Pg 1 Ln 1" Pos 6.21" │
│ ┌─────────── Word Not Found ───────────┐                        │
│   Word: anu                                                     │
│   ┌─ Suggestions: 1   of 13 ──┐   1. Skip Once                  │
│   A. Ainu                         2. Skip in this Document      │
│   B. nu                           3. Add to Dictionary          │
│   C. aeon                         4. Edit Word                  │
│   D. aiwain                       5. Look Up...                 │
│   E. an                           6. ☐ Ignore Numbers           │
│   F. anew                                                       │
│   G. ann                          7. Replace Word               │
│   H. anna                         8. Select Dictionary...       │
│   I. Anne                            WP{WP}US.SUP               │
│   J. Annie                                                      │
│                                                      Cancel     │
└─────────────────────────────────────────────────────────────────┘
```

The Word Not Found dialog box appears when Speller finds a word that's not in its vocabulary.

Speller not only points out misspelled words, but it's even kind enough to lay out a few suggested alternatives. If you want to use one of these words, highlight it in the Suggestions list and then select the **R**eplace Word option.

There are times, however, when a word that Speller doesn't recognize is perfectly legitimate (such as your name, your company's name, or too-hip words such as *cowabunga*). In these cases, Speller gives you four options:

- Select Skip Once to skip this instance of the word.
- Select Skip in this Document to skip all instances of the word in the document.
- Select Add to Dictionary to include the word in Speller's vocabulary.
- If the word has a number in it (such as *Fireball XL-5*), activate the Ignore Numbers check box to tell Speller not to flag these sorts of words.

> **By the Way . . .**
> Speller is good, but it's not *that* good. In particular, it won't flag words that are merely *misused* (as opposed to misspelled). For example, Speller is perfectly happy with either "we're going wrong" or "were going wrong," since everything is spelled correctly. For this grammatical stuff, see Chapter 21, "Painless Grammar Checking."

Editing Words

If Speller flags a word but you don't see the correct spelling in the suggestions (or if you string two words together accidentally, likethis), you can edit the text to make the correction yourself. Just select the Edit **W**ord option in the **Word Not Found** dialog box, and Speller puts the cursor beside the word. Make your changes, and then press **F7** or **Enter** when you're done.

Handling Weird Capitalizations

If you leave the Shift key down a split second too long, you'll end up with words like "SHift" and "TIerra del FUego." Speller will flag these unusual capitalizations and display the Irregular Case dialog box. You can choose

Skip Word to move on, or you can highlight one of the suggestions and then select Replace Word. If you'd like to just edit the word, there's also an Edit Word option.

Handling Duplicate Words

Another blunder that Speller looks out for is when you use the same word twice in in a row (like that). In this case, Speller highlights the second word, and displays the Duplicate Word Found dialog box. Select Delete Duplicate Word to fix it. If the duplication is okay (e.g., Pago Pago or "Tora, Tora, Tora!"), select the Skip Duplicate Word option instead.

> **OOPS!**
> While Speller is a handy tool, its big problem, of course, it that it won't tell you the meaning of a word. For that you're going to have to rely on a good old-fashioned dictionary. And since Speller isn't infallible, don't treat it as a substitute for a thorough proofreading.

Looking Up Words

If you're really not sure how to spell a word, you can use Speller to look it up in the dictionary. I know, I know, it's the old story: how do you look up a word that you can't spell? Well, that's the beauty of Speller: all you have to do is take a stab at it, and it displays any word that's even close.

To look up a word, start Speller and select the Look Up Word option to display the Look Up Word dialog box. Type how you think the word *might* be spelled in the **Word or Word Pattern** text box, and then press **Enter**. Speller consults its dictionary, and then produces a list of suggestions, as shown here.

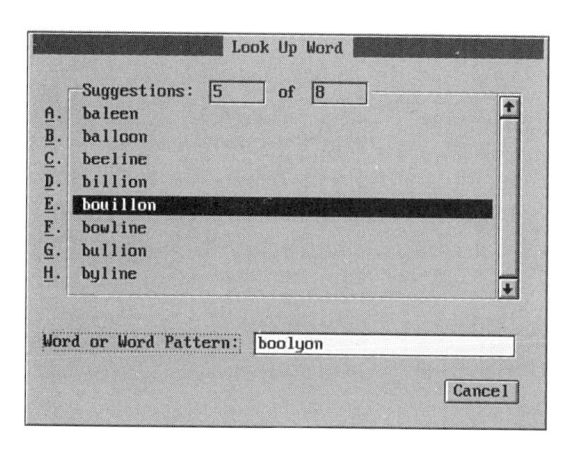

Speller lists every word in its dictionary that is even close to the word you entered.

If you see the word you want, highlight it and press **Enter**. When Speller asks if you want to add it to the text, select **Yes**. If the word isn't among the suggestions, press **Tab** and enter a new word, or just select **Cancel**.

You can even use things called *wildcards* to substitute for groups of letters. There are two wildcard characters: the question mark (**?**) and the asterisk (*****). The question mark substitutes for individual letters. So, for example, *?oof* finds all the words that begin with any letter and end with *oof* (such as *goof*, *hoof*, and *woof*). The asterisk substitutes for a group of letters. For example, if you can never remember the order of the last four letters of *onomatopoeia*, just look up *onomatop** to find out.

> You can also start the Thesaurus by pressing **Alt+F1** and selecting **Thesaurus** from the **Writing Tools** dialog box.

Using the Splendiferous Thesaurus

Did you know that the English language boasts about 616,500 words (plus about another 400,000-or-so technical terms)? So why use a boring word like *boring* when gems such as *prosaic* and *insipid* are available?

What's that? Vocabulary was never your best subject? No problemo. WordPerfect's built-in Thesaurus can supply you with enough synonyms (words with the same meaning) and even antonyms (words with the opposite meaning) to keep even the biggest word hound happy.

Starting the Thesaurus

> The word at the top of the column is called the *headword*. The words in the list are called *references*.

To see what the Thesaurus can do, place the cursor inside a word, pull down the Tools menu, select Writing Tools, and then select Thesaurus from the dialog box. WordPerfect highlights the word and then displays the Thesaurus dialog box, shown here.

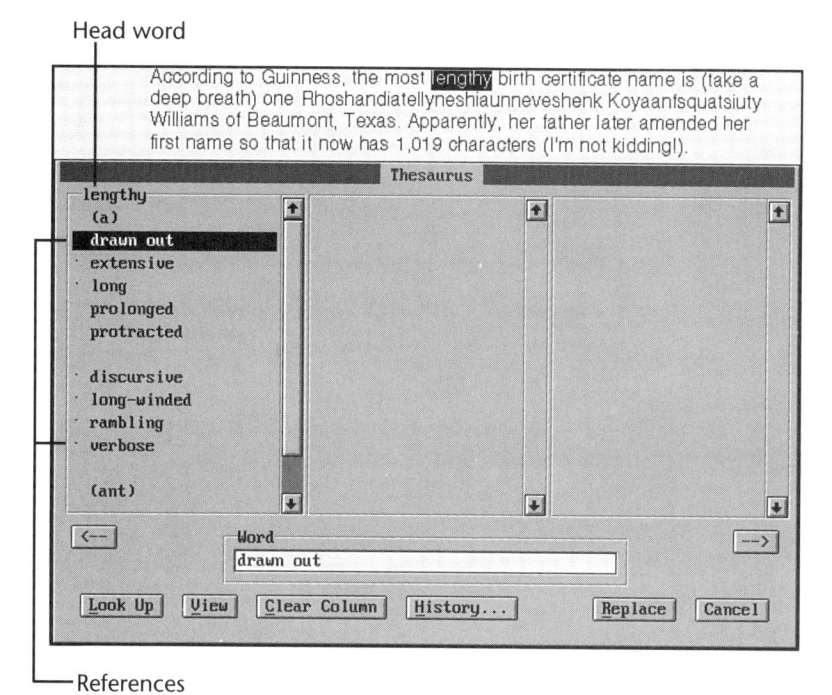

The Thesaurus dialog box.

The Thesaurus displays your word at the top of the first column, and displays a list of words beneath it. Depending on the word you used, the list will be divided in up to four different sections: adjectives, verbs (v), nouns (n), and antonyms (ant). You can use the **up** or **down arrow** keys or the scroll bar to navigate the list. If you see a word you'd like to use instead of the original, highlight it, and then select the **R**eplace option.

Displaying More Words

Not all of the reference words will have exactly the same meaning as the headword. You can often get more ideas by asking the Thesaurus to display the synonyms for one of the reference words. To do this, just highlight the reference word and press **Enter**, or double-click on it. The Thesaurus displays a new list of words in the next column.

> If you get lost among all the columns, select the **History** button to see a list of the headwords. Highlight the column you want, and choose the **Select** button. If you want to remove a column from the screen, highlight a word in the column, and then select the **Clear Column** button.

If you like, you can keep repeating this process to get new lists of words in other columns as well. To navigate between the columns of words, use the **left** and **right arrow** keys, or click on the **left** and **right arrows** in the **Thesaurus** dialog box.

> ### The Least You Need to Know
> This chapter showed you how to get control of your words with WordPerfect's Speller and Thesaurus utilities. Here's a quick review for the logofascinated:
>
> - To start Speller, select **W**riting Tools from the **T**ools menu, and then select **S**peller from the dialog box. (You can also just press **Ctrl+F2**.) Once the Speller dialog box appears, select how much of the document you want to check.
>
> - To correct a spelling mistake found by Speller, highlight the word you want to use and select **R**eplace Word.
>
> - If a word flagged by Speller is actually spelled correctly, you can select the Add to Dictionary option to include the word in Speller's vocabulary.
>
> - If you're not sure how to spell a word, start Speller and select the **L**ook Up Word option. Type how you think the word is spelled, and press **Enter**. Speller displays a list of possible words. If you see one you want to use, highlight it, press **Enter**, and then select **Y**es to add it to the text.
>
> - WordPerfect's Thesaurus can give you a list of synonyms and antonyms for a word. Just place the cursor inside the word, select the **T**ool menu's **W**riting Tools command, and then select Thesaurus.

Chapter 21
Painless Grammar Checking

In This Chapter

- About Grammatik, WordPerfect's grammar checker
- Using Grammatik to check your documents interactively
- Fixing (or ignoring) grammatical errors
- Allowing for different writing styles
- Idiot-proof grammar checking that absolutely *doesn't* require you to know a thing about predicates or prepositions

Grammar ranks right up there with *root canal* and *tax audit* on most people's Top Ten Most Unpleasant Things list. And it's no wonder, too: all those dangling participles, passive voices, and split infinitives. One look at that stuff and the usual reaction is "Yeah, well split *this*!"

If, like me, you couldn't tell a copulative verb from a correlative conjunction if your life depended on it, help is just around the corner. WordPerfect 6 comes with a tool *that will check your grammar for you*. That's right, this utility—it's called Grammatik—will actually analyze your document phrase by phrase, sentence by sentence, and tell you if things aren't right. It'll even tell you how to fix the problem, and often will be able to do it for you at the press of a key. It's about as painless as grammar gets, and it's the subject of this chapter.

Starting Grammatik

Before starting Grammatik, open or switch to the document you want to check (you can open files in Grammatik, but it's easier just to display the file first in WordPerfect). Now pull down the **T**ools menu, select the **W**riting Tools command, and then select the **G**rammatik command from the cascade menu. In a few moments, the main Grammatik screen will appear.

The Grammatik screen is not unlike the WordPerfect screen in text mode (Grammatik doesn't have a graphics mode). You have a menu bar across the top (it works just like WordPerfect's menu bar) that contains Grammatik's pull-down menus; there's a large work area where everything happens; and there's a status line (actually, the bottom *two* lines) that displays Grammatik's messages and shortcut keys.

The Basic Interactive Check

Grammatik has a number of ways to check your document, but the most straightforward is the *interactive* check. In this case, Grammatik scans your document and stops each time it thinks it has found a problem. It then shows you what's wrong, and gives you a chance to correct it on the spot.

> **By the Way . . .**
> Just because Grammatik says something is a problem, doesn't mean it actually *is* a problem. See the section "A Word About Grammatik's Accuracy," later in the chapter.

To start the interactive check, pull down the Checking menu and select the Interactive command. Whenever Grammatik finds a potential error, you'll see a screen like the one shown here.

Grammatik divides the work area into two boxes. The top box shows a section from your document, with the offending word or phrase highlighted. The bottom box is Grammatik's commentary on the problem, and it usually contains the following parts:

Chapter 21 • Painless Grammar Checking **213**

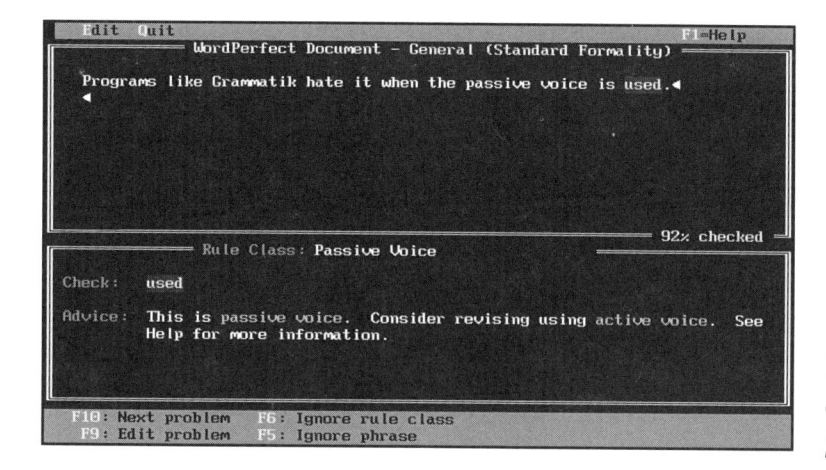

The screen you'll see each time Grammatik finds a possible error.

Rule Class Grammatik divides grammar problems into 72 different types or *classes*. This line tells you which class the current problem falls under.

Check This is the word or phrase in your document that caused Grammatik to go "tsk, tsk."

Advice This is what Grammatik thinks you ought to do about the problem.

Replacement This is Grammatik's suggested replacement for the errant prose. You'll see this only on certain types of problems.

You can also start Grammatik by pressing **Alt+F1** and then selecting the **G**rammatik option from the **Writing Tools** dialog box.

By the Way . . .

Some of Grammatik's explanations can get pretty technical. If you feel brave enough, you can look up some of the more arcane terms in Grammatik's glossary. Just press **F1** to pull down the **Help** menu, and select the **Glossary** command. In the list that appears, highlight the word or phrase and press **Enter**.

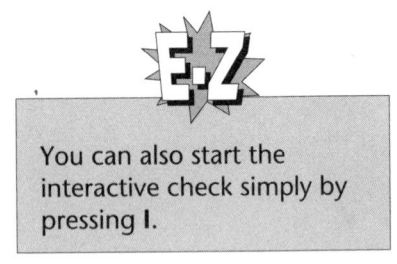

Handling Grammatik's Errors

> You can also start the interactive check simply by pressing **I**.

Once Grammatik displays an error, you need to decide what the heck to do with it. The Edit menu lists all your possible courses of action. Here's a rundown of the more common ones:

- **Skip to next problem** This command (one of my favorites) just ignores the problem altogether, and tells Grammatik to move on.

Shortcut key: F10

- **Edit this problem** Selecting this command places a cursor in the document area so you can make changes to the document yourself. When you're done, press **Esc**.

Shortcut key: F9

- **Replace problem** This command tells Grammatik to fix the problem using its suggested replacement. If the problem is a spelling error, you'll see a list of possible words. In this case, highlight the word you want, and press **Enter**.

Shortcut key: F2

- **Replace problem, skip to next** This is the same as above, except that Grammatik moves on to the next problem once it has finished the replacement.

Shortcut key: F3

- **Mark this problem** If you don't want to fix the problem, but you don't want to ignore it either, this command will insert Grammatik's advice into the document at the point of the error.

Shortcut key: F8

- **Ignore class from now on** This command instructs Grammatik to ignore any other instances of this rule class.

Shortcut key: F6

- **Learn misspelled word** For words that Grammatik flags as misspelled or unusual capitalization, use this command to add the word to Grammatik's dictionary.

Shortcut key: F7

☞ **Ignore phrase from now on** This command tells Grammatik not to flag any other instances of the highlighted phrase.

Shortcut key: F5

Quitting Interactive Check

Grammar checking is a complex business, so Grammatik can take a while to go through a large document. If important duties beckon (such as lunch), you can quit the interactive check at any time by selecting one the following four Quit menu commands:

☞ **Quit, Save work so far** This command quits the interactive check and saves any changes you've made so far.

Shortcut key: S

☞ **Quit, place Bookmark** Select this command if you want to pick up where you left off later on. (You can do that by selecting the Checking menu's **Resume interactive** command in the main Grammatik screen.)

Shortcut key: B

☞ **Quit, mark rest of document** This command continues checking, but just marks up the document with Grammatik's sage advice.

☞ **Cancel, ignore work so far** Use this command to quit, and restore the document to its original state. Grammatik will ask if you're sure you want to quit. Select Yes.

Shortcut key: Ctrl+C

Not all of these **Edit** menu commands will be available for each problem.

The grammar hounds in the audience might want to check out the **Edit** menu's **Show parts of speech** info command (the shortcut key is **F4**). This displays the various parts of speech (nouns, verbs, conjunctions, and so on) that Grammatik has assigned to the words in the problem sentence.

For quicker checks, you can narrow Grammatik's focus a little. For example, selecting the Grammar and Mechanics command (shortcut key: **G**) from the **C**hecking menu tells Grammatik to ignore style errors (e.g., clichés, passive voice, and wordiness). If you only want to check your spelling, choose the **C**hecking menu's **Spelling only** command (shortcut key: **E**).

A Word About Grammatik's Accuracy

Grammatik is probably one of the most sophisticated software programs on the market today. As you've seen, it can do some pretty amazing things—but in the end, it's no match for the English language. There are just too many strange rules, and too many ways to throw sentences together. As a result, Grammatik will often either miss some obvious problems, or flag things that are okay.

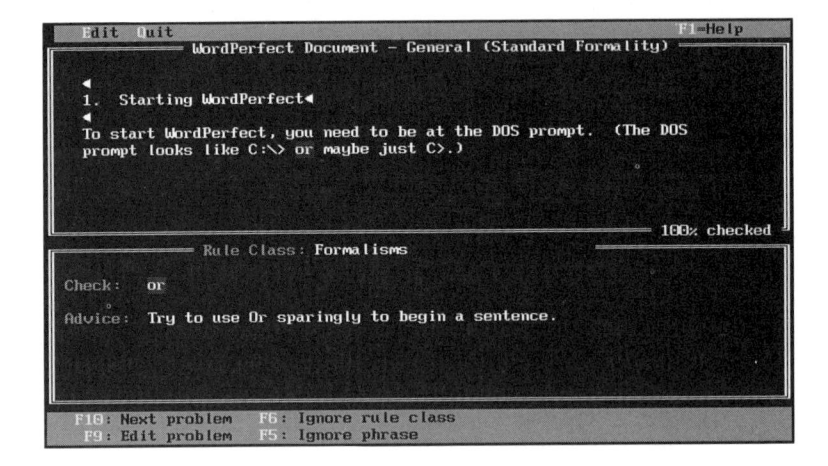

Grammatik is good, but it's no match for the complexity of English.

Here's an example where Grammatik missed a glaring error, but flagged something that was fine.

The phrase "it need to be" is bad English in anyone's books (except, possibly, for the bogus Indians in Grade-B westerns), but Grammatik missed it completely. On the other hand, it thinks that the "or" is starting a new sentence. (It was probably thrown off by the prompt symbol C:\>. It seems DOS messes with *everyone's* head!)

The lesson here is not that Grammatik is a lousy program, because it's not. It's just that you shouldn't lean on it too heavily. Take Grammatik's advice with a grain of salt, and always proofread your work yourself.

Working with Writing Styles

Obviously, not all documents are created equal. Some are stiff and formal, while others are relaxed and jaunty (and others, like portions of this book, are just downright silly). Each of these styles requires different standards of grammar. For example, in more relaxed writing, jargon and clichés are okay, whereas technical writing would have longer and more complex sentences.

For these different kettles of fish, Grammatik lets you choose from a number of different writing styles and levels of formality. And, if you're feeling spunky enough, you can even create your own custom styles. The next few sections tell you everything you need to know.

> To select the Writing style command quickly, just press **W**.

Selecting a Different Style

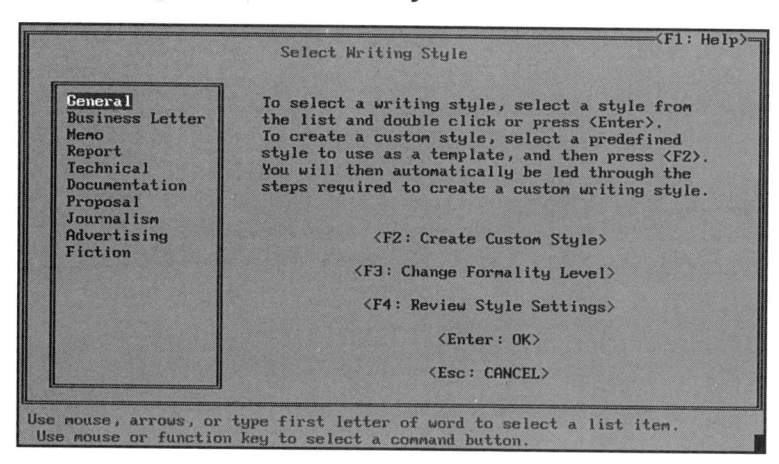

Use the Select Writing Style screen to choose a different writing style.

To select a different style, pull down the **Preferences** menu in Grammatik's main screen, and select the **Writing style** command. You'll see the Select Writing Style screen, shown here.

Before choosing a style, you might want to review its individual grammar settings. To do this, press **F4** or click on the **Review Style Settings** button. Grammatik displays the first of four screens that contain the various rule classes. To navigate the screens, use the following techniques:

☞ Press **Enter** or click on the **Enter: Next** button to go forward.

☞ Press **Backspace** or click on **Backspace: Previous** to go backward.

☞ Press **Esc** or click on **Esc: CANCEL** to return to the Select Writing Style screen.

> **E-Z**
> To navigate the style list faster, press the first letter of the style you want.

The first three screens (**Grammar Rules**, **Mechanical Rules**, and **Style Rules**) list various check boxes with scary-sounding names. If a check box is activated (i.e., it has an "X" in it), it means that Grammatik checks your document for that rule if you use this style. The fourth screen, **Thresholds**, lists this style's limits for things like sentence length and the number of sentences using passive voice.

To choose a different style, return to the **Select Writing Style** screen, use the **up** and **down arrow** keys to highlight a style, and then press **Enter**, or double-click on the style with a mouse.

Changing the Formality Level

The level of *formality* is a measure of how exacting Grammatik is when it checks your documents. The Informal level is the most easygoing (it'll accept contractions such as *it'll*, for example), while the Formal level won't let you get away with too much.

To change the formality level, press **F3** or click on the **Change Formality Level** button in the **Select Writing Style** screen. You'll see the Select Level of Formality screen with a list of the three levels: **Informal**, **Standard**, and **Formal**; select the one you want by highlighting it and pressing **Enter**, or by double-clicking on it.

Creating a Custom Style

Once you've used Grammatik for a while, you may notice certain types of ignorable errors keep cropping up. For example, Grammatik may complain about sentences being too long, or numbers that should be spelled out (i.e., using "two" instead of "2"). Believe me, it doesn't take long before these things get awfully annoying. The remedy isn't to chuck Grammatik out the window, but to create your own styles that don't check for these errors.

Here are the steps to follow to create your own custom style:

1. In the **Select Writing Style** screen, highlight the style upon which you want to base your custom style.

2. Press **F2** or click on the **Create Custom Style** button. The Select Style to Customize screen appears.

3. Grammatik lets you create up to three custom styles, so select one from the list. Grammatik prompts you to enter a name for the style.

4. Type in a name (no more than 23 characters) and press **Enter**. Grammatik displays the first of the rules screens.

5. Go through the rules on the screen, activating those you want to use, and deactivating those you want to ignore.

6. When you're done, press **Enter** to move to the next screen.

7. Repeat Steps 5 and 6 for each of the screens. When you press **Enter** on Screen 4, Grammatik asks if you're ready to save the style.

8. Press **Enter** to save it. Grammatik returns you to the Select Writing Style screen, and displays the new style at the bottom of the list.

> ### Put It To Work
> WordPerfect's Speller checks spelling, doubled words, and unusual capitalizations anyway (see Chapter 20), so you can speed up Grammatik by creating a custom style that doesn't use these checks. You'll find each of these rules on the Mechanical Rules screen.

Quitting Grammatik

When you've had enough of independent clauses and indefinite pronouns, you can quit Grammatik by returning to the main screen and selecting **Quit** from the File menu.

> You can select the Quit command quickly by simply pressing **Q**.

The Least You Need to Know

This chapter showed you the ins and outs of using Grammatik, WordPerfect 6's new grammar-checking program. Here's a recap:

- To start Grammatik, select **Writing Tools** from the **Tools** menu, and then select **Grammatik** from the dialog box.
- To start Grammatik's interactive check, select **Interactive** from the **Checking** menu (or just press **I**).
- When Grammatik flags a possible error, check out the **Edit** menu for a list of your options.
- To quit the interactive check, select one of the commands from the **Quit** menu.
- Grammatik can allow for different writing styles. To work with a different style, select the **Writing style** command from the **Preferences** menu (or just press **W**) and choose the style you want from the list that appears.
- To use a different level of formality, press **F3**, or click on the **Change Formality Level** button and then select the level you want from the list.

Glossary
Speak Like a Geek Glossary

acceleration factor   How quickly the mouse pointer moves across the screen when you move the mouse on its pad.

active window   The window you're currently slaving away in. You can tell a window is active if it has the blinking *cursor*, or if its title bar is a darker color than the other windows.

alphanumeric keypad   The keyboard area that contains the letters, numbers (the ones across the top row, not the ones on the *numeric keypad*), and other punctuation symbols.

ASCII text file   A file that uses only the American Standard Code for Information Interchange character set (which is just techno-lingo for the characters you see on your keyboard).

block   A selection of text in a document.

boilerplate   Text that you reuse over and over. It's the word processing equivalent of the old maxim, "Don't reinvent the wheel."

boot   Computer geeks won't tell you to start your computer they'll tell you to *boot* it. This doesn't mean you should punt your monitor across the room. The term *booting* comes from the phrase "pulling oneself up by one's own bootstraps" which just means that your computer can load everything it needs to operate properly without any help from the likes of you and me.

byte Computerese for a single character of information. So for example the phrase "This phrase is 28 bytes long" is, yes, 28 bytes long (you count the spaces too—but not the quotation marks).

cascade A cool way of arranging windows so that they overlap each other while still letting you see the top of each window.

cascade menu A menu that appears when you select certain *pull-down menu* commands.

character formatting Changing the attributes of individual characters by adding things such as bolding or italics, or by using different fonts.

character set A collection of related characters.

check box A square-shaped switch that toggles a *dialog box* option on or off. The option is toggled on when an "X" appears in the box.

click To quickly press and release the left mouse button.

clipboard An area that holds data temporarily during cut-and-paste operations.

command button A rectangular doohickey (usually found in *dialog boxes*) that, when chosen, runs whatever command is spelled out on its label.

commands The options you see in a *pull-down menu*. You use these commands to tell WordPerfect what you want it to do next.

cursor The vertical bar (it's horizontal in *text mode*) you see inside WordPerfect's typing area; it tells you where the next character you type will appear.

cursor control keys The keys (which you'll find on a separate keypad, or mixed in with the *numeric keypad*) that you use to navigate a document.

delay The amount of time it takes for a second character to appear when you press and hold down a key.

dialog boxes Ubiquitous windows that pop up on the screen to ask you for information, or to seek confirmation of an action you requested (or sometimes just to say "Hi").

directory A storage location on your hard disk for keeping related files together. If your hard disk is like a house, a directory is like a room inside the house. See also *subdirectory*.

disk See *floppy disk*.

double-click To quickly press and release the left mouse button *twice* in succession.

double-click interval The maximum amount of time between mouse clicks that WordPerfect will allow for a double-click to be registered.

drag To press and *hold down* the left mouse button and then move the mouse.

drop-down list A *dialog box* control that normally shows only a single item, but when selected, displays a list of options.

endnote A section of text placed at the end of a document that usually contains asides or comments that embellish something in the regular document text. See also *footnote*.

extension The three-character ending to a DOS file name. The extension is separated from the main name by a period.

file An organized unit of information inside your computer. If you think of your hard disk as a house, then files can be either servants (your programs) or things (data used by you or by a program).

floppy disk A portable storage medium that consists of a flexible disk protected by a plastic case. Floppy disks are available in a variety of sizes and capacities.

font A distinctive graphic design of letters, numbers, and other symbols.

footer A section of text that appears at the bottom margin of each page in a document. See also *header*.

footnote A section of text placed at the bottom of a page. It usually contains asides or comments that embellish something in the regular document text. See also *endnote*.

formatting The process of setting up a disk so it can read and write information. Not to be confused with *character formatting*.

frame A border that surrounds a *window* and lets you *maximize, minimize*, move, and size the window.

fritterware Any software that causes you to fritter away time fiddling with their various bells and whistles.

function keys The keys located either to the left of the *numeric keypad*, or across the top of the keyboard. There are usually 10 function keys (although some keyboards have 12), and they're labeled F1, F2, and so on. In WordPerfect, you use these keys either by themselves or as part of key combinations.

graphics mode A new mode introduced in version 6 that gives WordPerfect true *WYSIWYG* capabilities. The disadvantage is that it is slightly slower than *text mode*.

hard page break A *page break* that you insert yourself. Text always breaks at this point, regardless of the margin sizes.

header A section of text that appears at the top margin of each page in a document. See also *footer*.

hyphenation The process where WordPerfect splits larger words in two at the end of a line and inserts a hyphen. This can help improve the spacing in your paragraphs.

kilobyte 1,024 *bytes*. Usually abbreviated as just *K*.

landscape orientation When the lines on a page run across the long side of the page. See also *portrait orientation*.

margins The empty spaces that surround your text on the page. WordPerfect's standard margins are one inch high on the top and bottom edges of the page, and one inch wide on the left and right edges.

maximize To increase the size of a window to its largest extent. See also *minimize*.

megabyte 1,024 *kilobytes* or 1,048,576 *bytes*. The cognoscenti write this as *M* or *MB* and pronounce it *meg*.

menu bar The horizontal bar on the top line of the WordPerfect screen. The menu bar contains the *pull-down menus*.

minimize To reduce the size of a window to its smallest extent. See also *maximize*.

numeric keypad A separate keypad for entering numbers on most keyboards. It actually serves two functions: when the Num Lock key is on, you can use it to enter numbers; if Num Lock is off, the keypad cursor keys are enabled, and you can use them to navigate a document. Some keyboards (called extended keyboards) have a separate cursor keypad so you can keep Num Lock on all the time.

orphan A first line in a paragraph that appears by itself at the end of a page. See also *widow*.

page break A line that appears across the screen, telling you where one page ends and the next one begins.

page mode A mode that shows you page elements—such as page numbers, *headers*, and *footers*—that you normally only see once you print a document.

point To move the mouse pointer so it rests on a specific screen location.

port The connection you use to plug in the cable from a device such as a mouse or printer.

portrait orientation When the lines run across the short side of a page. This is the standard way most pages are oriented. See also *landscape orientation*.

pull-down menus Hidden menus that you open from WordPerfect's *menu bar* to access the program's commands and features.

radio buttons *Dialog box* options that appear as small circles in groups of two or more. Only one option from a group can be chosen.

RAM Stands for Random Access Memory. The memory in your computer that DOS uses to run your programs.

repeat rate After the initial *delay*, the rate at which characters appear when you press and hold down a key.

right ragged Left-justified text. The right side of each line doesn't line up, so it looks "ragged."

scroll bar A bar that appears at the bottom or on the right of a window whenever the window is too small to display all of its contents.

scrolling To move up or down through a document.

soft page break A *page break* inserted automatically by WordPerfect. The position of the break depends on the margin sizes.

subdirectory A *directory* within a directory.

text box A screen area you use to type in text information such as a description or a file name.

text mode WordPerfect's normal operating mode. It's faster, but you don't get *WYSIWYG* (or the cool 3-D effects you get with *graphics mode* or *page mode*).

type size A measure of the height of a font. Type size is measured in *points*; there are 72 points in an inch.

typeover mode A WordPerfect mode where your typing replaces characters instead of being inserted between them. Use the Insert key to toggle between this mode and normal typing.

watermark A translucent image or section of text that prints over the top of existing text on a page.

widow The last line in a paragraph that appears by itself at the top of a page. See also *orphan*.

window A screen area where WordPerfect displays your documents.

word processing Using a computer to write, edit, format, and print documents. A high-end word processor such as WordPerfect also lets you add complicated features such as *footnotes* and indexes, and even has desktop publishing options that let you do true page layout stuff.

word wrap A WordPerfect feature that starts a new line automatically as your typing reaches the end of the current line.

WYSIWYG What-You-See-Is-What-You-Get. The ability to see on your computer screen what you end up getting from your printer. It's pronounced *wizzy wig*.

Index

Symbols

– (minus key) on numeric keypad, 73
* (asterisk)
    marking
        files, 187
        print jobs for cancellation, 160
    wildcard, 208
+ (plus key) on numeric keypad, 73
. (dot), current directory, 184
.. (double dot), parent directories, 184
? (question mark) wildcard, 208
... (ellipsis), 46, 51
100% View (View menu) command, 163
200% View (View menu) command, 163

A

absolute tab stops, 124
acceleration factor, 221
active window, 170, 172, 221
Alignment (Layout menu) command, 126-127
    Hard Page, 134
Alignment list, Ribbon, 195
alphanumeric keypad, 30-31, 221
Alt key, 31-32
antonyms, 208-210
Appearance (Font menu) command, version 5.1, 114

Append To File (Edit menu) command, 95
appending text, 95
arrow keys, 33, 72
arrowheads after commands, 46
ASCII (American Standard Code for Information Interchange), 112
    text files, 221
asterisk (*)
    marking
        files, 187
        print jobs for cancellation, 160
    wildcard, 208
attributes, 112-114
automatically displaying documents at WordPerfect startup, 68

B

backing up files, 186
Backspace key, 4, 23, 35, 55, 82
Backward (Search menu) command, version 5.1, 101
Bad command or file name message, 20
base fonts, 118
Block (Edit menu) command, 6, 90
blocks of text, *see* text, blocks
boilerplate text, 67, 221
    appending, 95
bold text, 112-114
booting computers, 221
borders, 171-172

230 The Complete Idiot's Guide to WordPerfect

buffers, 85
Button Bar, 195-196
   Print Preview screen, 162
Button Bar (View menu) command, 195
Button Bar Setup (View menu)
  command, 196
buttons
   Cancel, 56
   command, 55-56
   OK, 56
   radio, 53-54
bytes, 182, 222

C

Cancel button, 56
canceling
   block selections, 92
   Copy command, 93
   moving windows, 174
   print jobs, 160-161
   resizing windows, 173
capitalization, 115
   correcting mistakes, 206-207
Caps Lock key, 31, 115
Cascade (Window menu) command, 174
cascade menus, 46, 222
cascading windows, 174-175, 222
center justification, 125
center tabs, 123
centering text vertically, 138
character sets, 119, 222
character-based mode, 112
characters
   attributes, 112-114
   capitalization, 115
   deleting, 82
   fonts, 116-119
   formatting, 6, 222
   navigating, 72
   resizing, 114-115
   subscript, 114-115
   superscript, 114-115
   symbols, 119
check boxes, 54-55, 222
child directories, 184
clicking, 4, 39, 222
Clipboard, 94, 222

Close (File menu) command, 69
closing
   documents, 69
   windows, 176
collating copies of print jobs, 158
colors, customizing, 199-200
columns, separating text into, 194-195
Columns (Layout menu) command, 195
Columns list, Ribbon, 194-195
command buttons, 55-56, 222
commands, 42, 222
   ... (ellipsis) after, 46
   100% View (View menu), 163
   200% View (View menu), 163
   Alignment (Layout menu), 126-127
      Hard Page, 134
   Append To File (Edit menu), 95
   arrowheads after, 46
   Block (Edit menu), 6, 90
   Button Bar (View menu), 195
   Button Bar Setup (View menu), 196
   Cascade (Window menu), 174
   Close (File menu), 69
   Columns (Layout menu), 195
   Comment (Layout menu), 146-147
   Convert Case (Edit menu), 115
   Copy (Edit menu), 92
   Copy and Paste (Edit menu), 93
   Cut (Edit menu), 93-94
   Cut and Paste (Edit menu), 94
   DATE, 145
   Date (Tools menu), 144
   Endnote (Layout menu), 145-146
   Exit WP (File menu), 7-8, 26-27
   Facing Pages (View menu), 163
   File Manager (File menu), 180
   Font (Font menu), 117-118
   Footnote (Layout menu), 145-146
   Frame (Window menu), 171
   Go to (Edit menu), 74
   Graphics Mode (View menu), 112
   Header/Footer/Watermark (Layout
     menu), 139-140
   Horizontal Scroll Bar (View menu), 76
   hot keys, 45
   in dialog boxes, 59
   Justification (Layout menu), 125
   Line (Layout menu), 126, 149
   Margins (Layout menu), 128, 133

Maximize (Window menu), 176
Minimize (Window menu), 176
New (File menu), 69
Next (Window menu), 168
Normal (Font menu), 113
Open (File menu), 5, 67-69
Other (Layout menu), 132
Page (Layout menu), 135-138, 151
Page Mode (View menu), 134
Pages menu, 163
Paste (Edit menu), 92-93
Previous (Window menu), 168
Print (File menu), 7, 157-164
Print Preview (File menu), 162-163
Repeat (Edit menu), 75, 84
Replace (Edit menu), 103-107
Retrieve (File menu), 69
Reveal Codes (View menu), 104
Ribbon (View menu), 192
Save (File menu), 5, 62
Save As (File menu), 66, 94
Screen Setup (View menu), 197-198
Search (Edit menu), 100-102
Select (Edit menu), 92
selecting, 5, 43-44
Setup (File menu)
    Display, 199-200
    Mouse, 198-199
shortcut keys, 46
Size/Position (Font menu), 114
Styles (Layout menu), 194
Switch (Window menu), 168
Switch To (Window menu), 168
Tab Set (Layout menu), 122-124
Thumbnails (View menu), 163
Tile (Window menu), 175
Undelete (Edit menu), 7, 85-86
Undo (Edit menu), 6-7, 96
version 5.1
    Appearance (Font menu), 114
    Backward (Search menu), 101
    Exit (File menu), 65, 69
    Forward (Search menu), 101
    Line (Layout menu), 123-124, 126
    Page (Layout menu), 138
    Page Numbering (Page Numbering menu), 138
    Paste (Edit menu), 93
    Print (File menu), 134
    Retrieve (File menu), 68-69
    Save (File menu), 62, 66
    Spell (Tools menu), 205
    Switch Document (Edit menu), 170
    Undelete (Edit menu), 85
    Window (Edit menu), 170
    Vertical Scroll Bar (View menu), 75-76
WP, 3, 19
WP Characters (Font menu), 119
Writing Tools (Tools menu)
    Grammatik, 212
    Speller, 204-205
    Thesaurus, 208-210
Zoom (View menu), 193
Zoom In (View menu), 163
Zoom Out (View menu), 163
Comment (Layout menu) command, 146-147
comments, 146-147
computers, booting, 221
context-sensitive help, 25
controls, *see* dialog boxes, controls
Convert Case (Edit menu) command, 115
Copy (Edit menu) command, 92
Copy and Paste (Edit menu) command, 93
copying
    blocks of text, 92-93
    files, 185-186
Ctrl key, 31-32
current date, 144-145
current directory, . (dot), 184
cursor, 21, 222
cursor-control keys, 32-33, 72-75, 222
Cut (Edit menu) command, 93-94
Cut and Paste (Edit menu) command, 94

D

Date (Tools menu) command, 144
DATE command, 145
dates, 144-145
decimal tabs, 123
decorative fonts, 117
delay, 72, 222
Delete key, 35, 82
deleting
    blocks of text, 94-95
    characters, 82

files, 187
hard page breaks, 134
lines of text, 83
pages, 84
repeating, 84
searching for text and, 105
tabs, 124-125
words, 82-83
device drivers, mouse, 198
dialog boxes, 223
accessing, 51
Append To, 95
Button Bar Options, 196
Colors, 200
commands in, 59
Control Printer, 160-161
controls
check boxes, 54-55, 222
command buttons, 55-56, 222
drop-down lists, 57-58, 223
navigating, 52-53
pop-up lists, 56
radio buttons, 53-54, 226
text boxes, 55, 226
Copy, 185-186
Display, 199-200
Document on Disk, 160
Duplicate Word Found, 207
Edit Graphics Screen Colors, 200
Exit WordPerfect, 7-8, 26-27
Font, 117-118
Go to, 74
Graphics Mode Screen Type/Colors, 199-200
guidelines, 51-52
Header/Footer/Watermark, 139-140
Irregular Case, 206-207
Line Format, 126, 149
Look Up Word, 207-208
Margin Format, 128, 133
Mouse, 198-199
Move/Rename, 186
Open Document, 5, 67-69
Page Format, 151
Page Number Position, 135-136
Page Numbering, 135-138
Paper Size/Type, 151
Position Hyphen, 149-150
Print, 7, 157-164
Print Multiple Pages, 158-159

Repeat, 75, 84
Retrieve Document, 69
Save Block, 94
Save Document, 5, 63
Screen, 173-174
Screen Setup, 197-198
Search, 100-102
Search and Replace, 103-106
Select Printer, 156, 164
Set Page Number, 137
Specify File Manager List, 180
Speller, 205-208
Switch To Document, 168
Tab Set, 122-124
Thesaurus, 208-210
Undelete, 7, 85-86
Window, 173-174
Word Not Found, 205-206
WordPerfect Characters, 119
dictionaries, looking up words, 207-208
directories, 181-182, 223
child, 184
current, . (dot), 184
parent, .. (double dot), 184
subdirectories, 182, 226
documents
closing, 69
comments, 146-147
creating, 69
dates and times, inserting, 144
deleting pages, 84
footnotes and endnotes, 145-146
grammar checking, 212-219
hyphenation, 148-150
navigating, 72-77
opening, 5, 66-69, 184
previewing, 161-163
printing, 156-160
retrieving, 66-69, 184
saving, 61-66
spell checking, 204-208
switching between, 168-170
text
entering, 4, 22-23
separating into columns, 194-195
viewing contents without opening, 184-185
zooming, 192-193
see also files

DOS prompt, 3, 18
    returning to, 18-19
dot (.), current directory, 184
dot leaders, 123
double dot (..), parent directories, 184
double-click interval, 223
double-clicking, 39, 223
down arrow key, 33, 72
Down scroll arrow, 77
dragging, 39, 223
drop-down lists, 57-58, 223

E

editing
    comments, 147
    footnotes or endnotes, 146
    spelling mistakes, 206
    with word processors, 10-11
ellipsis (...), 46, 51
End key, 73
Endnote (Layout menu) command, 145-146
endnotes, 145-146, 223
Enhanced keyboards, 31
Enter key, 4, 34-35
Esc key, 7, 32, 85
Exit (File menu) command, version 5.1, 65, 69
Exit Control button, 172, 176
Exit WP (File menu) command, 7-8, 26-27
exiting
    Grammatik, 219
    interactive grammar checks, 215
    menus without selecting commands, 44
    Print Preview, 163
    WordPerfect, 7-8, 26-27, 65-66
extended keyboards, 33
extensions, 63-65

F

Facing Pages (View menu) command, 163
File Manager
    documents
        opening and retrieving, 184
        viewing contents without opening, 184-185
    file list, 182-184

files
    copying, 185-186
    deleting, 187
    moving/renaming, 186
    selecting multiple, 187-188
    starting, 180-181
File Manager (File menu) command, 180
files, 181-182, 223
    ASCII text, 221
    copying, 185-186
    deleting, 187
    displaying lists of, 68-69
    extensions, 223
    marking, 187
    moving, 186
    naming, 63-65
    printing, 7
    renaming, 186
    saving, 5-6
    selecting multiple, 187-188
    see also documents
floppy disks, 223
Font (Font menu) command, 117-118
Font list, Ribbon, 195
fonts, 116-119, 223
    type size, 226
footers, 138-140, 224
Footnote (Layout menu) command, 145-146
footnotes, 145-146, 224
formatting, 224
    capitalization, 115
    centering text vertically, 138
    character attributes, 112-114
    characters, 6, 222
    dates and times, 144
    fonts, 116-119
    footnotes or endnotes, 145-146
    guidelines, 122
    headers and footers, 138-140
    hyphenation, 148-150
    indenting paragraphs, 126-127
    justifying, 124-126
    line spacing, 126
    margins
        pages, 132-133
        paragraphs, 127-128
    numbering pages, 135-138
    page breaks, 133-134

resizing characters, 114-115
styles, 194
subscript, 114-115
superscript, 114-115
tabs, 122-124
watermarks, 139
widows and orphans, 132
with word processors, 11
formatting codes, 104
Forward (Search menu) command,
 version 5.1, 101
Frame (Window menu) command, 171
frames, 224
framing windows, 170-171
fritterware, 13, 224
full justification, 125
function keys, 33, 224

G

Go to (Edit menu) command, 74
Grammatik
 exiting, 219
 handling errors, 214-215
 interactive checks, 212-213
  exiting, 215
 shortcomings, 216
 starting, 212
 writing styles, 216-219
graphics mode, 23-25, 112, 224
Graphics Mode (View menu)
 command, 112

H

hard page breaks, 134, 224
Header/Footer/Watermark (Layout menu)
 command, 139-140
headers, 138-140, 224
headwords, 208-209
Help, 25
Help menu, 25
highlighting blocks of text, 6
Home key, 7
horizontal (landscape) orientation, 150, 224
Horizontal Scroll Bar (View menu)
 command, 76

hot keys
 commands, 45
 pull-down menus, 43
hyphenation, 148-150, 224
hyphenation zones, 150

I-J

indenting paragraphs, 126-127
 with tabs, 122-124
Insert key, 35-36, 82
installing
 printers, 156
 WordPerfect, 18
interactive grammar checks, 212-213
 exiting, 215
Invalid drive/path specification message, 64
italic text, 112-114

Justification (Layout menu) command, 125
justifying text, 124-126

K

keyboard shortcuts, *see* shortcut keys
keyboards
 components, 29-36
 delay, 72, 222
 Enhanced, 31
 extended, 33
 navigating documents, 72-75
 repeat rate, 72, 226
keypads
 alphanumeric, 30-31, 221
 numeric, 33, 225
keys
 – (minus), numeric keypad, 73
 + (plus), numeric keypad, 73
 alphanumeric, 30
 Alt, 31-32
 Backspace, 4, 23, 35, 55, 82
 Caps Lock, 31, 115
 Ctrl, 31-32
 cursor-control, 32-33, 72-75, 222
 Delete, 35, 82
 down arrow, 33, 72
 End, 73
 Enter, 4, 34-35

Esc, 7, 32, 85
function, 33, 224
hot, 43, 45
Insert, 35-36, 82
left arrow, 33, 72
Num Lock, 33-34
Page Down, 33, 73
Page Up, 33, 73
right arrow, 33, 72
Shift, 31
Shift+Tab, 53
Tab, 53, 122
up arrow, 33, 72
kilobytes (K), 224

L

landscape (horizontal) orientation, 150, 224
laptop keyboards, 34
leaders, 123
left arrow key, 33, 72
left justification, 125
left ragged text, 126
left tabs, 123
Line (Layout menu) command, 126, 149
    Justification (version 5.1), 126
    Tab Set (version 5.1), 123-124
line spacing, 126
lines of text
    deleting, 83
    justifying, 126
    navigating, 72-73
lists
    drop-down, 57-58
    pop-up, 56
lowercase, converting to, 115

M

margins, 22, 225
    pages, 132-133
    paragraphs, 127-128
    top and bottom, centering text between, 138
Margins (Layout menu) command, 128, 133
marking
    files, 187
    print jobs for cancellation, 160

Maximize (Window menu) command, 176
maximize arrow, 172, 176
maximizing windows, 176, 225
megabytes (M or MB), 225
memory, RAM (Random Access Memory), 226
menu bar, 4, 21, 42, 225
    Print Preview screen, 162
menus
    cascade, 46, 222
    exiting without selecting commands, 44
    Help, 25
    hot keys, 43
    pull-down, 4-5, 42, 226
    selecting commands, 43-44
    WordPerfect 5.1, 49-50
messages
    Bad command or file name, 20
    Invalid drive/path specification, 64
Minimize (Window menu) command, 176
minimize arrow, 172, 176
minimizing windows, 175-176, 225
minus key (–) on numeric keypad, 73
modes
    graphics, 23-25, 112, 224
    page, 134-135, 225
    text, 112, 226
    typeover, 35-36, 82, 226
mouse
    clicking, 4, 222
    customizing, 198-199
    double-clicking, 223
    dragging, 223
    navigating documents with, 75-76
    operations, 36-39
mouse pointer, 36
    acceleration factor, 221
moving
    blocks of text, 93-94
    files, 186
    windows, 173-174

N-O

naming files, 63-65
New (File menu) command, 69
Next (Window menu) command, 168
Normal (Font menu) command, 113

notebook keyboards, 34
Num Lock key, 33-34
numbering pages, 135-138
numbers beside controls, 53
numeric keypad, 33, 225
    – (minus key), 73
    + (plus key), 73
    troubleshooting typing numbers, 34

OK button, 56
Open (File menu) command, 5, 67-69
opening documents, 5, 66-69, 184
orientation, 150
    landscape (horizontal), 224
    portrait (vertical), 225
orphans, 132, 225
Other (Layout menu) command, 132

P

Page (Layout menu) command, 135-138, 151
page breaks, 133-134, 225
    hard, 224
    soft, 226
    viewing on-screen, 23
Page Down key, 33, 73
page mode, 134-135, 225
Page Mode (View menu) command, 134
Page Numbering (Page Numbering menu) command, version 5.1, 138
Page Up key, 33, 73
pages
    centering text vertically, 138
    deleting, 84
    headers and footers, 138-140
    margins, 132-133
    navigating, 73
    numbering, 135-138
    printing multiple, 158-159
    widows and orphans, 132
    zooming, 192-193
Pages menu commands, 163
pangrams, 30
paper sizes, 150-151
paragraphs
    formatting guidelines, 122
    indenting, 126-127
    justifying, 124-126

line spacing, 126
margins, 127-128
navigating, 72-73
tabs, 122-124
parent directories, .. (double dot), 184
Paste (Edit menu) command, 92-93
pixels, 112
plus key (+) on numeric keypad, 73
pointing, 39
points, 118, 225
pop-up lists, 56
portrait (vertical) orientation, 150, 225
ports, 225
previewing documents before printing, 161-163
Previous (Window menu) command, 168
primary names, files, 63-65
Print (File menu) command, 7, 157-164
    View Document (version 5.1), 134
Print Preview (File menu) command, 162-163
printers
    installing, 156
    selecting, 164
printing
    canceling jobs, 160-161
    collating copies, 158
    documents, 156-158
        previewing before, 161-163
        unopened, 160
    files, 7
    multiple pages, 158-159
    with word processors, 11-12
programs
    fritterware, 13, 224
    Grammatik, 212-219
    Speller, 204-208
pull-down menus, 4-5, 42, 226
    hot keys, 43
    selecting commands, 43-44

Q-R

question mark (?) wildcard, 208
radio buttons, 53-54, 226
RAM (Random Access Memory), 226
references, 208
relative tab stops, 124

remarks, 146-147
renaming files, 186
Repeat (Edit menu) command, 75, 84
repeat rate, 72, 226
repeating, 75
    deletions, 84
Replace (Edit menu) command, 103-106
replacing text, 103-106
resizing
    characters, 114-115
    windows, 172-173
restoring deleted text, 85-86
Retrieve (File menu) command, 68-69
retrieving documents, 66-69, 184
Return key, *see* Enter key
Reveal Codes
    [chpt #], 137
    [page #], 136-138
Reveal Codes (View menu) command, 104
Ribbon
    Alignment list, 195
    Columns list, 194-195
    displaying, 192
    Font list, 195
    selecting items from, 192
    Size list, 195
    Style list, 194
    Zoom list, 192-193
Ribbon (View menu) command, 192
right arrow key, 33, 72
right justification, 125
right ragged text, 126, 226
right tabs, 123

S

sans-serif fonts, 117
Save (File menu) command, 5, 62
    version 5.1, 62, 66
Save As (File menu) command, 66, 94
saving
    blocks of text, 94
    documents, 61-66
    files, 5-6
Screen Setup (View menu) command, 197-198
screens
    colors, customizing, 199-200
    navigating, 73

Print Preview, 162-163
    WordPerfect, elements, 20-22
scroll arrows, 77
scroll bars, 75-77, 226
    in drop-down lists, 58
scroll box, 58
scrolling, 72, 226
Search (Edit menu) command, 100-102
searching for text, 100-102
    and deleting, 105
    and replacing, 103-106
Select (Edit menu) command, 92
selecting
    blocks of text, 6, 90-92
    commands, 5, 43-44
    drop-down list items, 57-58
    fonts, 117-118
    multiple files, 187-188
    printers, 164
serial mouse, 198
serif fonts, 117
Setup (File menu) command
    Display, 199-200
    Mouse, 198-199
Shift key, 31
Shift+Tab keys, 53
shortcut keys, 26, 31-32, 46
    Block (F12 or Alt+F4), 6, 90
    Bold (F6), 112
    Center (Shift+F6), 128
    Columns (Alt+F7), 195
    Copy (Ctrl+C), 92
    Copy and Paste (Ctrl+Insert), 93
    Current/previous document toggle
      (Shift+F3), 168
    Cut (Ctrl+X), 93
    Cut and Paste (Ctrl+Del), 94
    Date (Shift+F5), 144
    Delete line (Ctrl+End), 83
    Delete to beginning of word
      (Home,Backspace), 83
    Delete to end of page
      (Ctrl+Page Down), 84
    Delete to end of word (Home,Delete), 83
    Delete word (Ctrl+Backspace), 82
    entering, 36
    Exit WP (Home, F7), 7, 27
    File Manager (F5), 68, 180
    File Manager navigation, 183

Font (Ctrl+F8), 117
Go to (Ctrl+Home), 74
Grammatik error-handling, 214-215
Hard page break (Ctrl+Enter), 134
Help (F1), 25
Indent from both margins
 (Shift+F4), 128
Indent paragraph (F4), 128
Italics (Ctrl+I), 112
Mark/unmark file toggle (Spacebar), 187
Move down one paragraph (Ctrl+down
 arrow), 73
Move left one word (Ctrl+left arrow), 72
Move right one word (Ctrl+right
 arrow), 72
Move to beginning of document
 (Home,Home,up arrow), 73
Move to beginning of line (Home,left
 arrow), 73
Move to bottom of screen (Home,down
 arrow or plus key [+] on numeric
 keypad), 73
Move to end of document
 (Home,Home,down arrow), 73
Move to end of line (Home,right
 arrow), 73
Move to top of screen (Home,up
 arrow or minus key [–] on numeric
 keypad), 73
Move up one paragraph (Ctrl+up
 arrow), 73
Normal (Ctrl+N), 114
Open/Retrieve toggle (Shift+F10), 5,
 67-68
Paste (Ctrl+V), 92
Print (Shift+F7), 157
Repeat (Ctrl+R), 75
Replace (Alt+F2), 103
Reveal Codes (Alt+F3), 104
Right-justify (Alt+F6), 128
Save (Ctrl+F12), 5, 62
Save As (F10), 66
Screen (Ctrl+F3), 173
Search (F2), 100
Search Backward (Shift+F2), 101
Setup (Shift+F1), 199
Soft hyphen (Ctrl+-), 150
Speller (Ctrl+F2), 204
Styles (Alt+F8), 194

Switch To (Home,0), 168
Undelete (Escape), 85
Underline (F8), 112
Undo (Ctrl+Z), 7, 96
version 5.1
 Exit WP (F7), 7, 27
 Extended Search Backward
  (Home,Shift+F2), 103
 Extended Search Forward
  (Home,F2), 103
 Help (F3), 25
 menu bar (Alt+=), 4, 21, 43
 Repeat (Escape), 75
 Save (F10), 5
 Spell (Ctrl+F2), 205
 Switch Document (Shift+F3), 170
 Undelete (F1), 7, 85
 Window (Ctrl+F3), 170
 WordPerfect Characters (Ctrl+W), 119
 Writing Tools (Alt+F1), 208
Size list, Ribbon, 195
Size/Position (Font menu) command, 114
soft hyphens, 150
soft page breaks, 134, 226
spacing, line, 126
Spell (Tools menu) command,
 version 5.1, 205
Speller, 204
 capitalization mistakes, 206-207
 duplicate words, 207
 editing words, 206
 looking up words, 207-208
 spelling mistakes, 205-206
 starting, 204-205
starting
 File Manager, 180-181
 Grammatik, 212
 Speller, 204-205
 Thesaurus, 208-209
 WordPerfect, 3-4, 19
  displaying documents
   automatically, 68
  preparing for, 18-19
status line, 21-22
 Print Preview screen, 163
Style list, Ribbon, 194
styles, 194
 of writing, 216-219
Styles (Layout menu) command, 194

subdirectories, 182, 226
subscript, 114-115
superscript, 114-115
Switch (Window menu) command, 168
Switch Document (Edit menu) command, version 5.1, 170
Switch To (Window menu) command, 168
switching between documents, 168-170
symbols, 119
synonyms, 208-210

T

Tab key, 53, 122
Tab Set (Layout menu) command, 122-124
tabs, 122-123
    absolute, 124
    deleting, 124-125
    relative, 124
    setting, 124
    types, 123
text
    attributes, 112-114
    blocks, 89-90, 221
        appending, 95
        canceling selections, 92
        copying, 92-93
        deleting, 94-95
        extending selections, 92
        moving, 93-94
        saving, 94
        selecting, 6, 90-92
    boilerplate, 67, 221
        appending, 95
    bold, 112-114
    capitalization, 115
    centering vertically, 138
    comments, 146-147
    deleting, 82-83
    entering, 4
        guidelines for, 22-23
    fonts, 116-119
    footnotes and endnotes, 145-146
    grammar checking, 212-219
    hyphenation, 148-150
    italic, 112-114
    left ragged, 126
    navigating, 72-73

    paragraphs
        formatting guidelines, 122
        indenting, 126-127
        justifying, 124-126
        line spacing, 126
        margins, 127-128
        tabs, 122-124
    resizing, 114-115
    right ragged, 126
    searching for, 100-102
        and deleting, 105
        and replacing, 103-106
    separating into columns, 194-195
    spell checking, 204-208
    subscript, 114-115
    superscript, 114-115
    symbol characters, 119
    undeleting, 7, 85-86
    underlined, 112-114
    word wrap, 4, 227
text boxes, 55, 226
text files, ASCII, 221
text mode, 112, 226
Thesaurus, 208-210
Thumbnails (View menu) command, 163
Tile (Window menu) command, 175
tiling windows, 175
time, 144-145
title bar, 171
    moving windows with, 174
titles, windows, 171
type size, 226
typeover mode, 35-36, 82, 226
typewriters versus word processors, 10
typing area, 21

U-V

Undelete (Edit menu) command, 7, 85-86
undeleting text, 7, 85-86
underlined text, 112-114
Undo (Edit menu) command, 6-7, 96
undoing
    last action, 6-7, 96
    text-typing mistakes, 23
unopened documents, printing, 160
up arrow key, 33, 72
Up scroll arrow, 77
uppercase, converting to, 115

vertical (portrait) orientation, 150, 225
Vertical Scroll Bar (View menu) command,
   75-76
video cards, 113
viewing area, Print Preview screen, 162

W

watermarks, 139, 226
widows, 132, 227
wildcards, 208
Window (Edit menu) command,
   version 5.1, 170
windows, 170, 227
   active, 170, 172, 221
   cascading, 174-175, 222
   closing, 176
   components, 171-172
   customizing, 196-198
   frames, 224
   framing, 170-171
   maximizing, 176, 225
   minimizing, 175-176, 225
   moving, 173-174
   resizing, 172-173
   tiling, 175
word processors, 10, 227
   disadvantages, 12-14
   editing with, 10-11
   formatting with, 11
   printing with, 11-12
   versus typewriters, 10
word wrap, 4, 22-23, 34-35, 227
WordPerfect
   exiting, 7-8, 26-27, 65-66
   features, 14-15
   installing, 18
   screen elements, 20-22
   starting, 3-4, 19
      displaying documents
         automatically, 68
      preparing for, 18-19
   version 5.1
      commands, *see* commands,
         version 5.1
      menus, 49-50
words
   deleting, 82-83
   hyphenation, 148-150
   looking up in dictionaries, 207-208
   navigating, 72
WP Characters (Font menu) command, 119
WP command, 3, 19
writing styles, 216-219
Writing Tools (Tools menu) command
   Grammatik, 212
   Speller, 204-205
   Thesaurus, 208-210
WYSIWYG (What-You-See-Is-What-You-
   Get), 24, 227

X-Z

zones, hyphenation, 150
Zoom (View menu) command, 193
Zoom In (View menu) command, 163
Zoom list, Ribbon, 192-193
Zoom Out (View menu) command, 163